PRINCE
Freya

5

STORY AND ART BY
KEIKO ISHIHARA

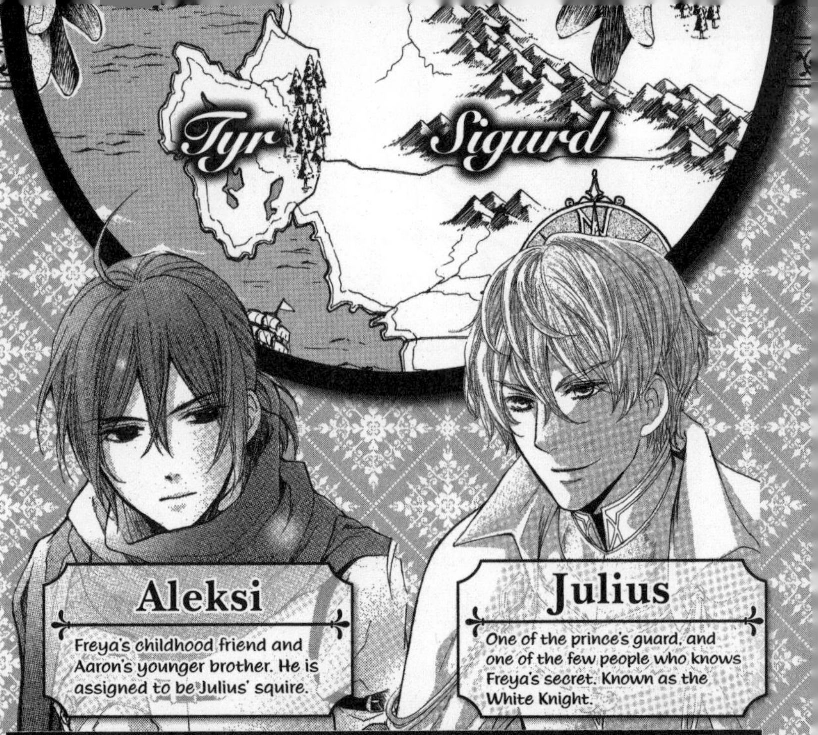
Tyr
Sigurd

Aleksi

Freya's childhood friend and Aaron's younger brother. He is assigned to be Julius' squire.

Julius

One of the prince's guard, and one of the few people who knows Freya's secret. Known as the White Knight.

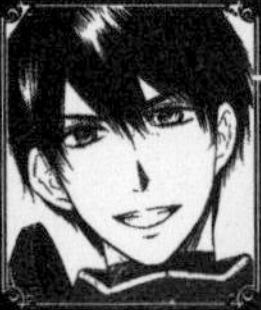

Aaron

Freya's childhood friend and the part of the prince's personal guard. Known as the Black Knight. Slain by a villain's sword.

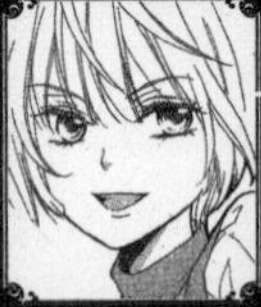

Prince Edvard

Crown prince of Tyr. He was recently assassinated via poison.

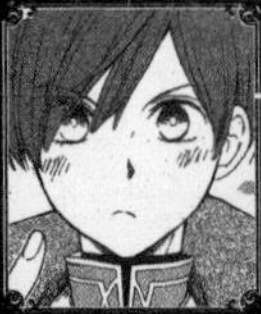

Mikal

A member of the prince's personal guard. He's an impulsive red-head who's infatuated with the prince.

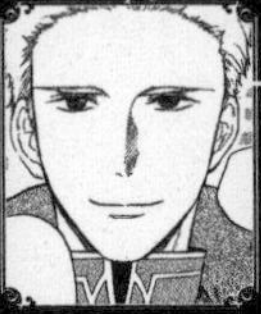

Yngvi

A member of the prince's personal guard. He's known to be a master of cooking outside.

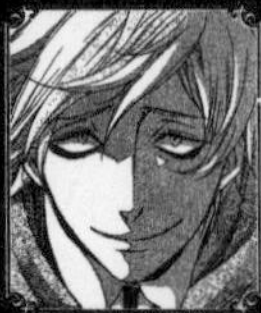

Sable Nerasof

A Sigurdian officer and Aaron's killer.

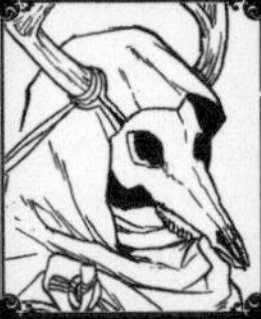

Forest People

An ancient tribe that resists the rule of the Sigurdian Empire. They helped Alek when he fell off a cliff and nearly died.

Characters & Story

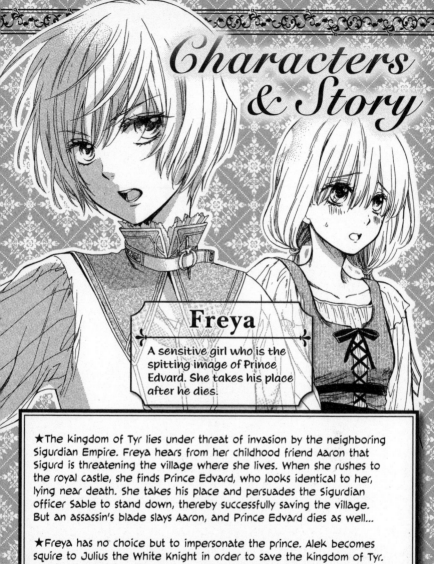

Freya

A sensitive girl who is the spitting image of Prince Edvard. She takes his place after he dies.

★The kingdom of Tyr lies under threat of invasion by the neighboring Sigurdian Empire. Freya hears from her childhood friend Aaron that Sigurd is threatening the village where she lives. When she rushes to the royal castle, she finds Prince Edvard, who looks identical to her, lying near death. She takes his place and persuades the Sigurdian officer Sable to stand down, thereby successfully saving the village. But an assassin's blade slays Aaron, and Prince Edvard dies as well...

★Freya has no choice but to impersonate the prince. Alek becomes squire to Julius the White Knight in order to save the kingdom of Tyr. Word arrives of an attack by Sigurdian forces on Fort Leren near the border. The fort is on the brink of falling, but Freya rushes to its defense. Alek, previously thought dead in an enemy attack, arrives with the Forest People, who help Tyr successfully repel Sigurd. After driving the enemy from their borders, Freya and company set out bearing the Royal Jewel on a journey to enlist the aid of Tyr's four former allies.

5
CONTENTS

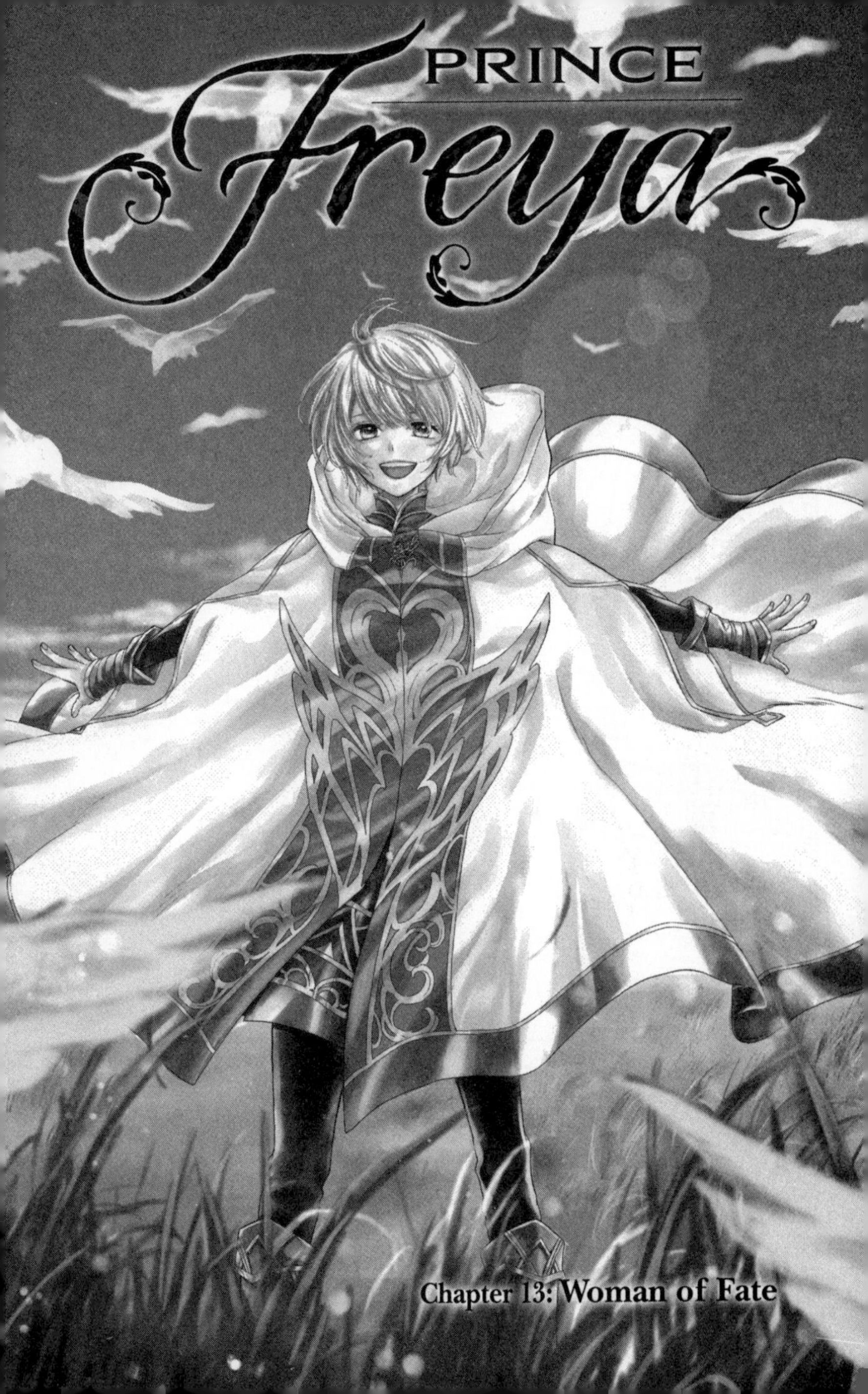
PRINCE
Freya
Chapter 13: Woman of Fate

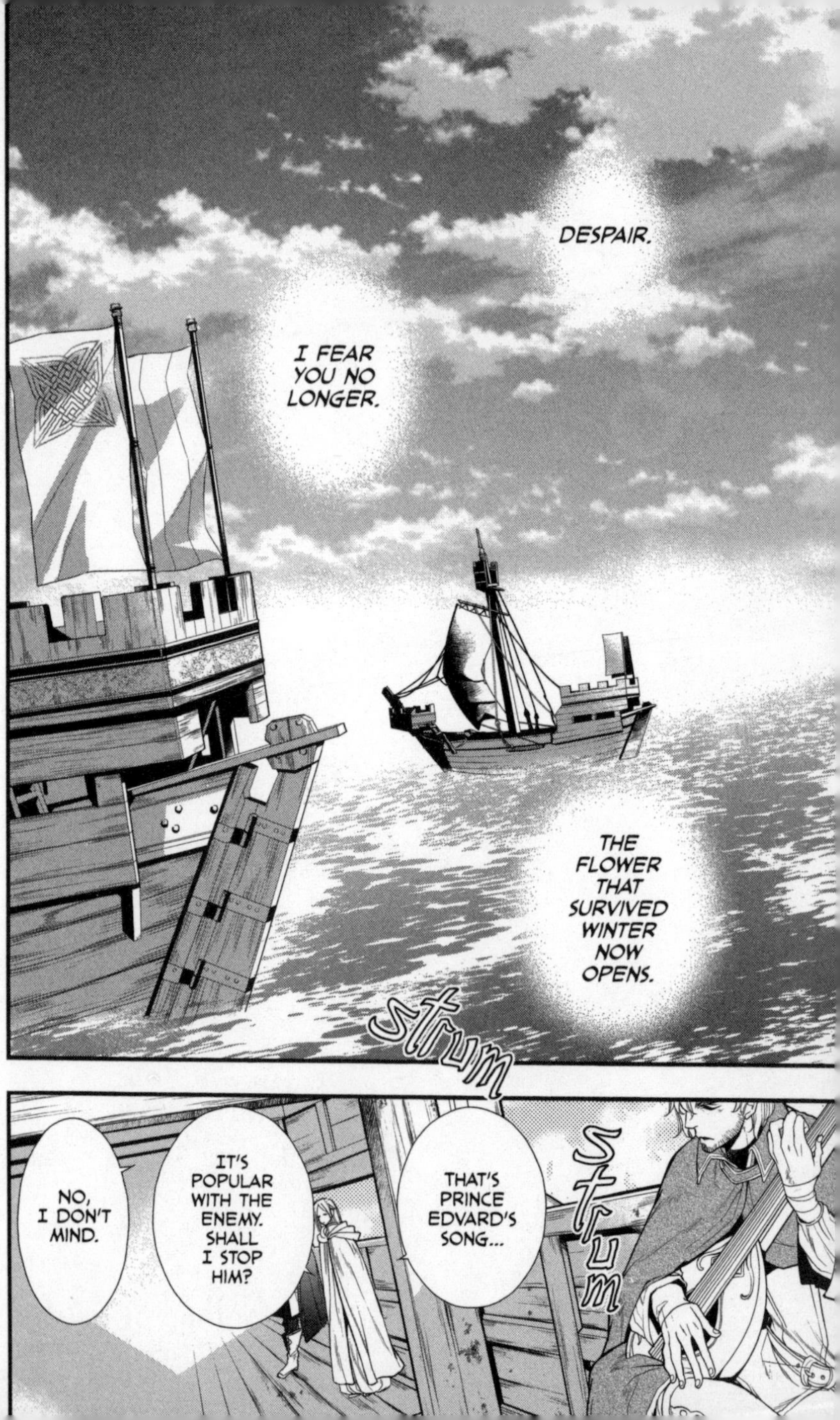
DESPAIR.
I FEAR YOU NO LONGER.
THE FLOWER THAT SURVIVED WINTER NOW OPENS.
strum
strum
THAT'S PRINCE EDVARD'S SONG...
IT'S POPULAR WITH THE ENEMY. SHALL I STOP HIM?
NO, I DON'T MIND.

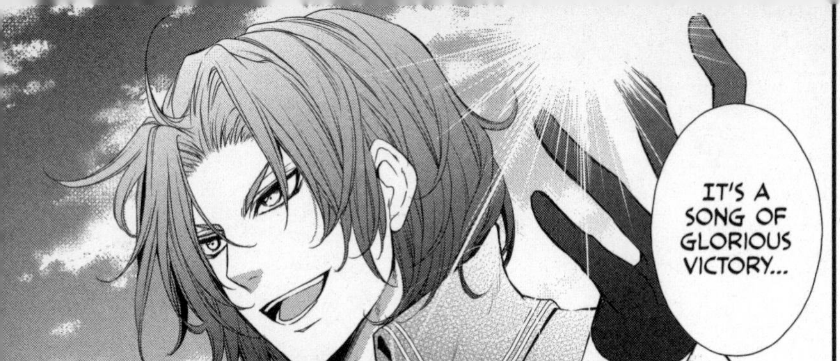
IT'S A SONG OF GLORIOUS VICTORY...
...NOW THAT TYR HAS REPELLED US.

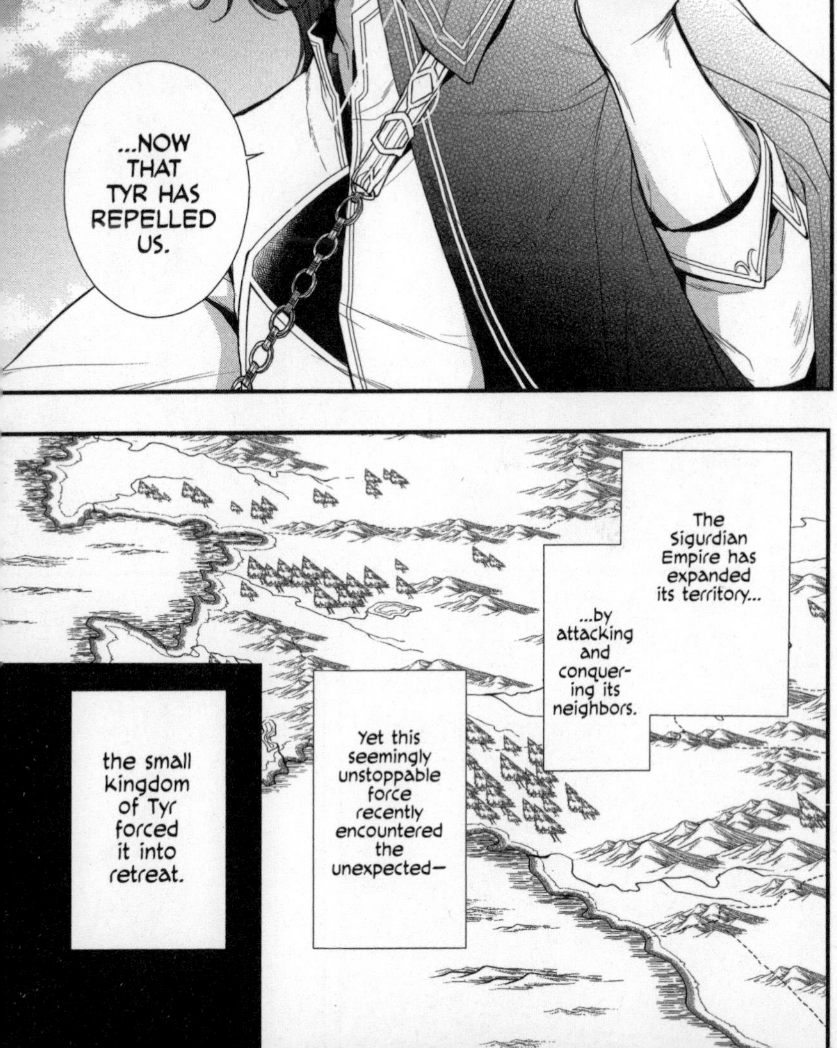
The Sigurdian Empire has expanded its territory...
...by attacking and conquer-ing its neighbors.
Yet this seemingly unstoppable force recently encountered the unexpected—
the small kingdom of Tyr forced it into retreat.

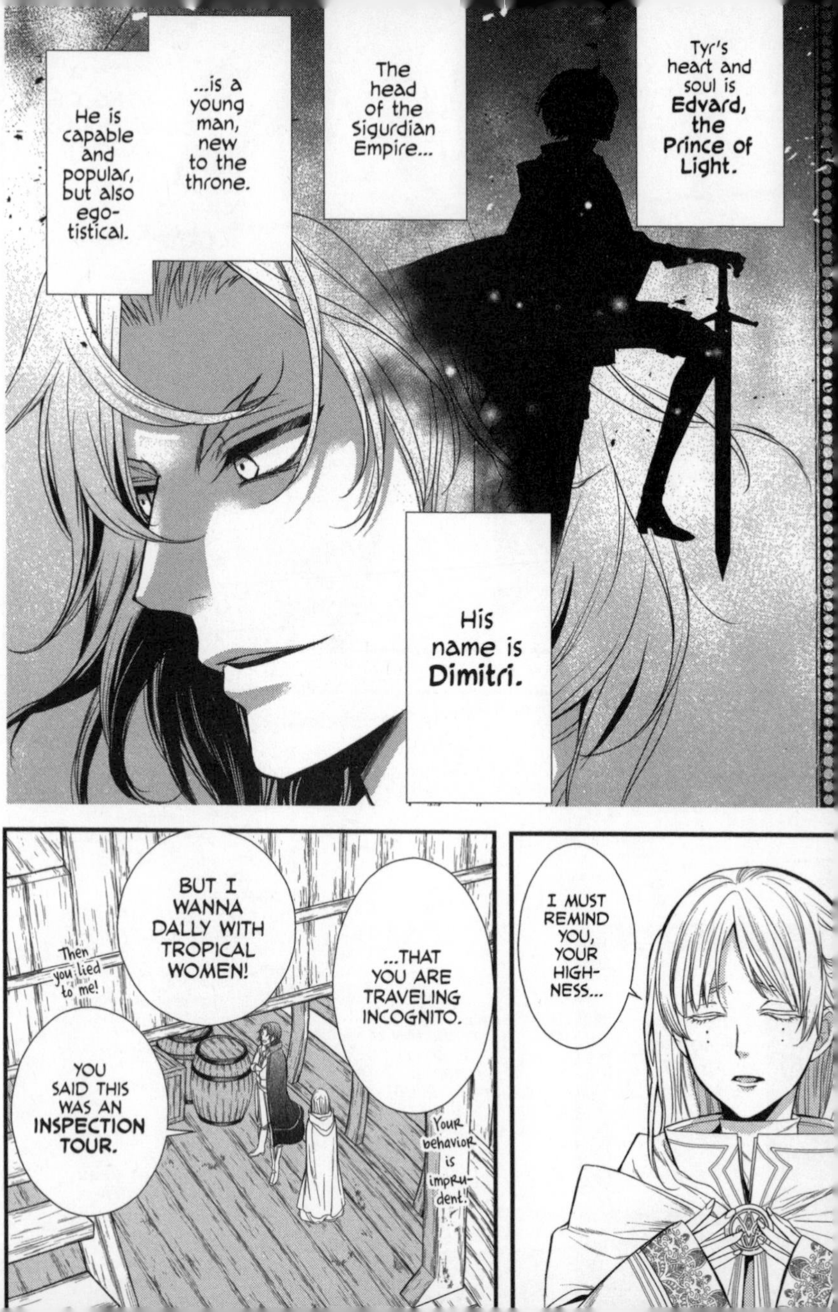

Tyr's heart and soul is **Edvard, the Prince of Light.**
The head of the Sigurdian Empire...
...is a young man, new to the throne.
He is capable and popular, but also ego-tistical.
His name is **Dimitri.**
I MUST REMIND YOU, YOUR HIGH-NESS...
...THAT YOU ARE TRAVELING INCOGNITO.
BUT I WANNA DALLY WITH TROPICAL WOMEN!
Then you lied to me!
YOU SAID THIS WAS AN **INSPECTION TOUR.**
Your behavior is impru-dent!

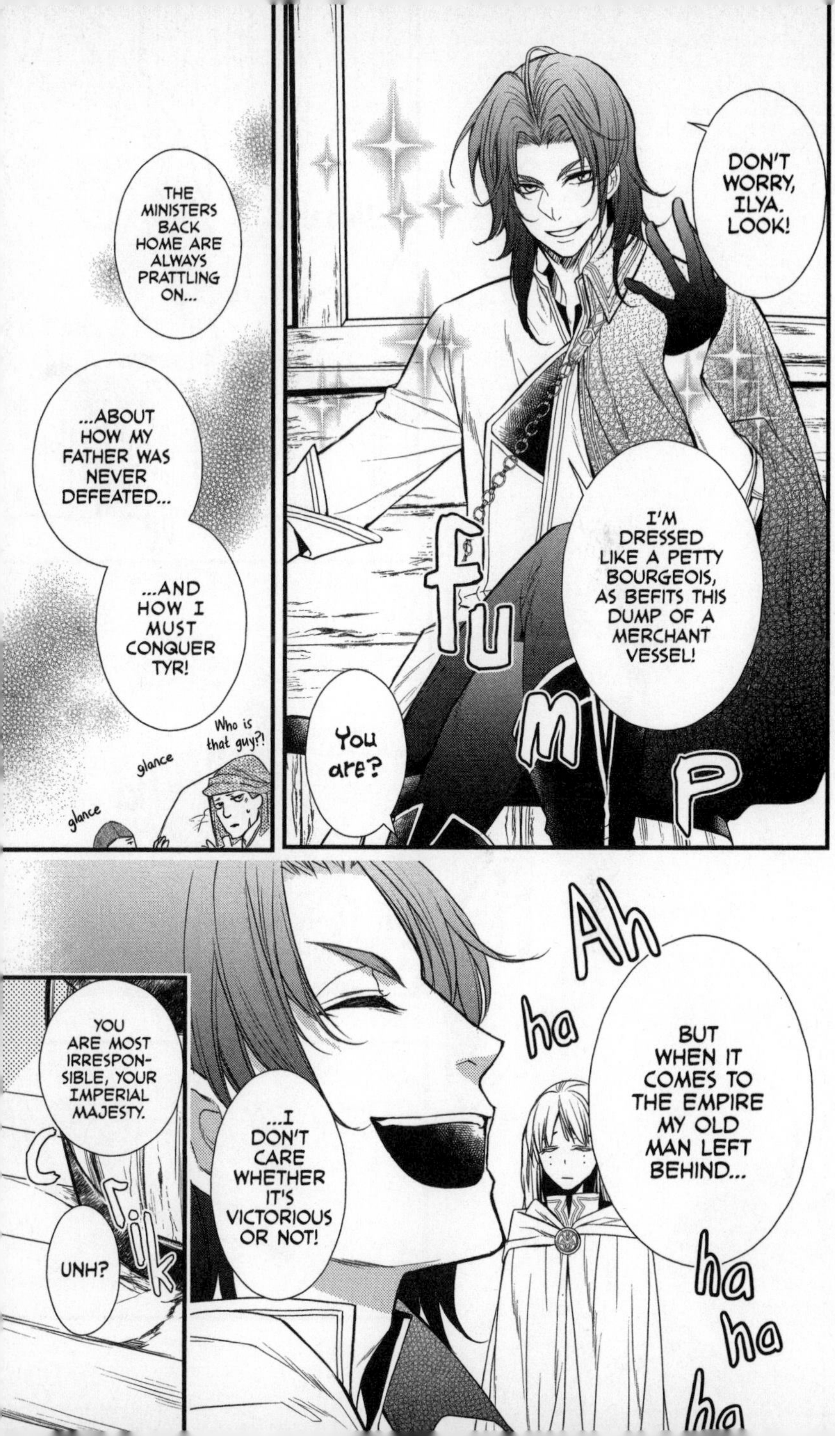
DON'T WORRY, ILYA. LOOK!
I'M DRESSED LIKE A PETTY BOURGEOIS, AS BEFITS THIS DUMP OF A MERCHANT VESSEL!
fumP
You are?
THE MINISTERS BACK HOME ARE ALWAYS PRATTLING ON...
...ABOUT HOW MY FATHER WAS NEVER DEFEATED...
...AND HOW I MUST CONQUER TYR!
Who is that guy?!
glance
glance
Ah ha
BUT WHEN IT COMES TO THE EMPIRE MY OLD MAN LEFT BEHIND...
...I DON'T CARE WHETHER IT'S VICTORIOUS OR NOT!
ha ha ha
YOU ARE MOST IRRESPON-SIBLE, YOUR IMPERIAL MAJESTY.
Crik
UNH?

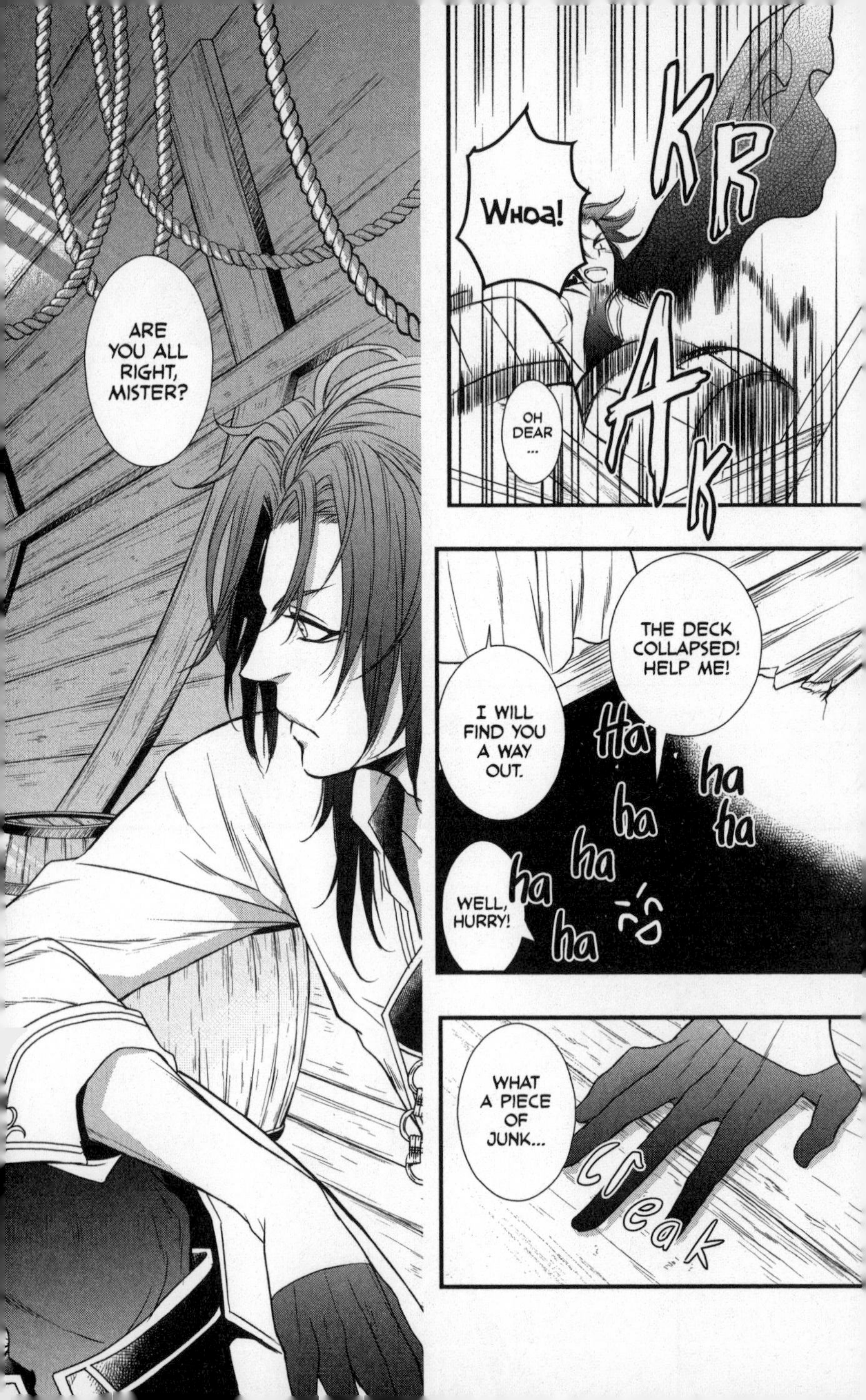
KRAK
WHOA!
OH DEAR ...
THE DECK COLLAPSED! HELP ME!
I WILL FIND YOU A WAY OUT.
ha ha ha ha ha ha ha
WELL, HURRY!
WHAT A PIECE OF JUNK...
creak
ARE YOU ALL RIGHT, MISTER?

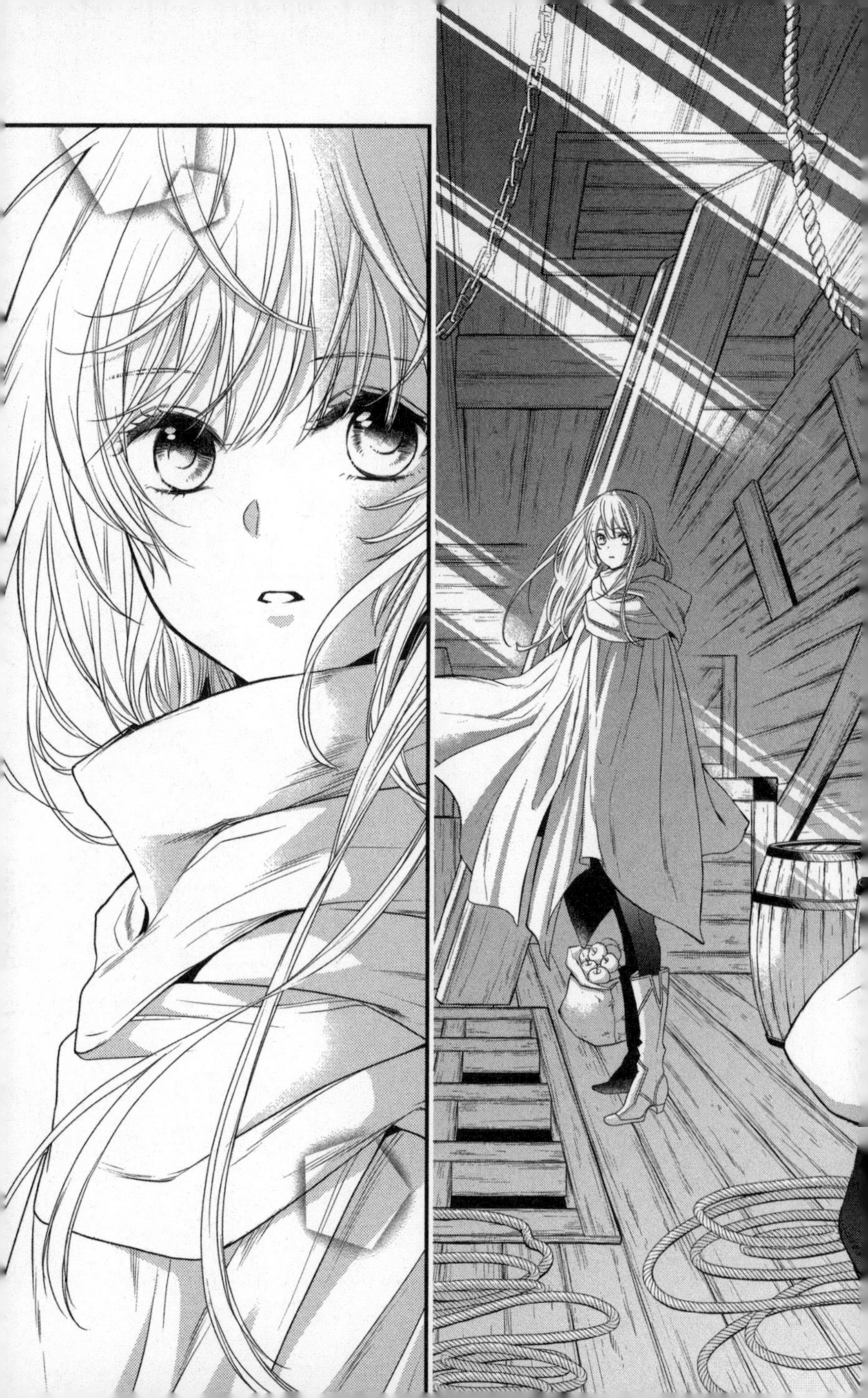

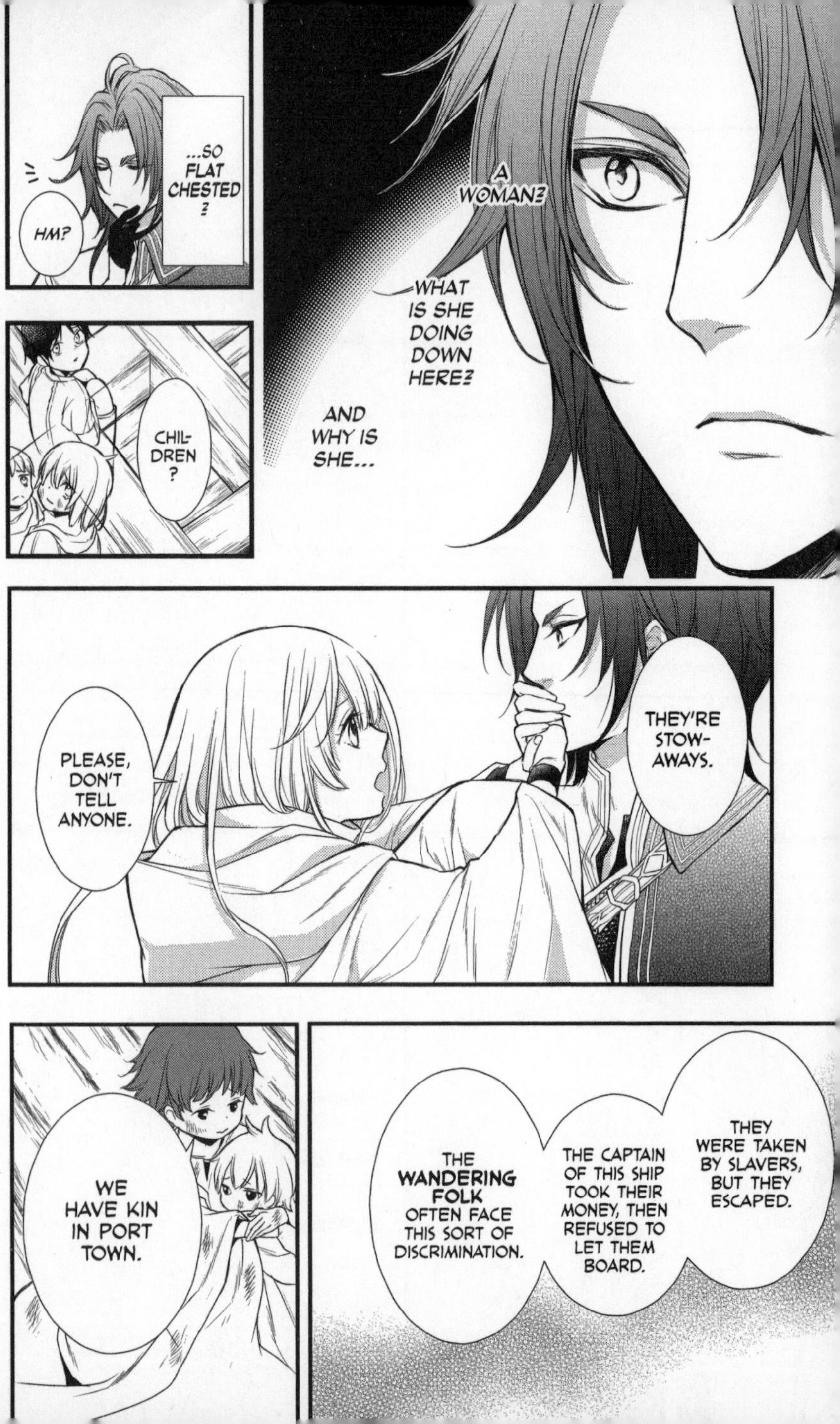
A WOMAN?
WHAT IS SHE DOING DOWN HERE?
AND WHY IS SHE...
...SO FLAT CHESTED?
HM?
CHILDREN?
THEY'RE STOWAWAYS.
PLEASE, DON'T TELL ANYONE.
THEY WERE TAKEN BY SLAVERS, BUT THEY ESCAPED.
THE CAPTAIN OF THIS SHIP TOOK THEIR MONEY, THEN REFUSED TO LET THEM BOARD.
THE **WANDERING FOLK** OFTEN FACE THIS SORT OF DISCRIMINATION.
WE HAVE KIN IN PORT TOWN.

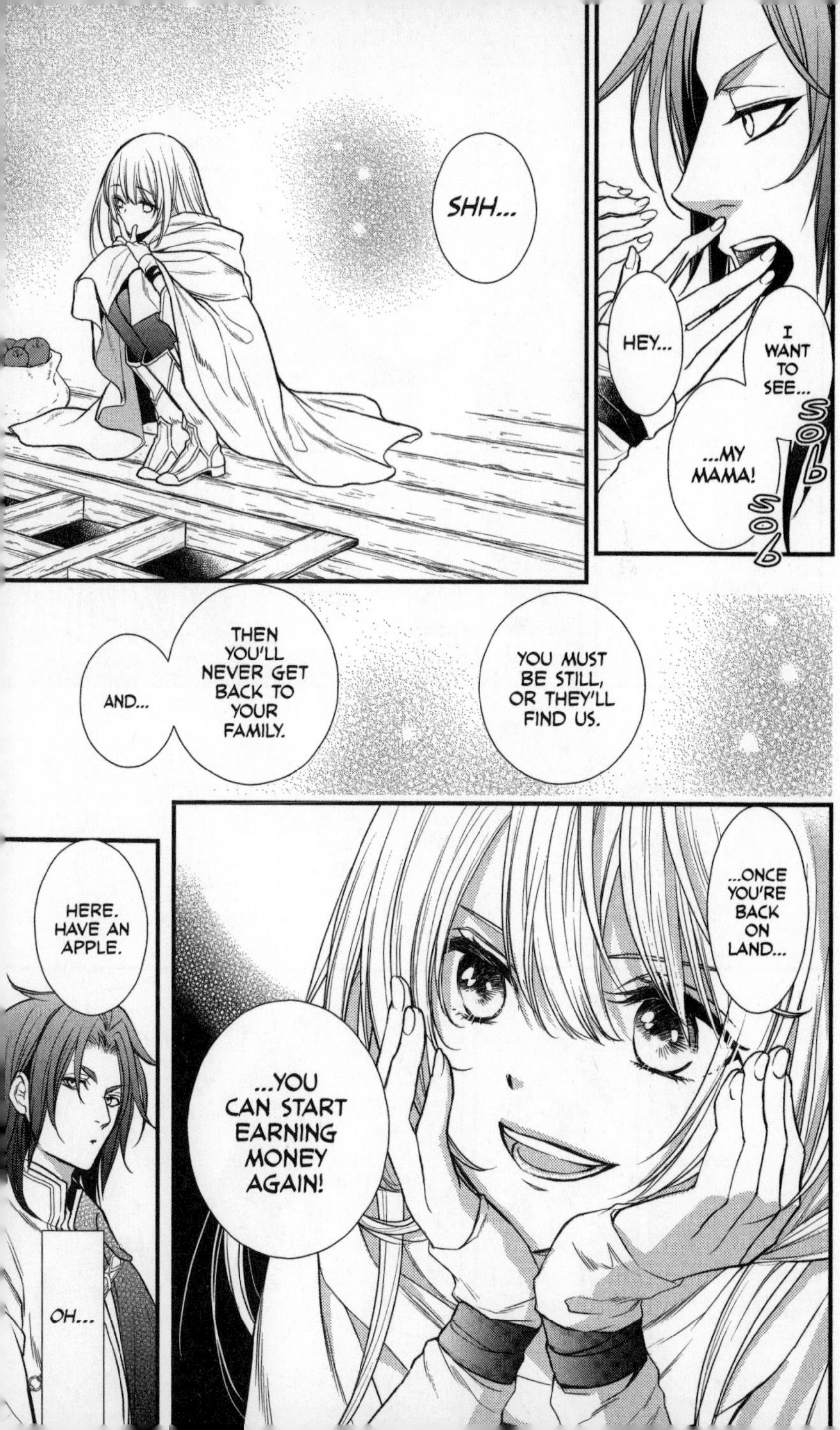
I WANT TO SEE...
SOB
HEY...
...MY MAMA!
SOB
SHH...
YOU MUST BE STILL, OR THEY'LL FIND US.
THEN YOU'LL NEVER GET BACK TO YOUR FAMILY.
AND...
...ONCE YOU'RE BACK ON LAND...
...YOU CAN START EARNING MONEY AGAIN!
HERE. HAVE AN APPLE.
OH...

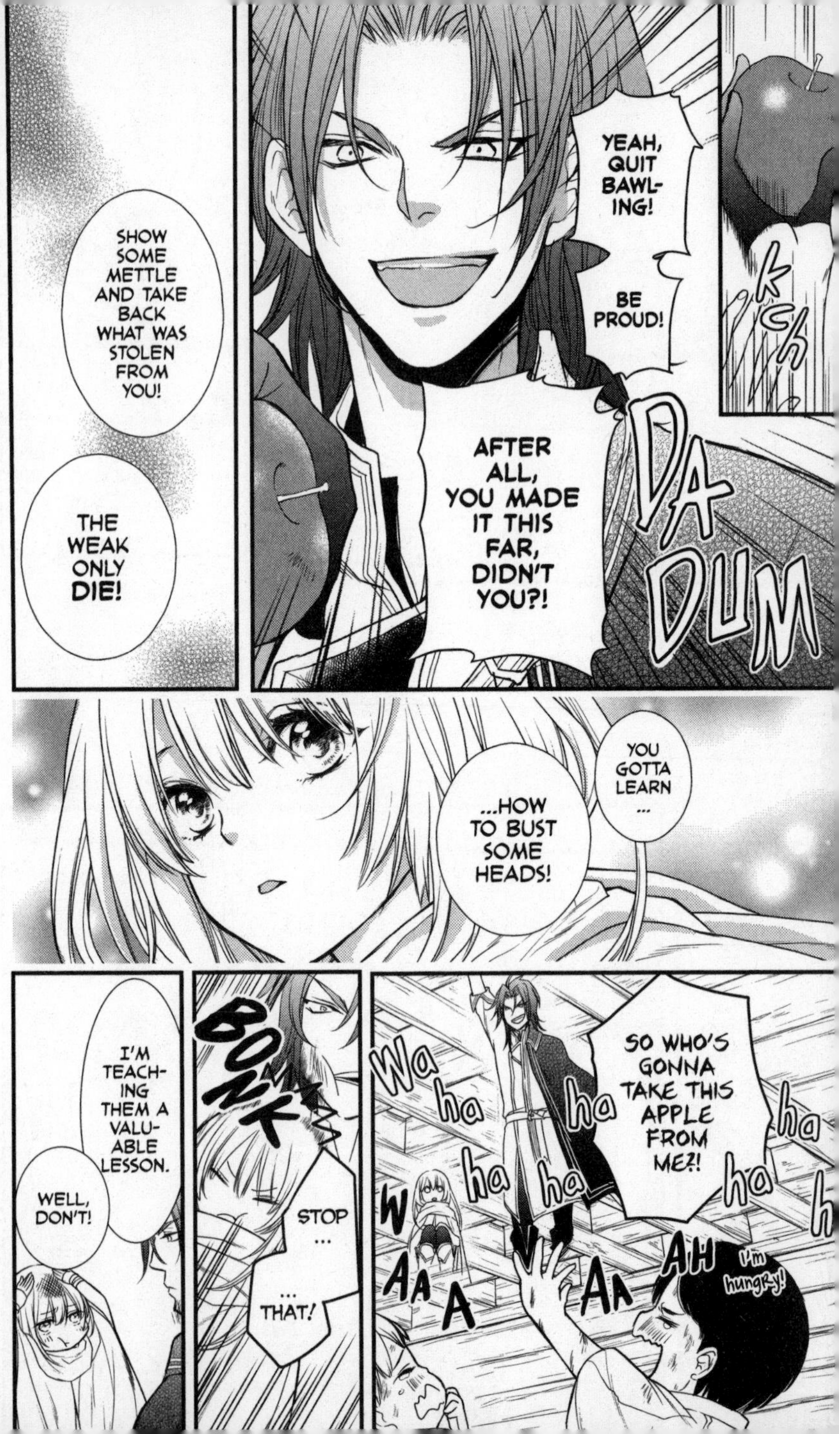
kch
YEAH, QUIT BAWL-ING!
BE PROUD!
AFTER ALL, YOU MADE IT THIS FAR, DIDN'T YOU?!
DA DUM
SHOW SOME METTLE AND TAKE BACK WHAT WAS STOLEN FROM YOU!
THE WEAK ONLY DIE!
YOU GOTTA LEARN...
...HOW TO BUST SOME HEADS!
SO WHO'S GONNA TAKE THIS APPLE FROM ME?!
Wa ha ha ha ha ha ha ha h
WAAAAAH
I'm hungry!
BONK
STOP...
...THAT!
I'M TEACH-ING THEM A VALU-ABLE LESSON.
WELL, DON'T!

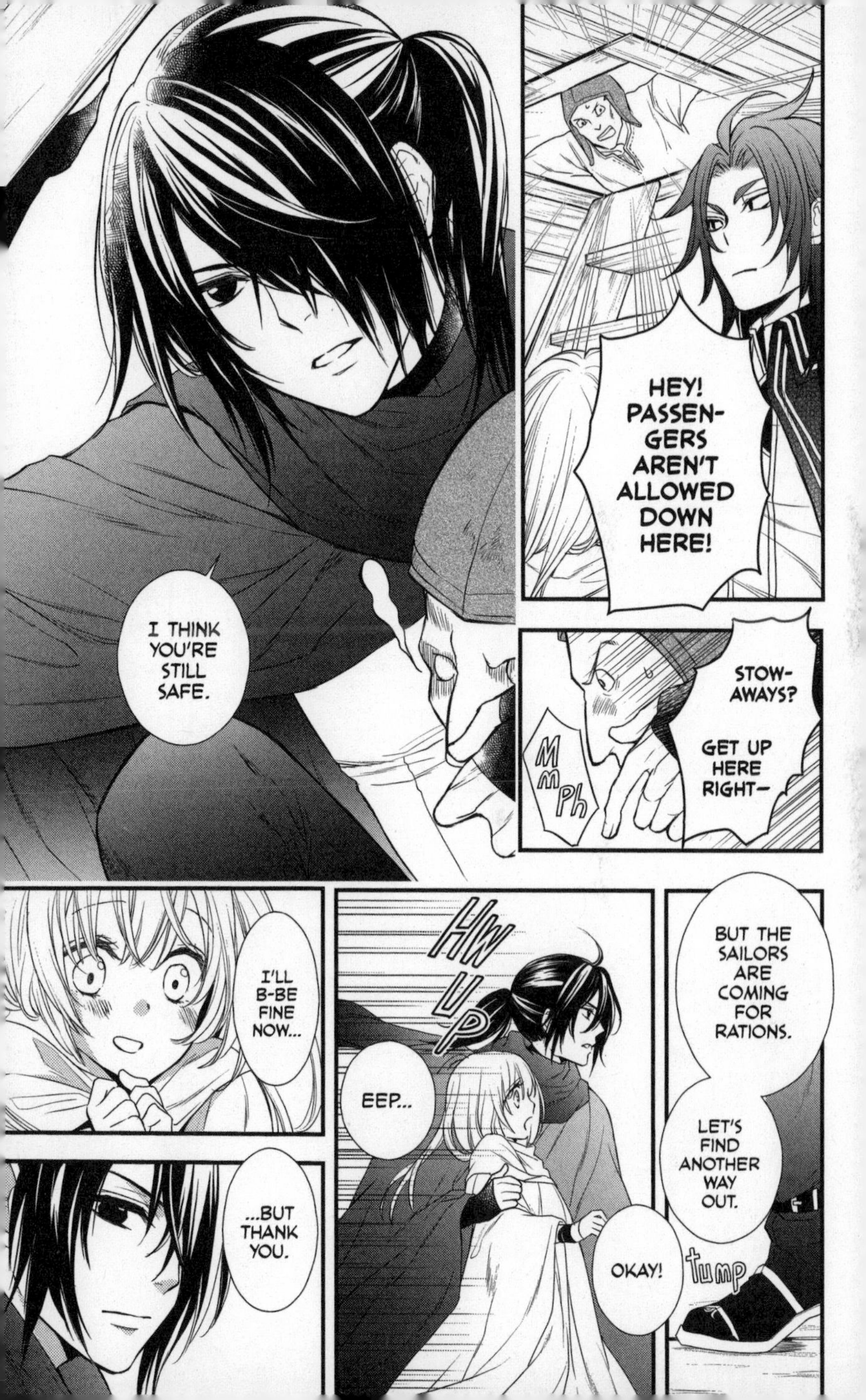
HEY! PASSENGERS AREN'T ALLOWED DOWN HERE!
STOW-AWAYS?
GET UP HERE RIGHT—
MMPH
I THINK YOU'RE STILL SAFE.
BUT THE SAILORS ARE COMING FOR RATIONS.
LET'S FIND ANOTHER WAY OUT.
TUMP
HWUP
EEP...
OKAY!
I'LL B-BE FINE NOW...
...BUT THANK YOU.

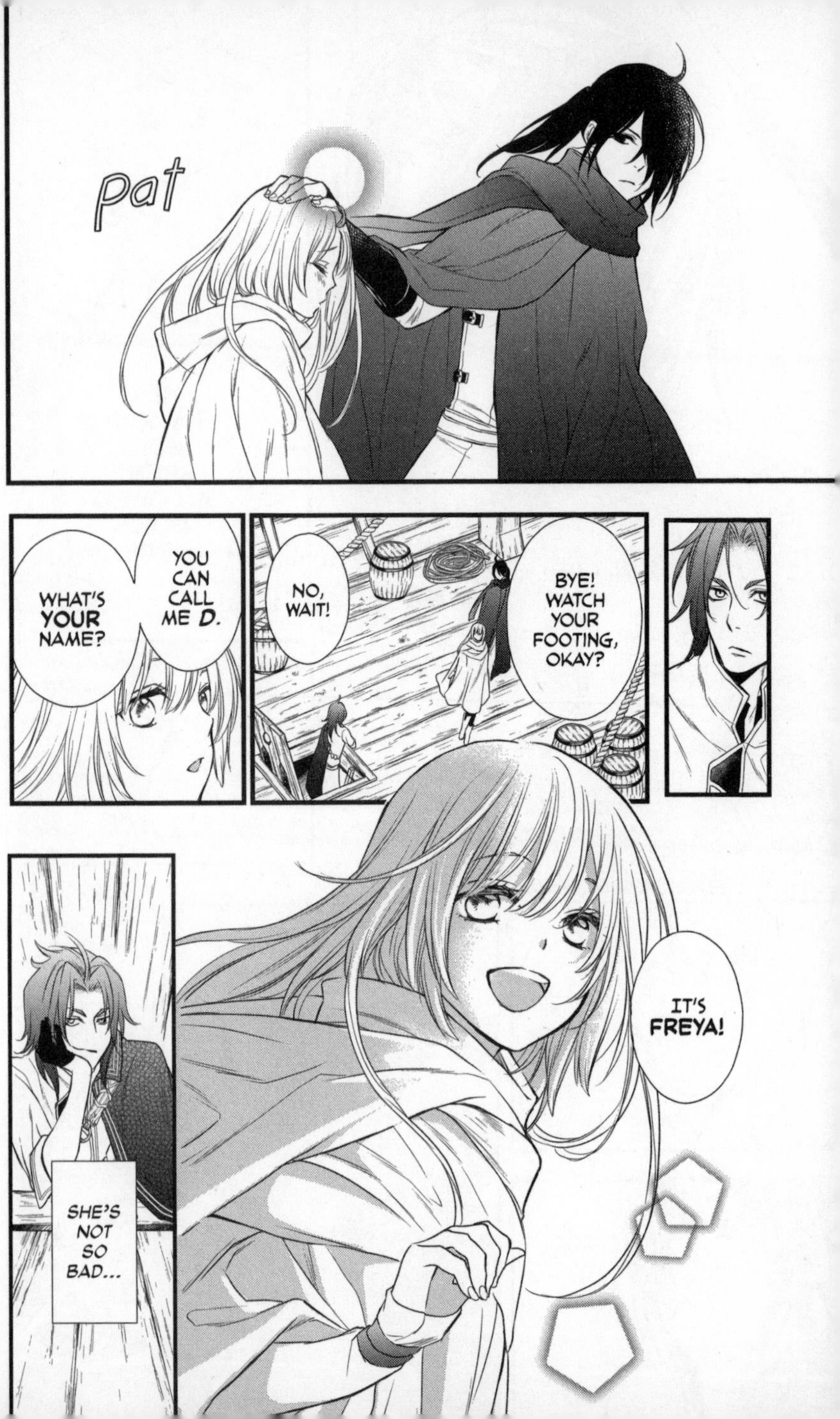
pat
BYE! WATCH YOUR FOOTING, OKAY?
NO, WAIT!
YOU CAN CALL ME D.
WHAT'S YOUR NAME?
IT'S FREYA!
SHE'S NOT SO BAD...

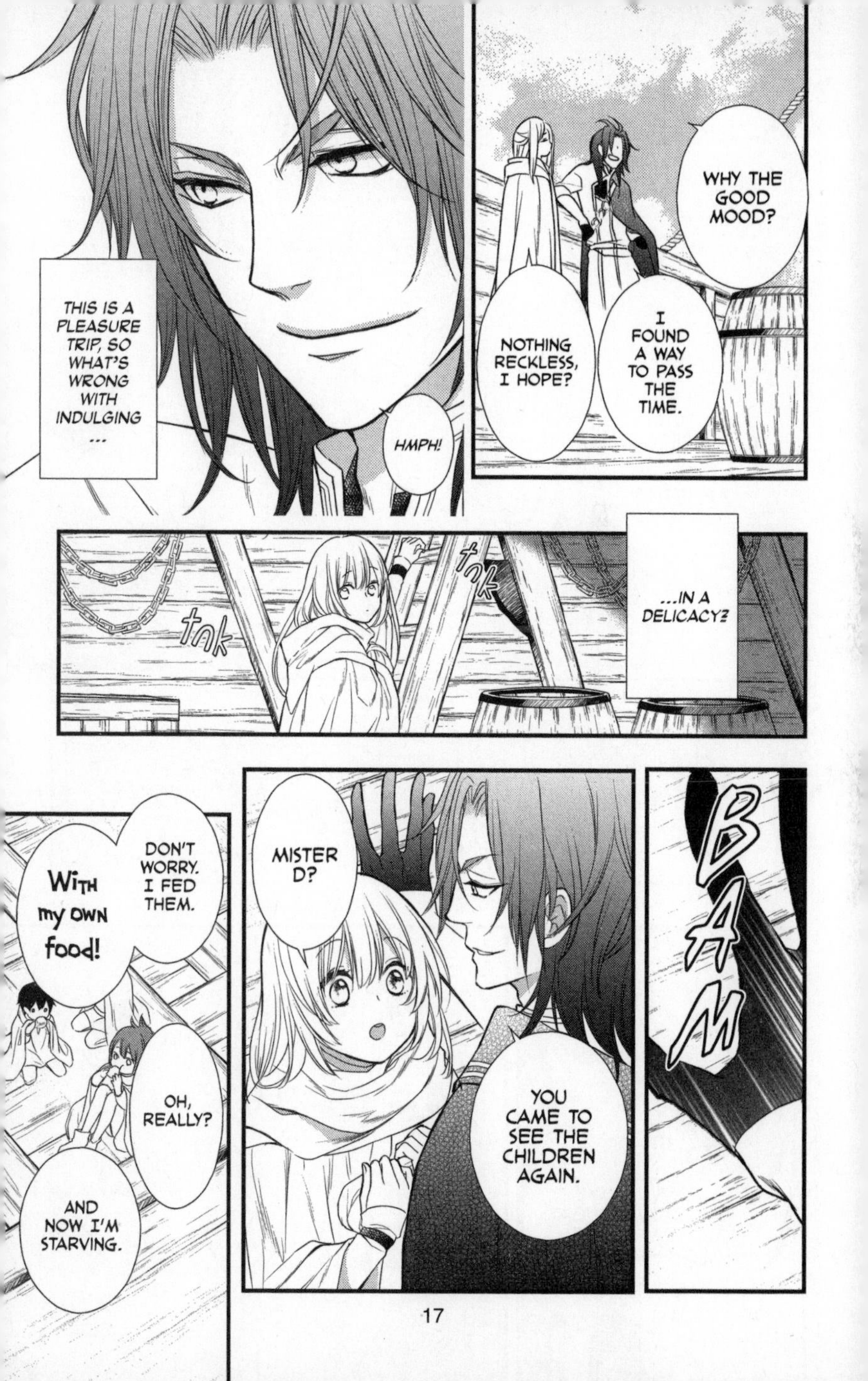
WHY THE GOOD MOOD?
I FOUND A WAY TO PASS THE TIME.
NOTHING RECKLESS, I HOPE?
HMPH!
THIS IS A PLEASURE TRIP, SO WHAT'S WRONG WITH INDULGING ...
...IN A DELICACY?
tnk
tnk
BAM
MISTER D?
YOU CAME TO SEE THE CHILDREN AGAIN.
DON'T WORRY. I FED THEM.
With my own food!
OH, REALLY?
AND NOW I'M STARVING.

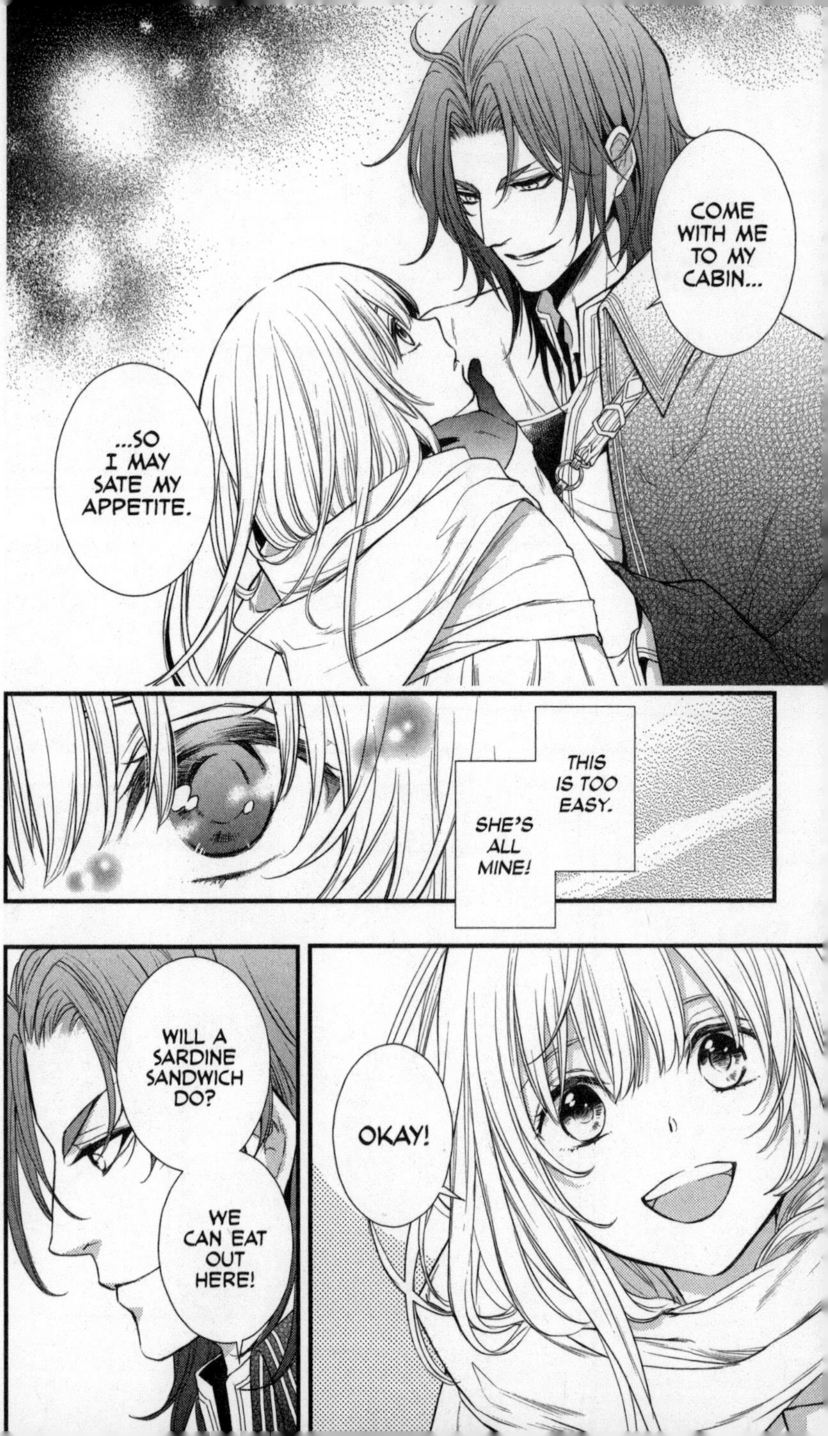
COME WITH ME TO MY CABIN...
...SO I MAY SATE MY APPETITE.
THIS IS TOO EASY.
SHE'S ALL MINE!
OKAY!
WILL A SARDINE SANDWICH DO?
WE CAN EAT OUT HERE!

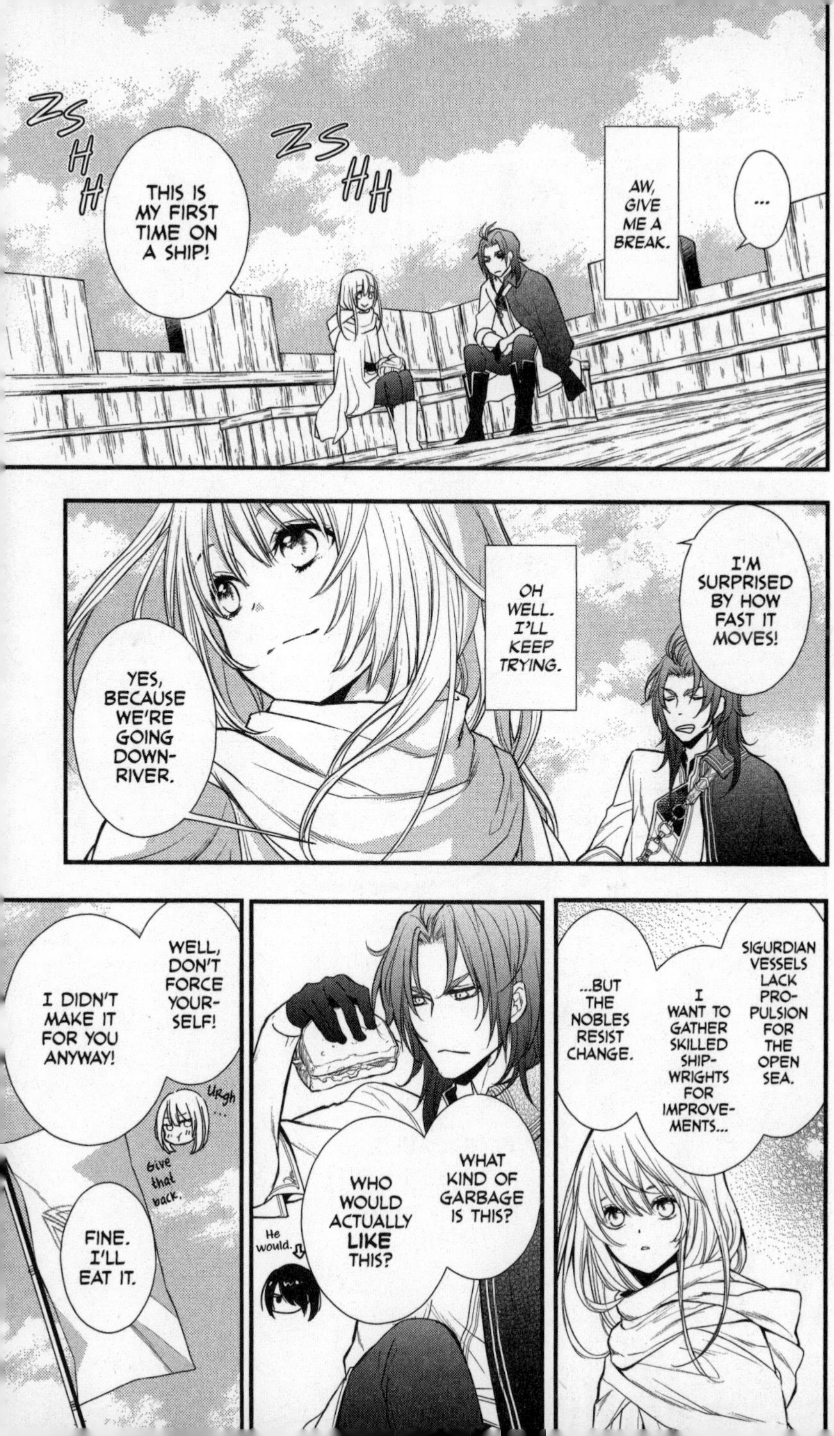
...
AW, GIVE ME A BREAK.
ZSHH
THIS IS MY FIRST TIME ON A SHIP!
ZSHH
I'M SURPRISED BY HOW FAST IT MOVES!
OH WELL. I'LL KEEP TRYING.
YES, BECAUSE WE'RE GOING DOWNRIVER.
SIGURDIAN VESSELS LACK PROPULSION FOR THE OPEN SEA.
I WANT TO GATHER SKILLED SHIPWRIGHTS FOR IMPROVEMENTS...
...BUT THE NOBLES RESIST CHANGE.
WHAT KIND OF GARBAGE IS THIS?
WHO WOULD ACTUALLY **LIKE** THIS?
He would.
WELL, DON'T FORCE YOURSELF!
I DIDN'T MAKE IT FOR YOU ANYWAY!
Urgh...
Give that back.
FINE. I'LL EAT IT.

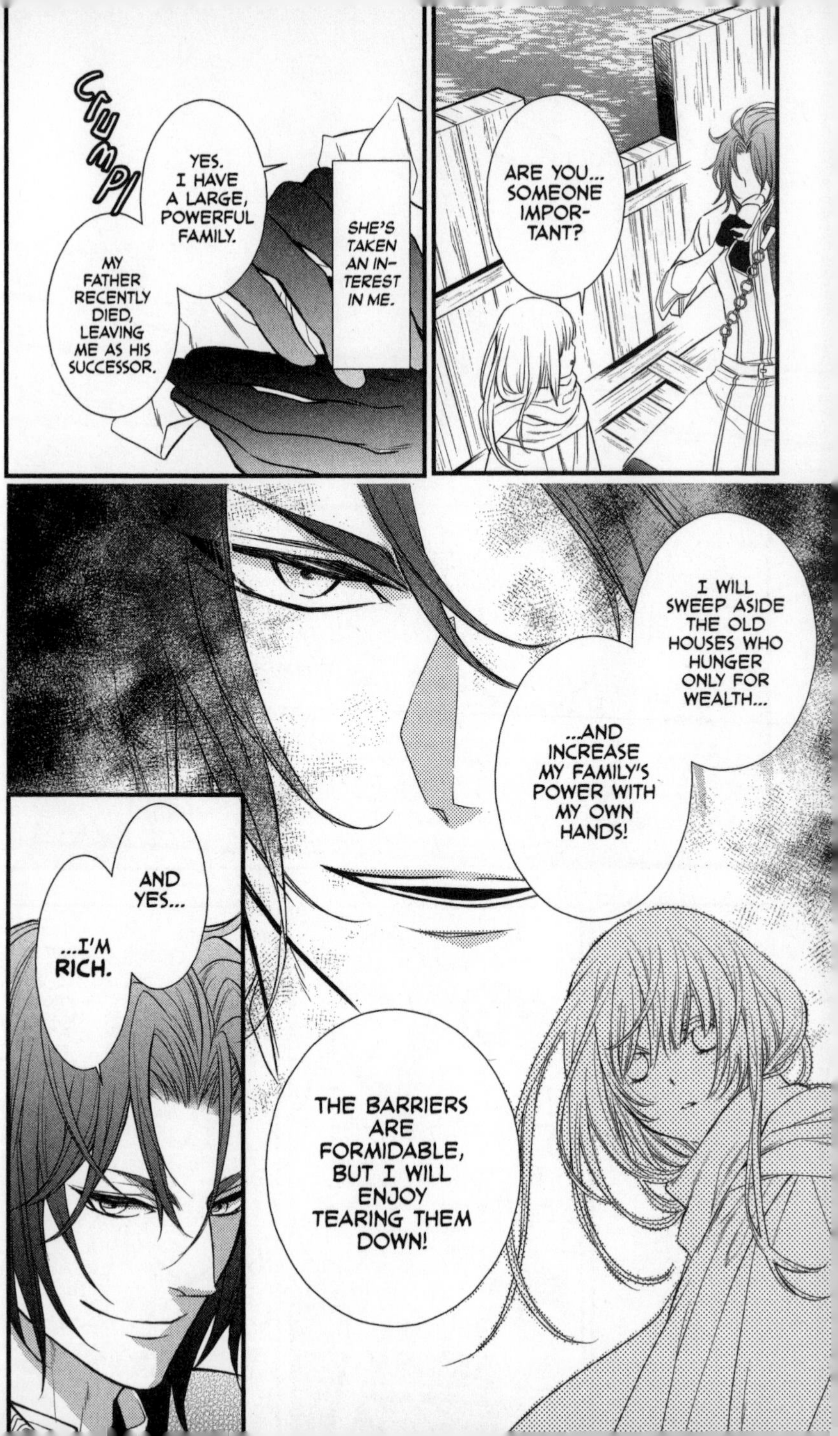
ARE YOU... SOMEONE IMPORTANT?
SHE'S TAKEN AN INTEREST IN ME.
YES. I HAVE A LARGE, POWERFUL FAMILY.
MY FATHER RECENTLY DIED, LEAVING ME AS HIS SUCCESSOR.
CRUMP!
I WILL SWEEP ASIDE THE OLD HOUSES WHO HUNGER ONLY FOR WEALTH...
...AND INCREASE MY FAMILY'S POWER WITH MY OWN HANDS!
THE BARRIERS ARE FORMIDABLE, BUT I WILL ENJOY TEARING THEM DOWN!
AND YES...
...I'M RICH.

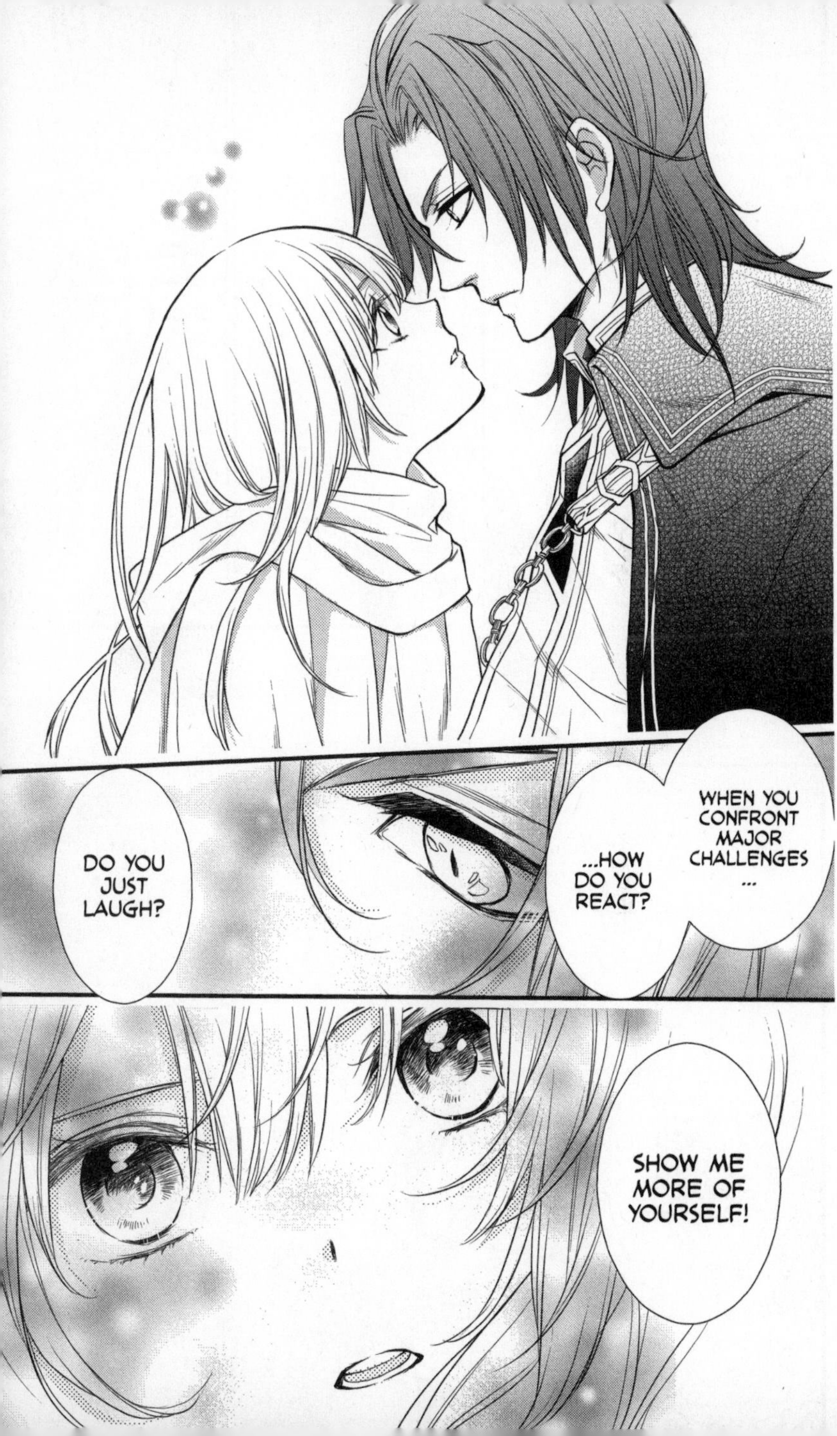
WHEN YOU CONFRONT MAJOR CHALLENGES ...
...HOW DO YOU REACT?
DO YOU JUST LAUGH?
SHOW ME MORE OF YOURSELF!

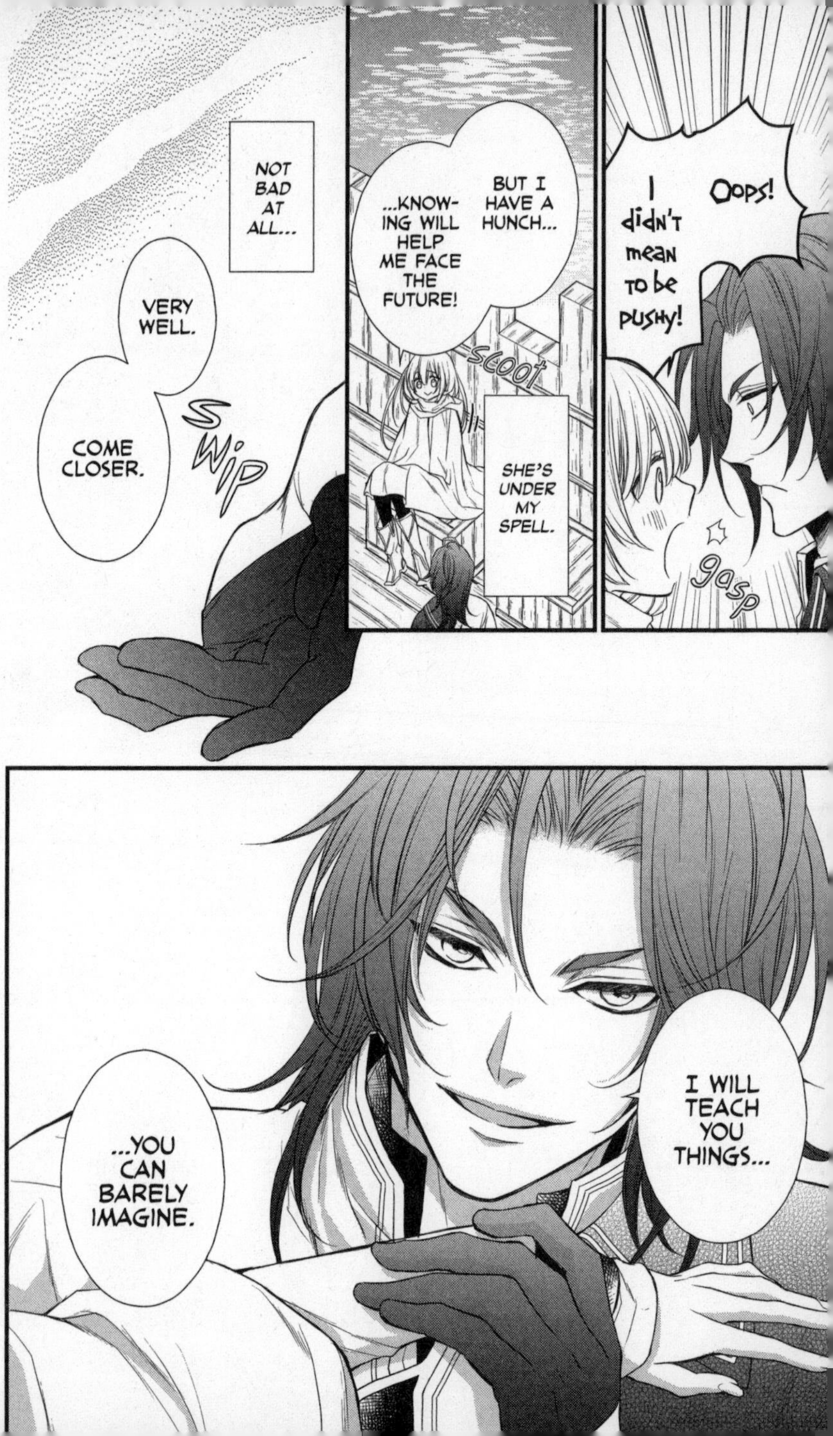
Oops!
I didn't mean to be pushy!
gasp
BUT I HAVE A HUNCH...
...KNOW-ING WILL HELP ME FACE THE FUTURE!
scoot
SHE'S UNDER MY SPELL.
NOT BAD AT ALL...
VERY WELL.
COME CLOSER.
SWIP
I WILL TEACH YOU THINGS...
...YOU CAN BARELY IMAGINE.

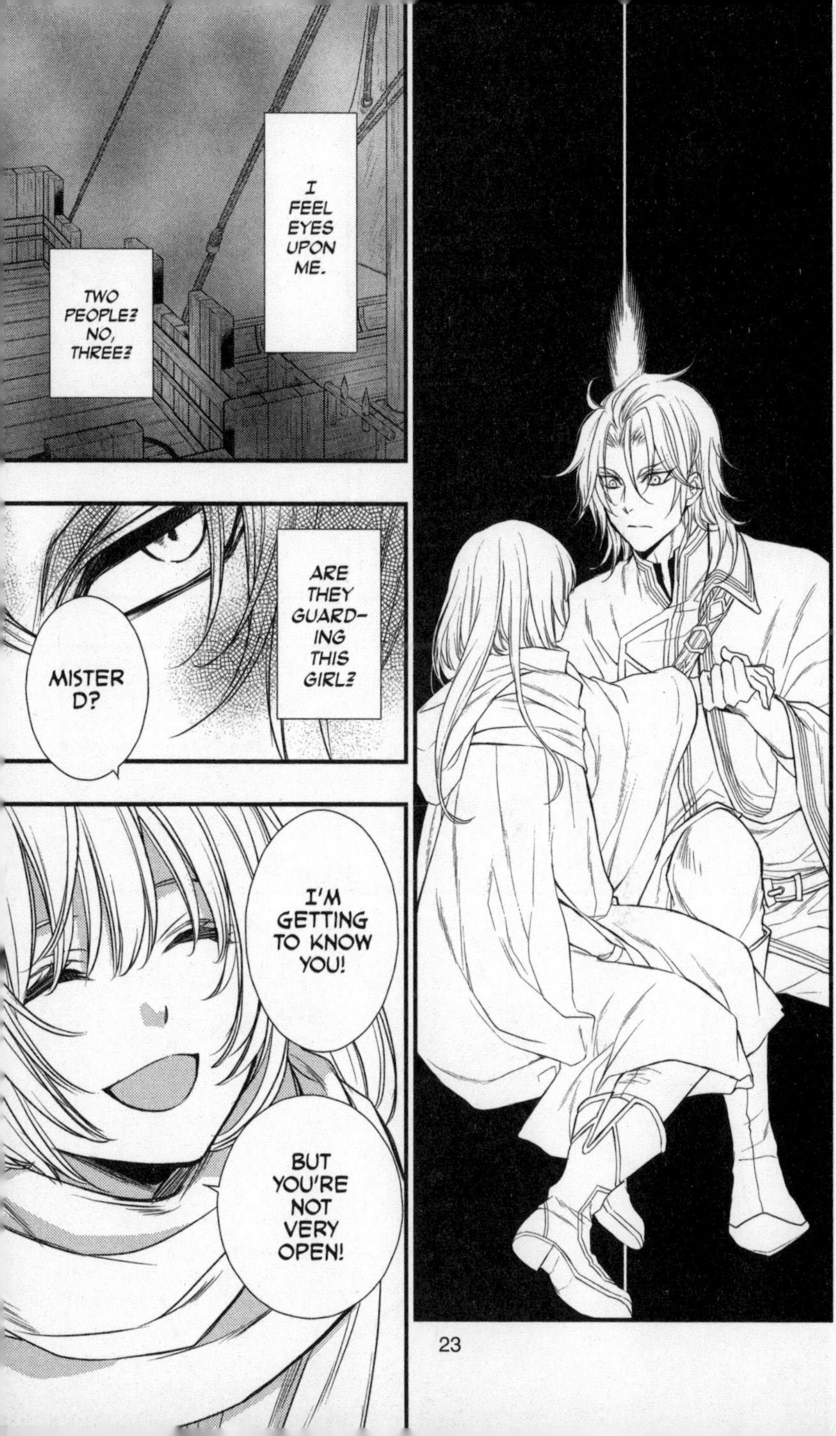
I FEEL EYES UPON ME.
TWO PEOPLE? NO, THREE?
ARE THEY GUARDING THIS GIRL?
MISTER D?
I'M GETTING TO KNOW YOU!
BUT YOU'RE NOT VERY OPEN!

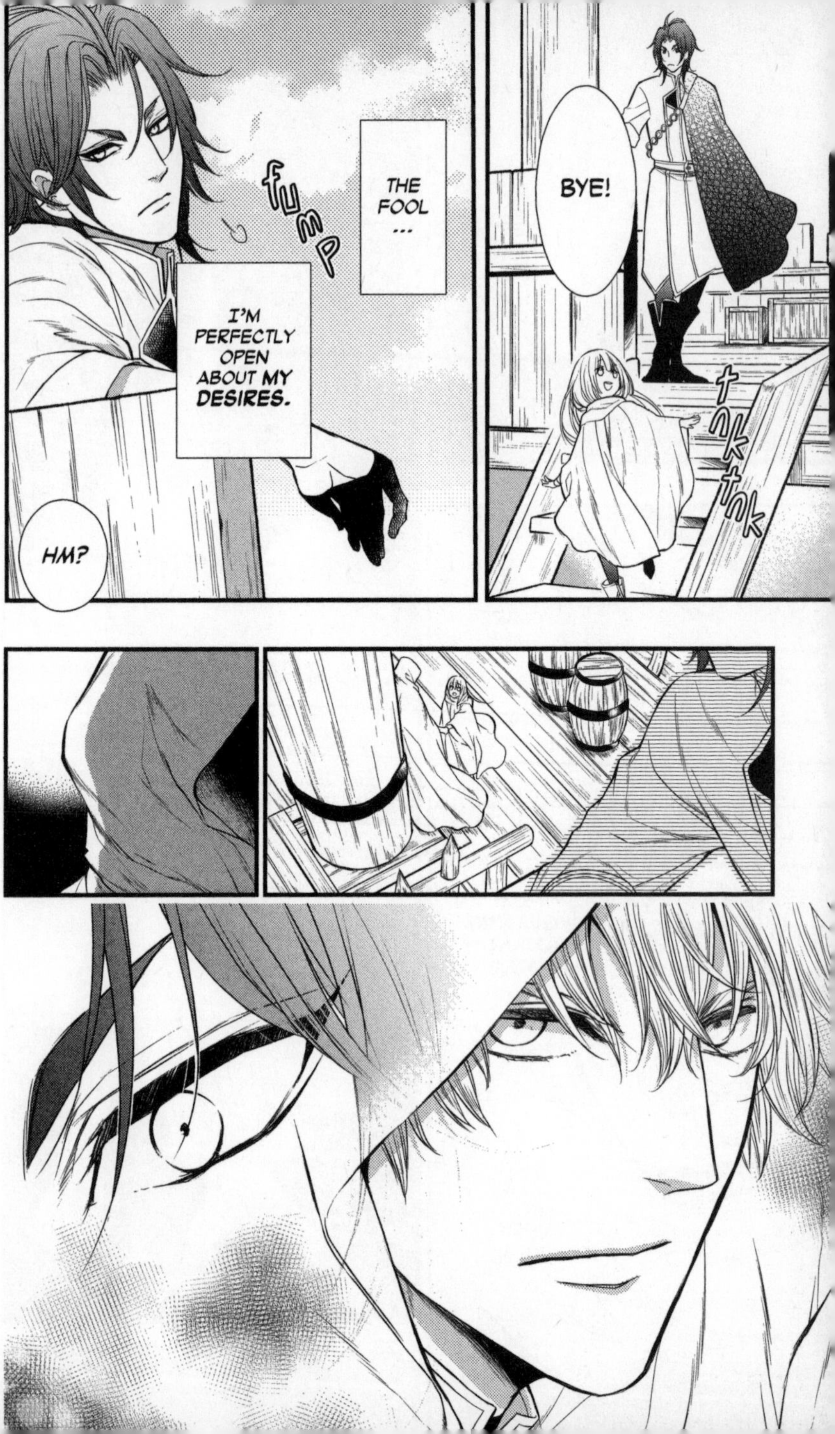
BYE!
tnk tnk
THE FOOL ...
fump
I'M PERFECTLY OPEN ABOUT MY DESIRES.
HM?

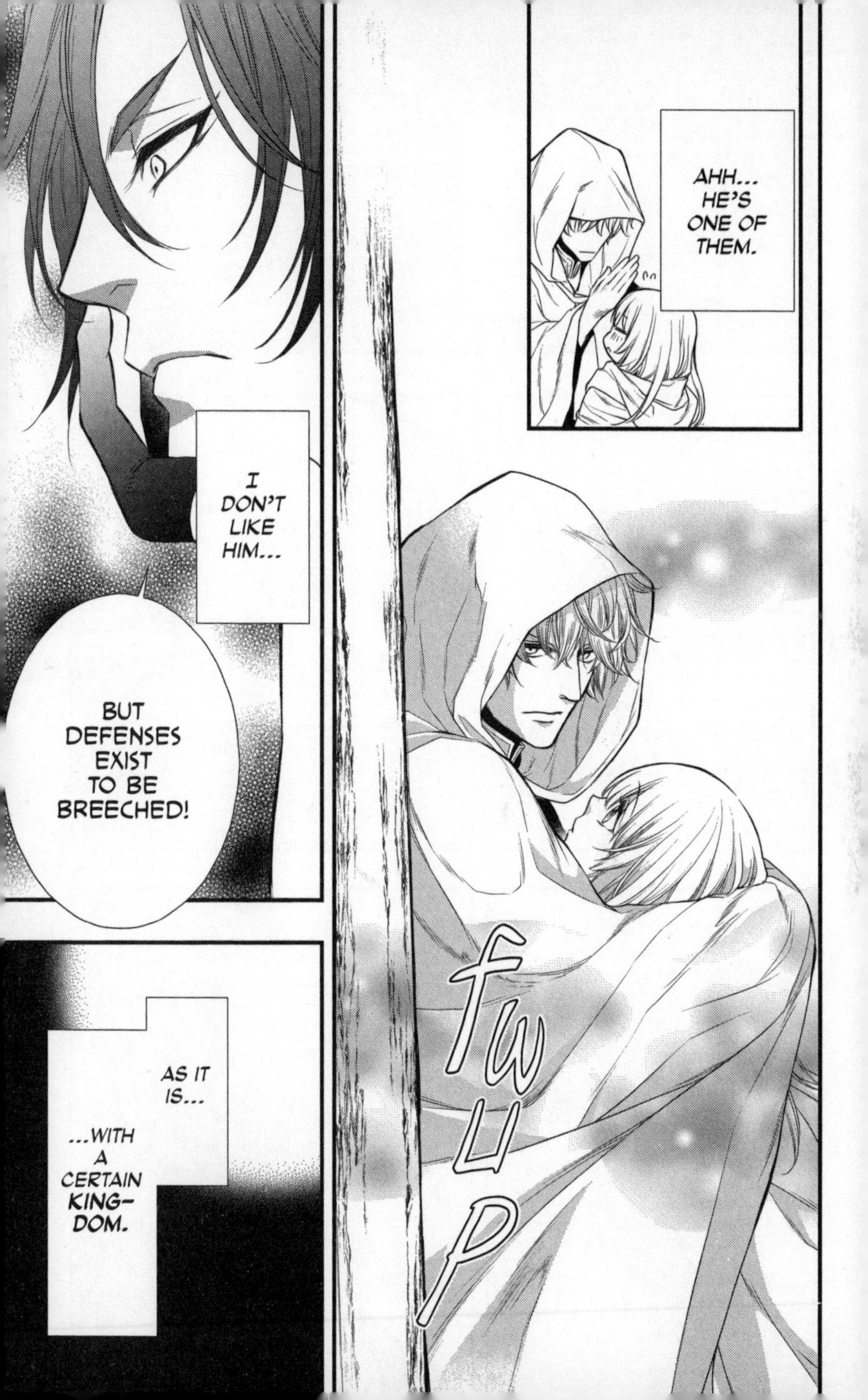
AHH... HE'S ONE OF THEM.
fwup
I DON'T LIKE HIM...
BUT DEFENSES EXIST TO BE BREECHED!
AS IT IS...
...WITH A CERTAIN KINGDOM.

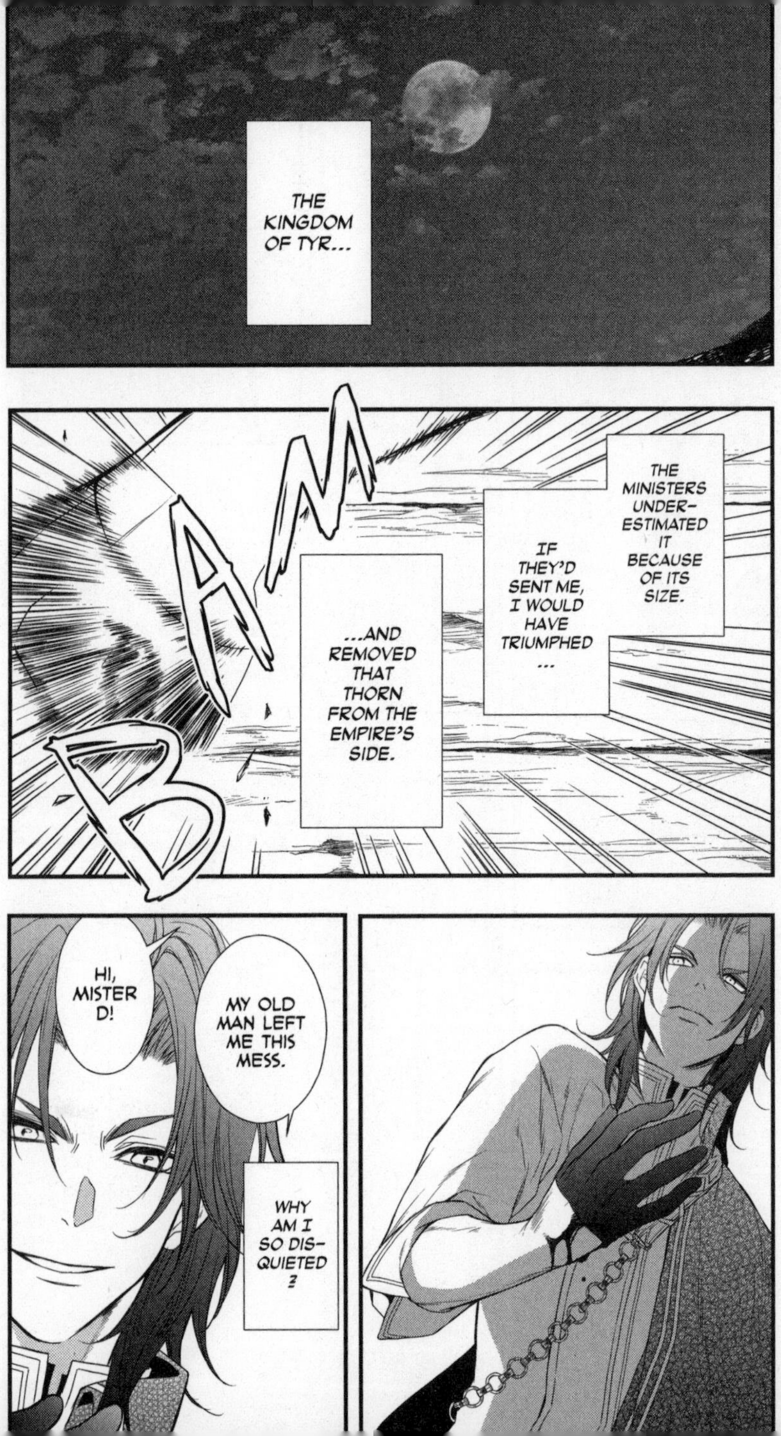
THE KINGDOM OF TYR...
THE MINISTERS UNDER-ESTIMATED IT BECAUSE OF ITS SIZE.
IF THEY'D SENT ME, I WOULD HAVE TRIUMPHED...
...AND REMOVED THAT THORN FROM THE EMPIRE'S SIDE.
BAM
HI, MISTER D!
MY OLD MAN LEFT ME THIS MESS.
WHY AM I SO DIS-QUIETED?

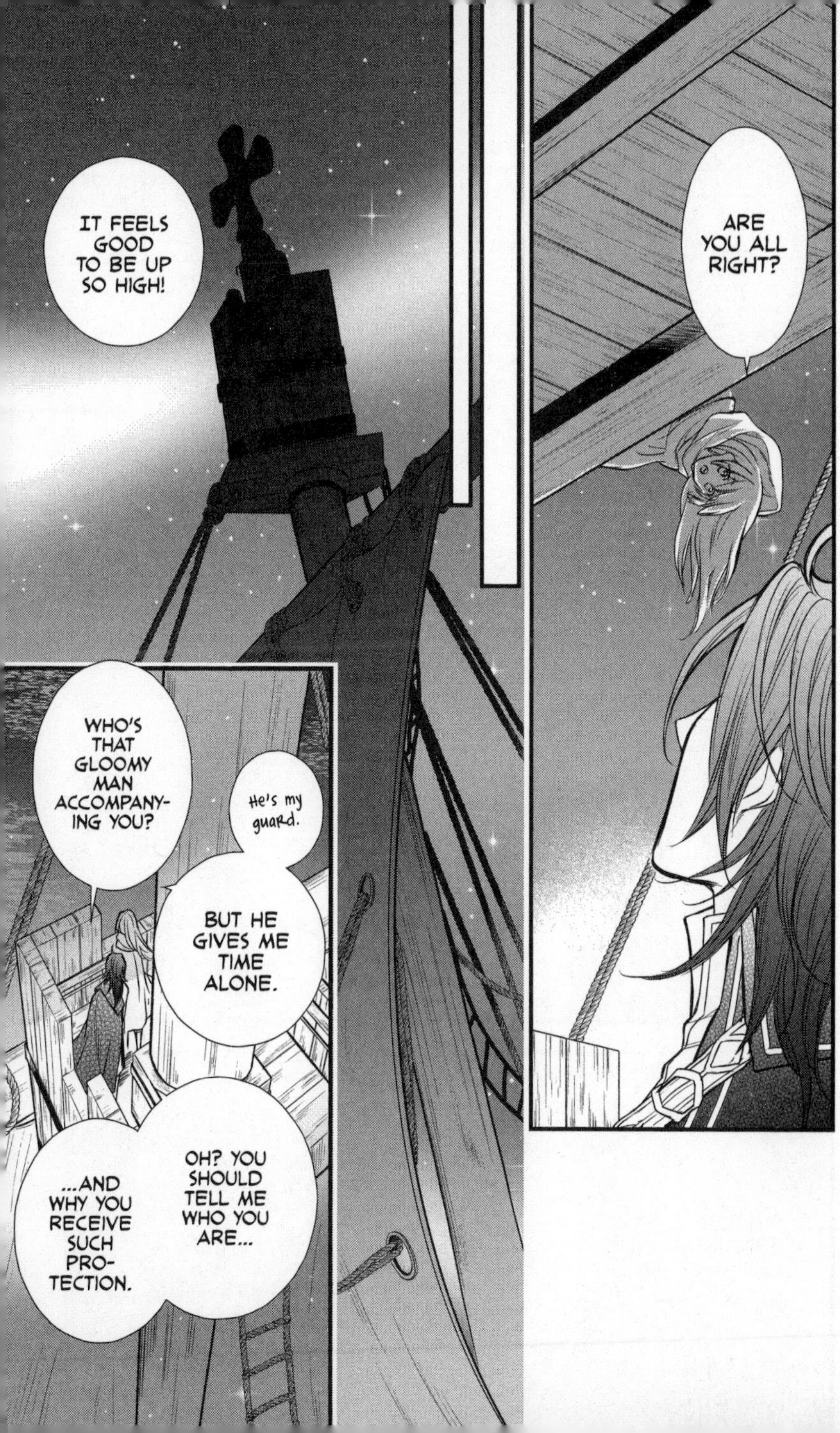
ARE YOU ALL RIGHT?
IT FEELS GOOD TO BE UP SO HIGH!
WHO'S THAT GLOOMY MAN ACCOMPANYING YOU?
He's my guard.
BUT HE GIVES ME TIME ALONE.
OH? YOU SHOULD TELL ME WHO YOU ARE...
...AND WHY YOU RECEIVE SUCH PROTECTION.

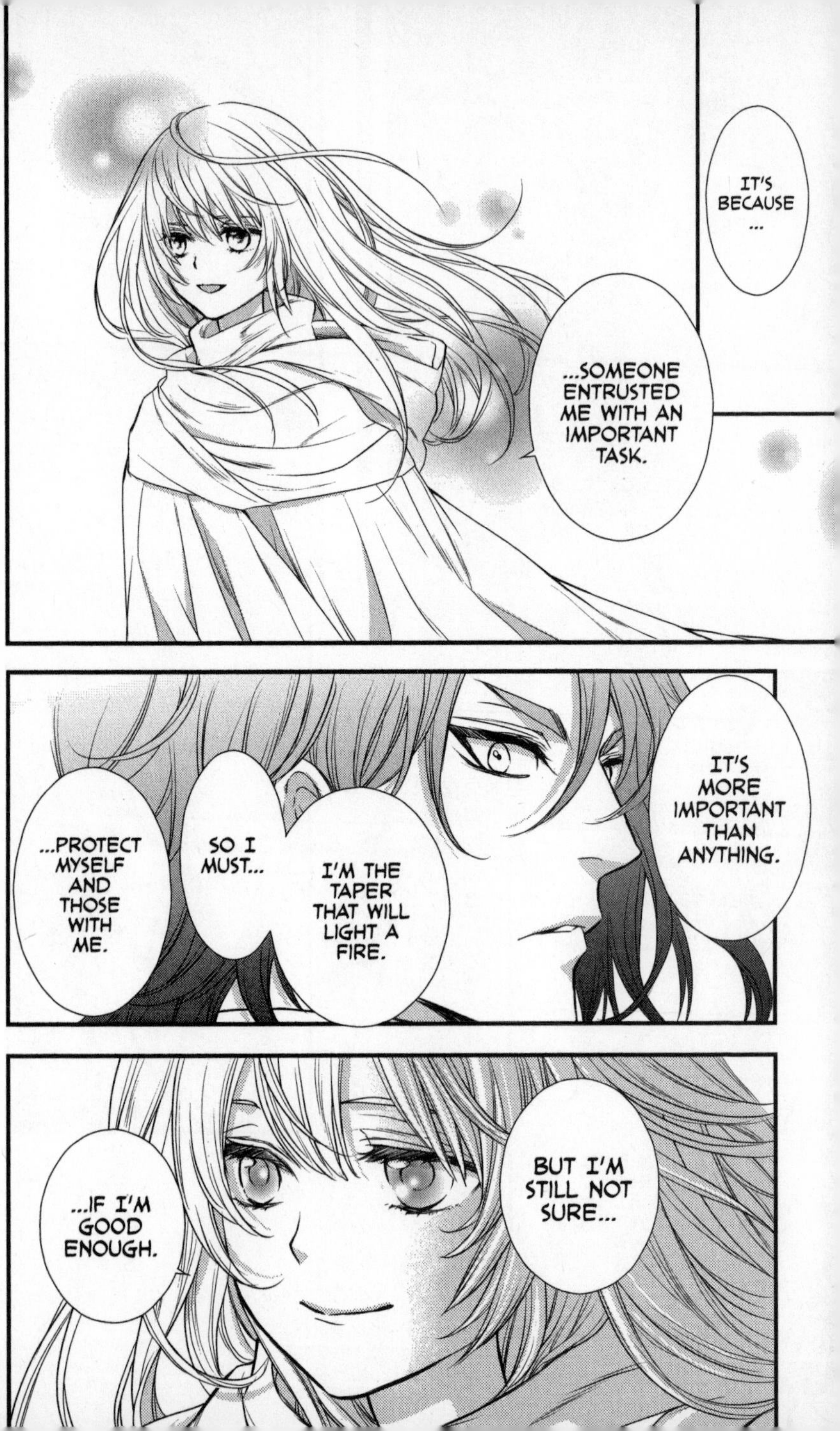
IT'S BECAUSE ...
...SOMEONE ENTRUSTED ME WITH AN IMPORTANT TASK.
IT'S MORE IMPORTANT THAN ANYTHING.
I'M THE TAPER THAT WILL LIGHT A FIRE.
SO I MUST...
...PROTECT MYSELF AND THOSE WITH ME.
BUT I'M STILL NOT SURE...
...IF I'M GOOD ENOUGH.

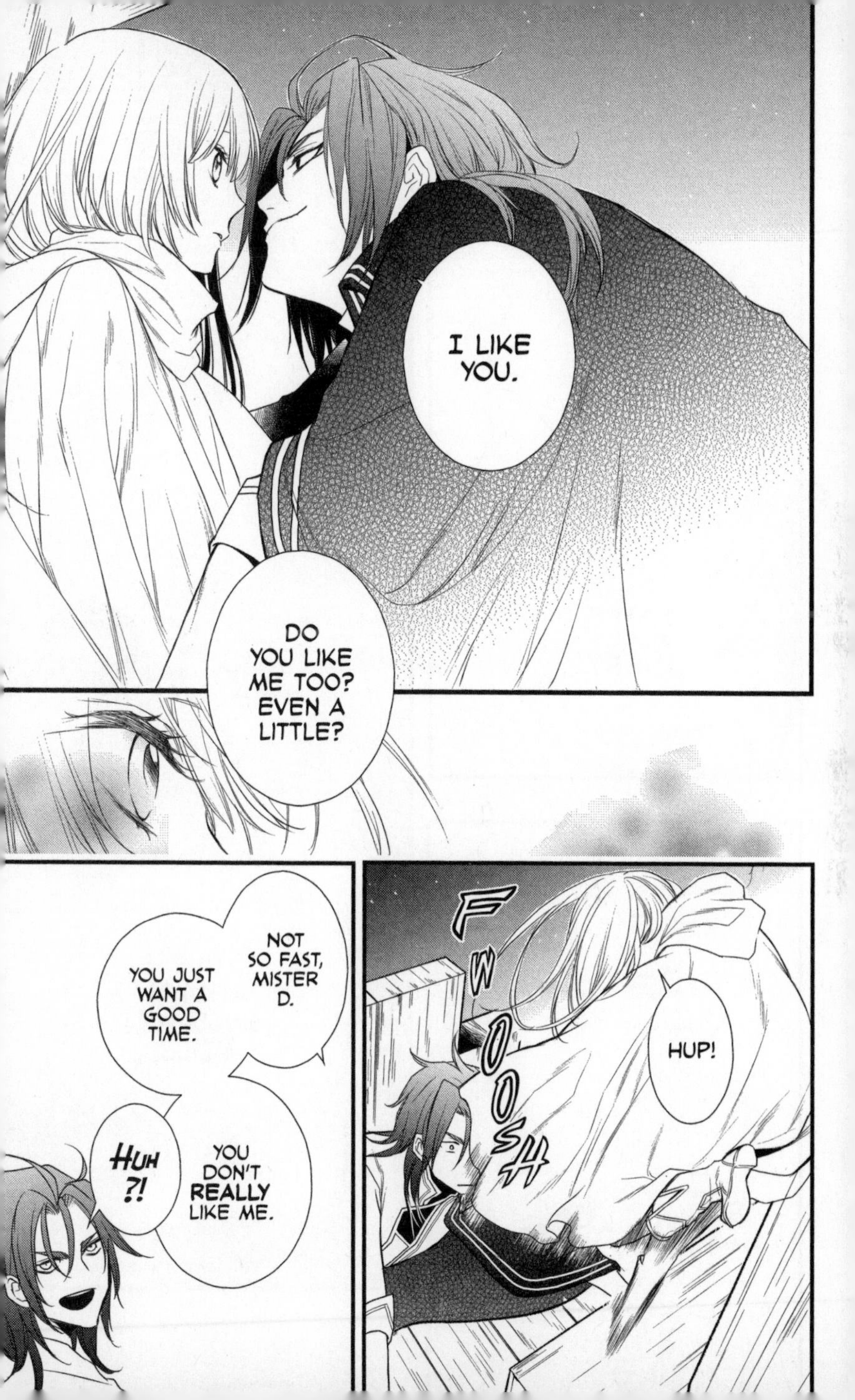
I LIKE YOU.
DO YOU LIKE ME TOO? EVEN A LITTLE?
FWOOSH
HUP!
NOT SO FAST, MISTER D.
YOU JUST WANT A GOOD TIME.
YOU DON'T REALLY LIKE ME.
HUH ?!

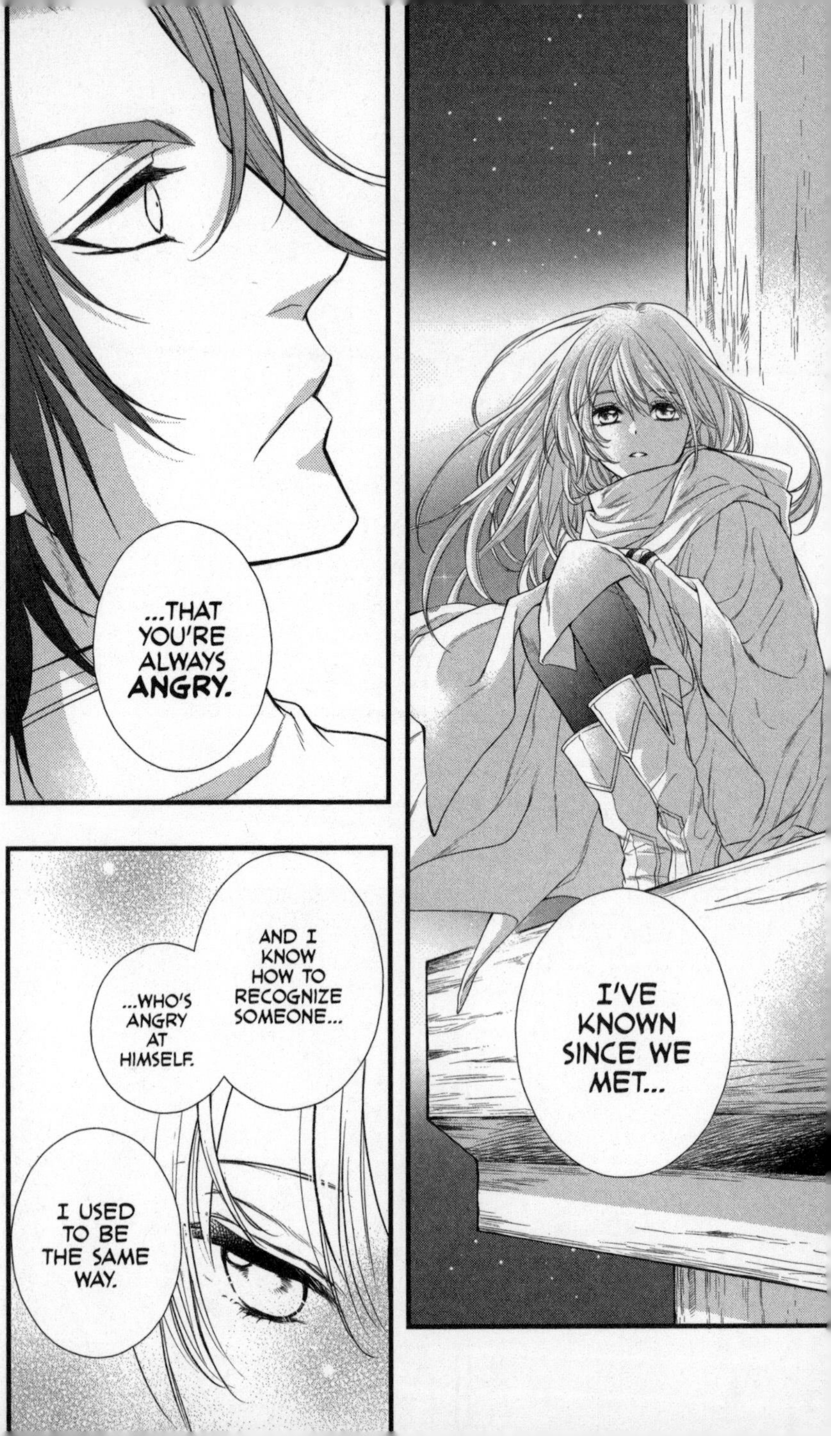
I'VE KNOWN SINCE WE MET...
...THAT YOU'RE ALWAYS **ANGRY.**
AND I KNOW HOW TO RECOGNIZE SOMEONE...
...WHO'S ANGRY AT HIMSELF.
I USED TO BE THE SAME WAY.

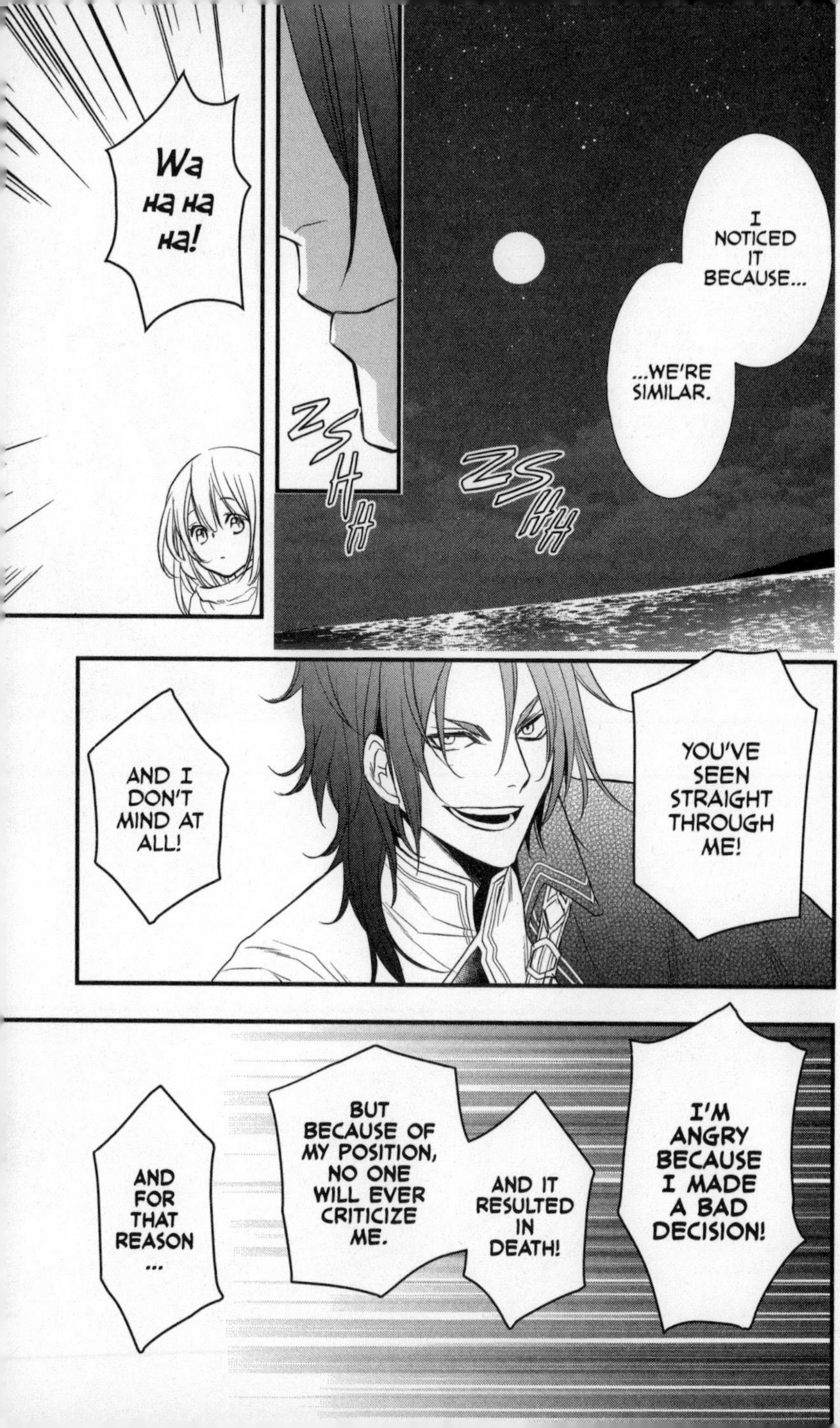
I NOTICED IT BECAUSE...
...WE'RE SIMILAR.
ZSHH
ZSHH
Wa ha ha ha!
YOU'VE SEEN STRAIGHT THROUGH ME!
AND I DON'T MIND AT ALL!
I'M ANGRY BECAUSE I MADE A BAD DECISION!
AND IT RESULTED IN DEATH!
BUT BECAUSE OF MY POSITION, NO ONE WILL EVER CRITICIZE ME.
AND FOR THAT REASON...

...I MUST STAY ANGRY AT **MYSELF.**

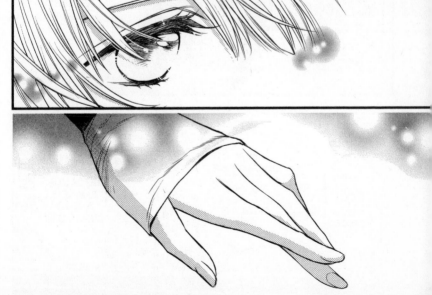

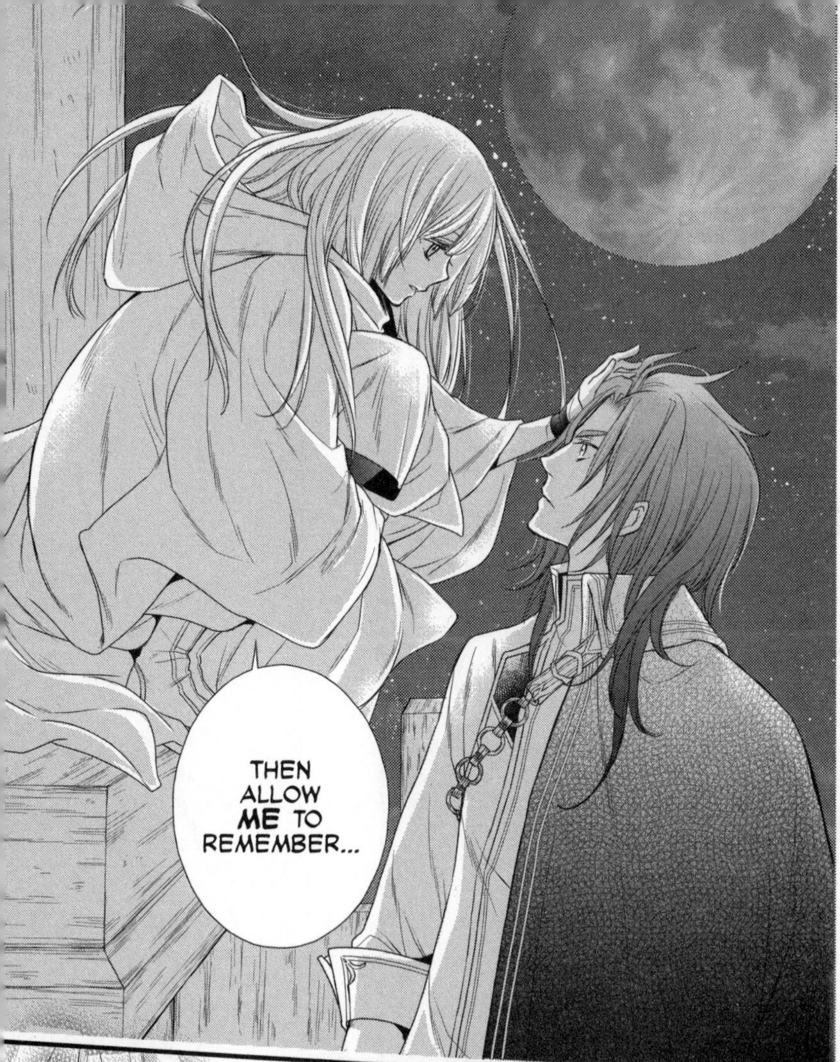
THEN ALLOW ME TO REMEMBER...
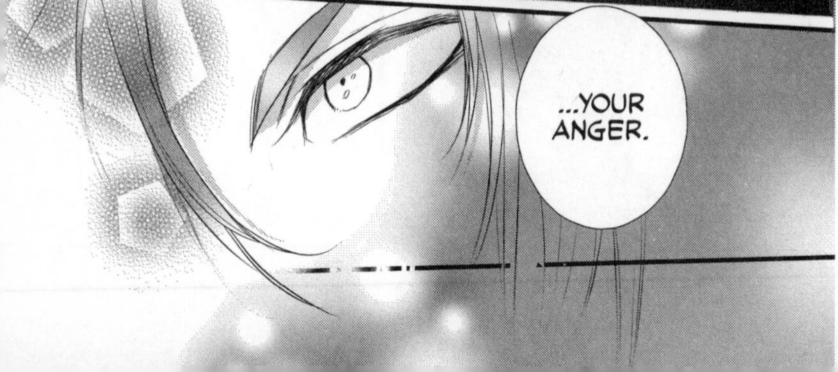
...YOUR ANGER.

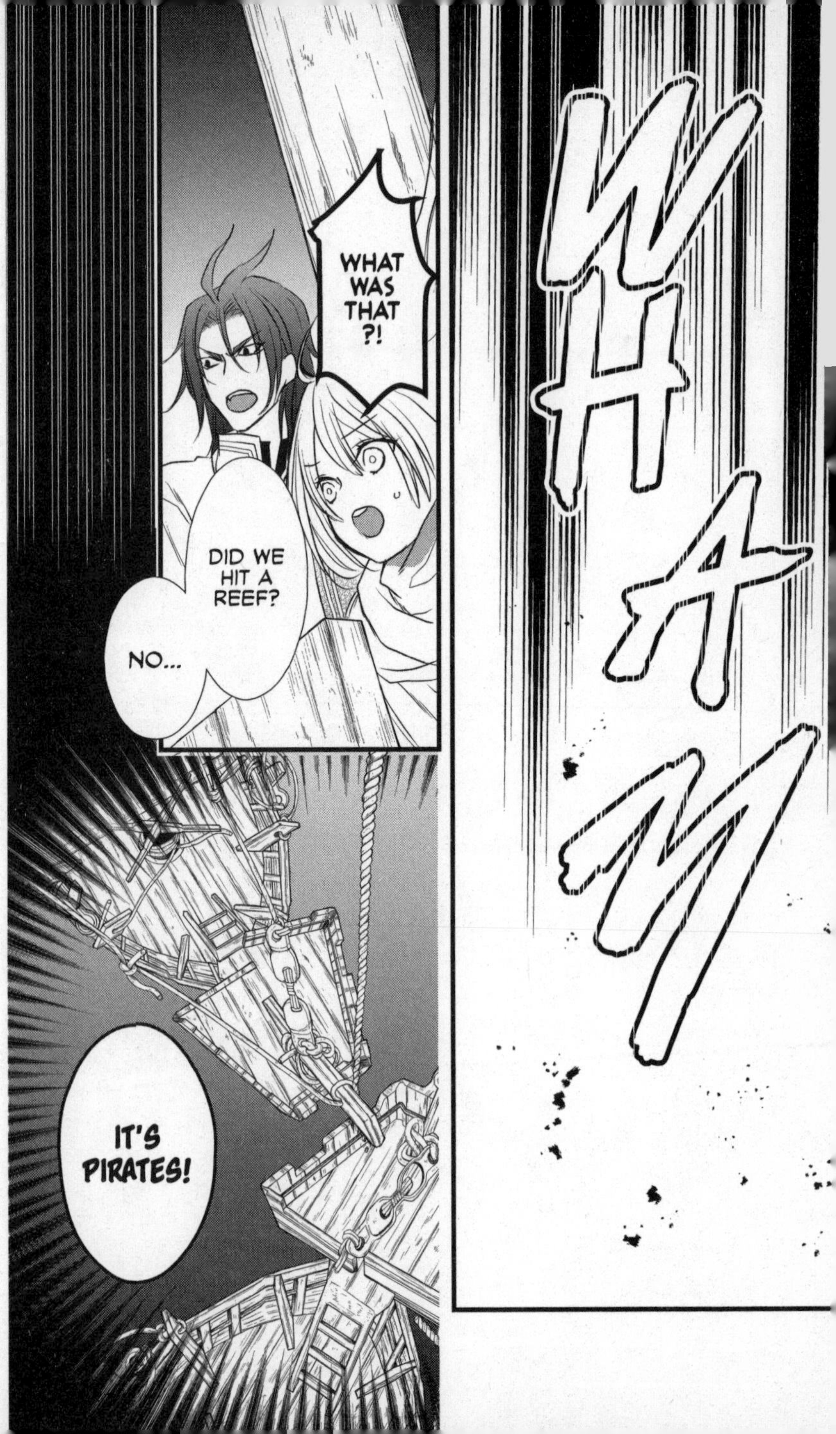
WHAM
WHAT WAS THAT ?!
DID WE HIT A REEF?
NO...
IT'S PIRATES!

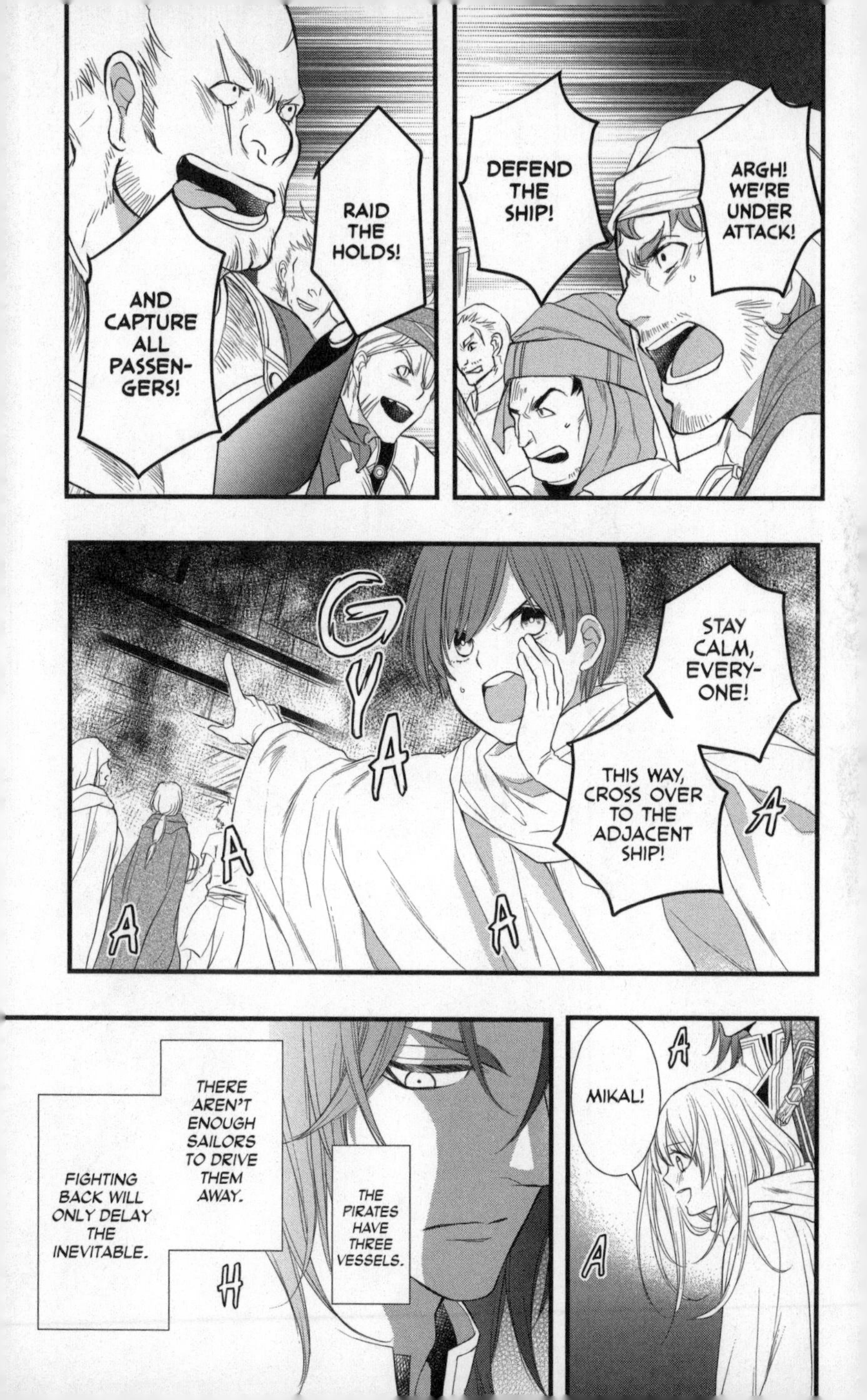
ARGH! WE'RE UNDER ATTACK!
DEFEND THE SHIP!
RAID THE HOLDS!
AND CAPTURE ALL PASSEN-GERS!
STAY CALM, EVERY-ONE!
THIS WAY, CROSS OVER TO THE ADJACENT SHIP!
A
GYA
A
A
A
A
MIKAL!
A
THE PIRATES HAVE THREE VESSELS.
THERE AREN'T ENOUGH SAILORS TO DRIVE THEM AWAY.
FIGHTING BACK WILL ONLY DELAY THE INEVITABLE.
H

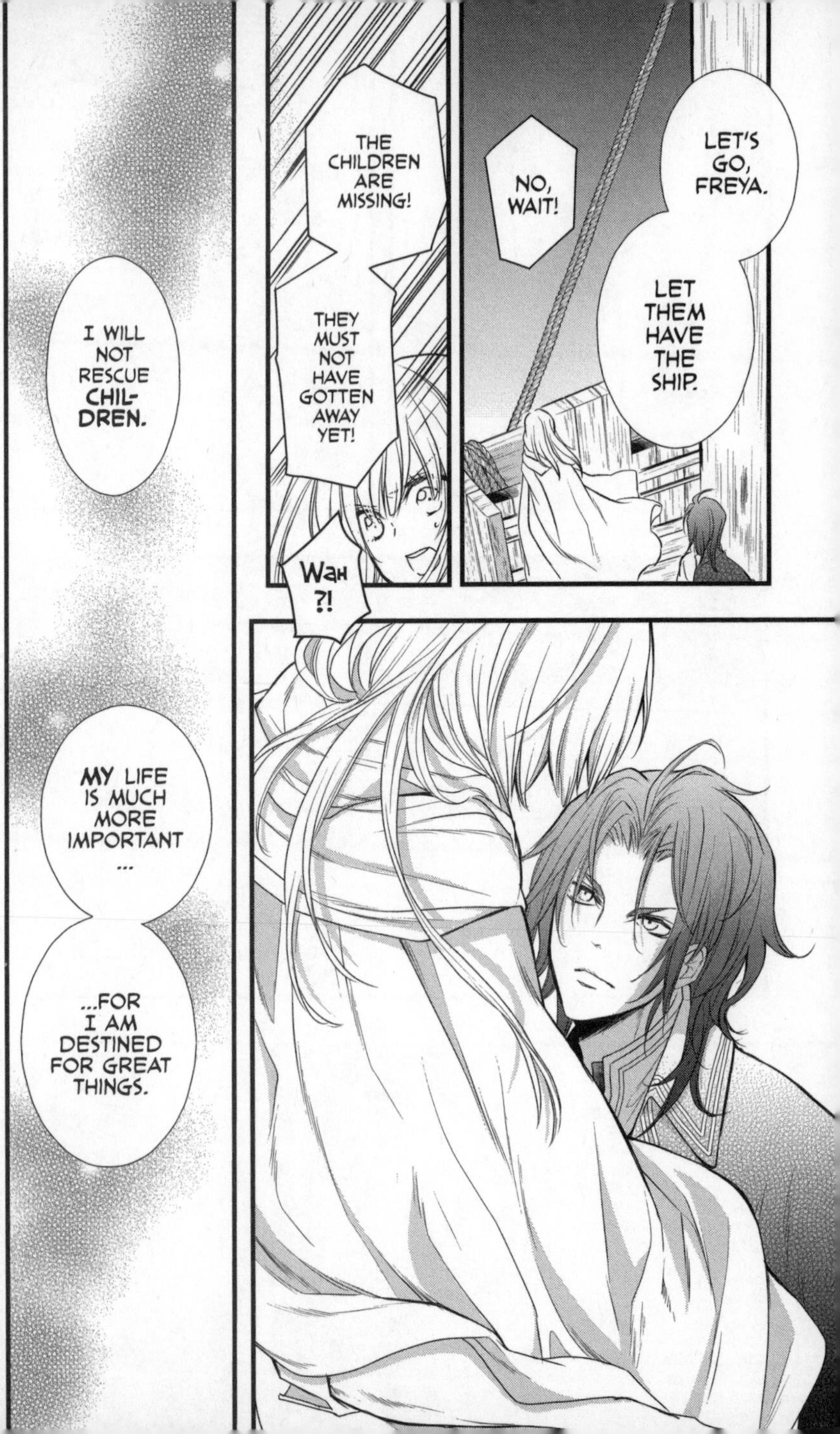
LET'S GO, FREYA.
LET THEM HAVE THE SHIP.
NO, WAIT!
THE CHILDREN ARE MISSING!
THEY MUST NOT HAVE GOTTEN AWAY YET!
WAH ?!
I WILL NOT RESCUE CHIL-DREN.
MY LIFE IS MUCH MORE IMPORTANT ...
...FOR I AM DESTINED FOR GREAT THINGS.

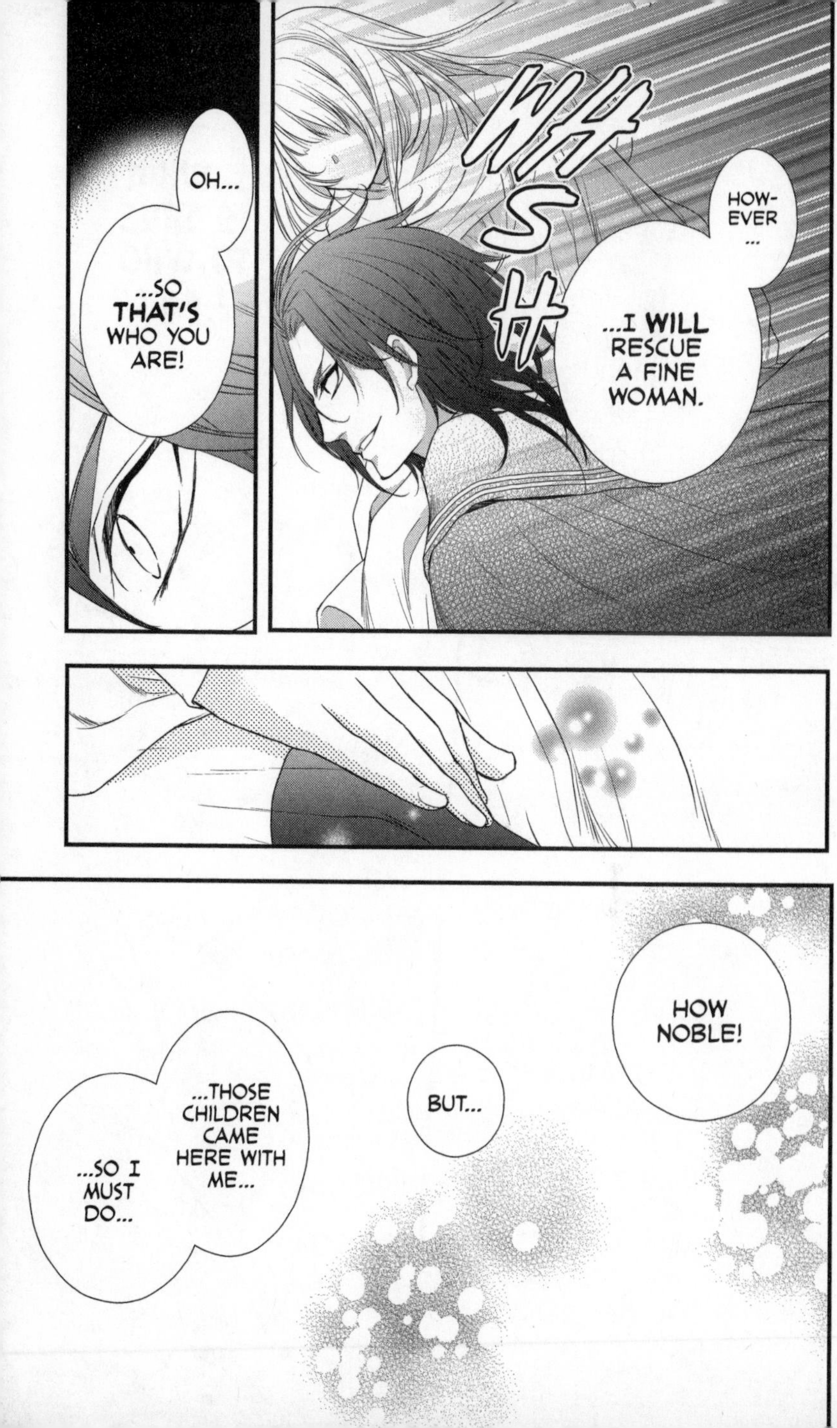
WHSH
HOW-EVER...
...I WILL RESCUE A FINE WOMAN.
OH...
...SO THAT'S WHO YOU ARE!
HOW NOBLE!
BUT...
...THOSE CHILDREN CAME HERE WITH ME...
...SO I MUST DO...

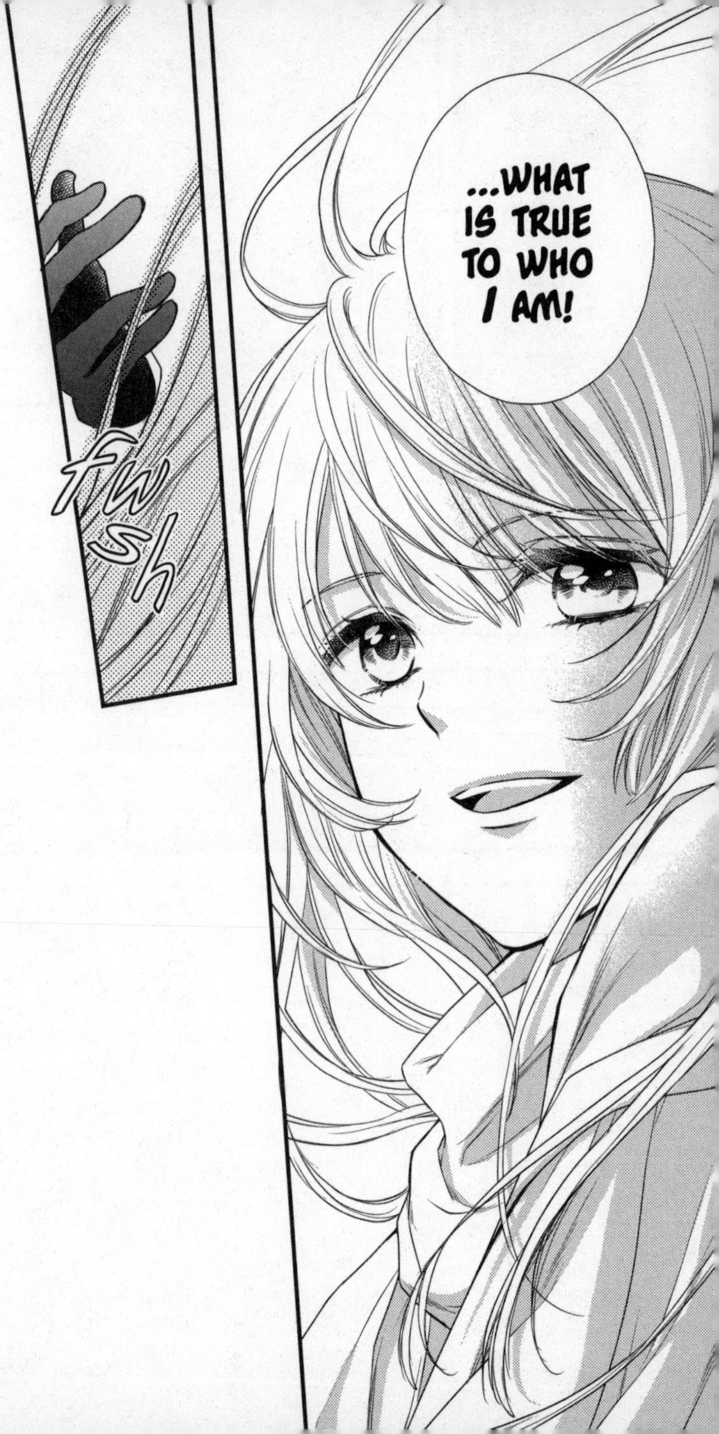
...WHAT IS TRUE TO WHO I AM!
fwsh

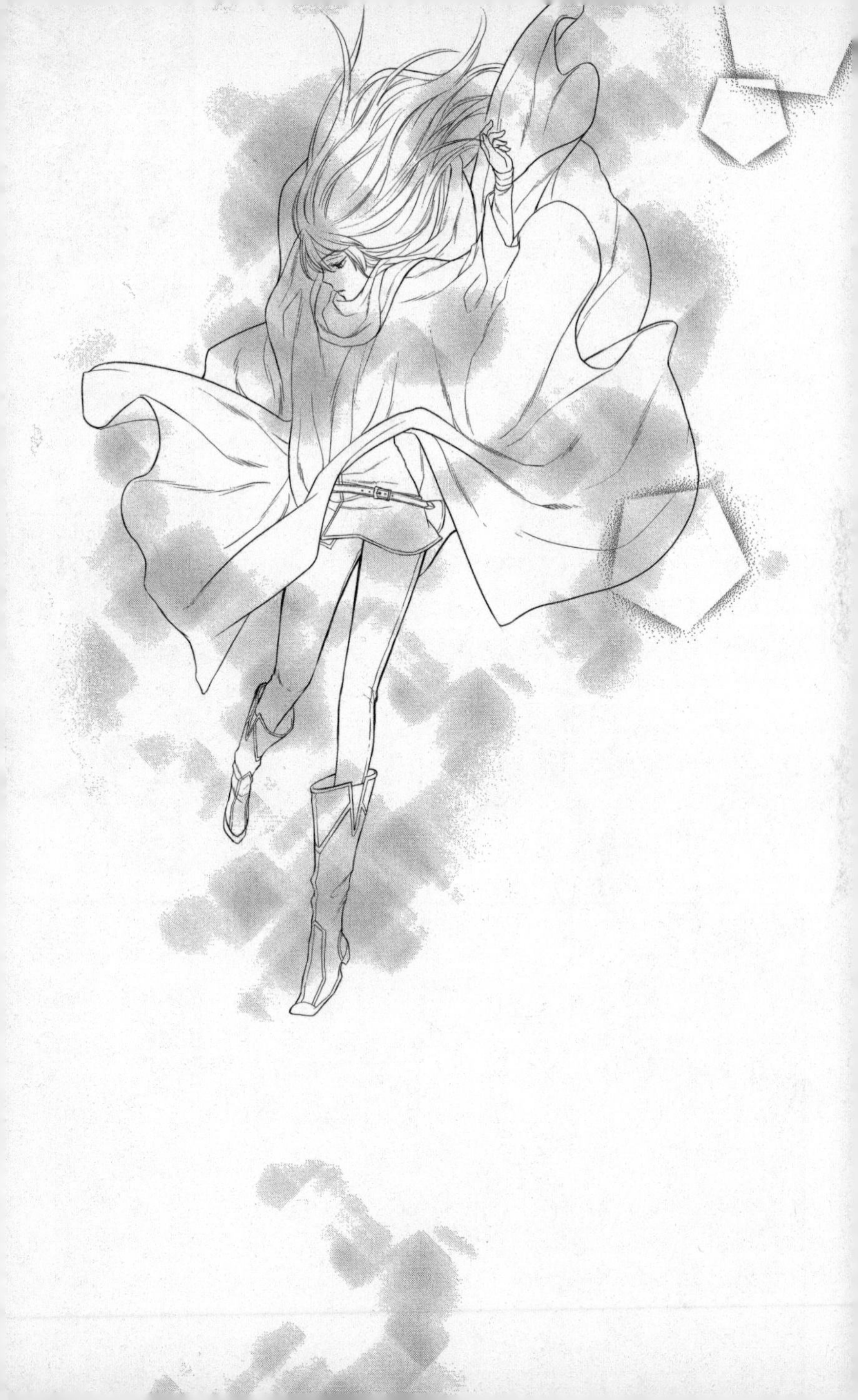

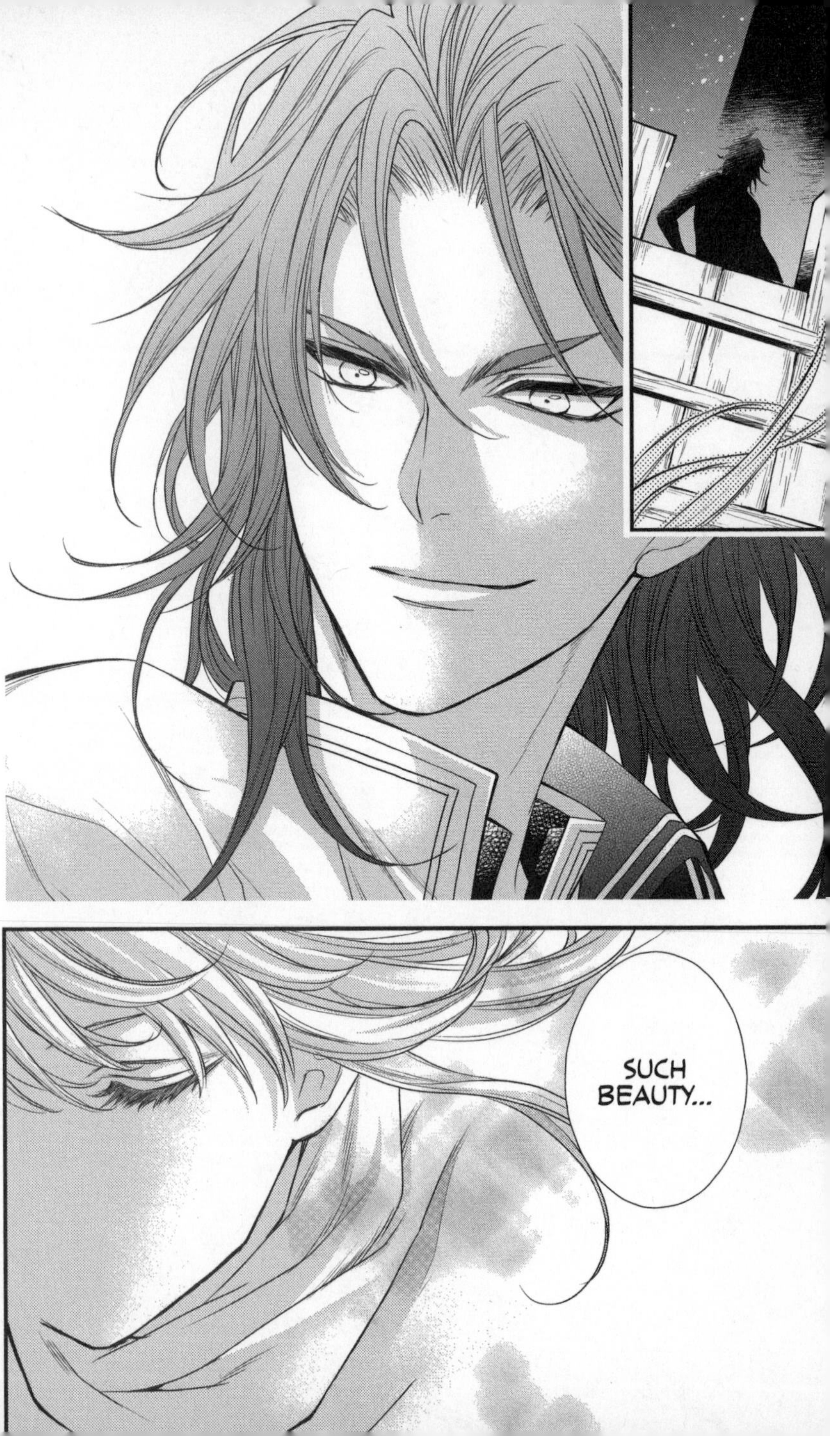
SUCH BEAUTY...

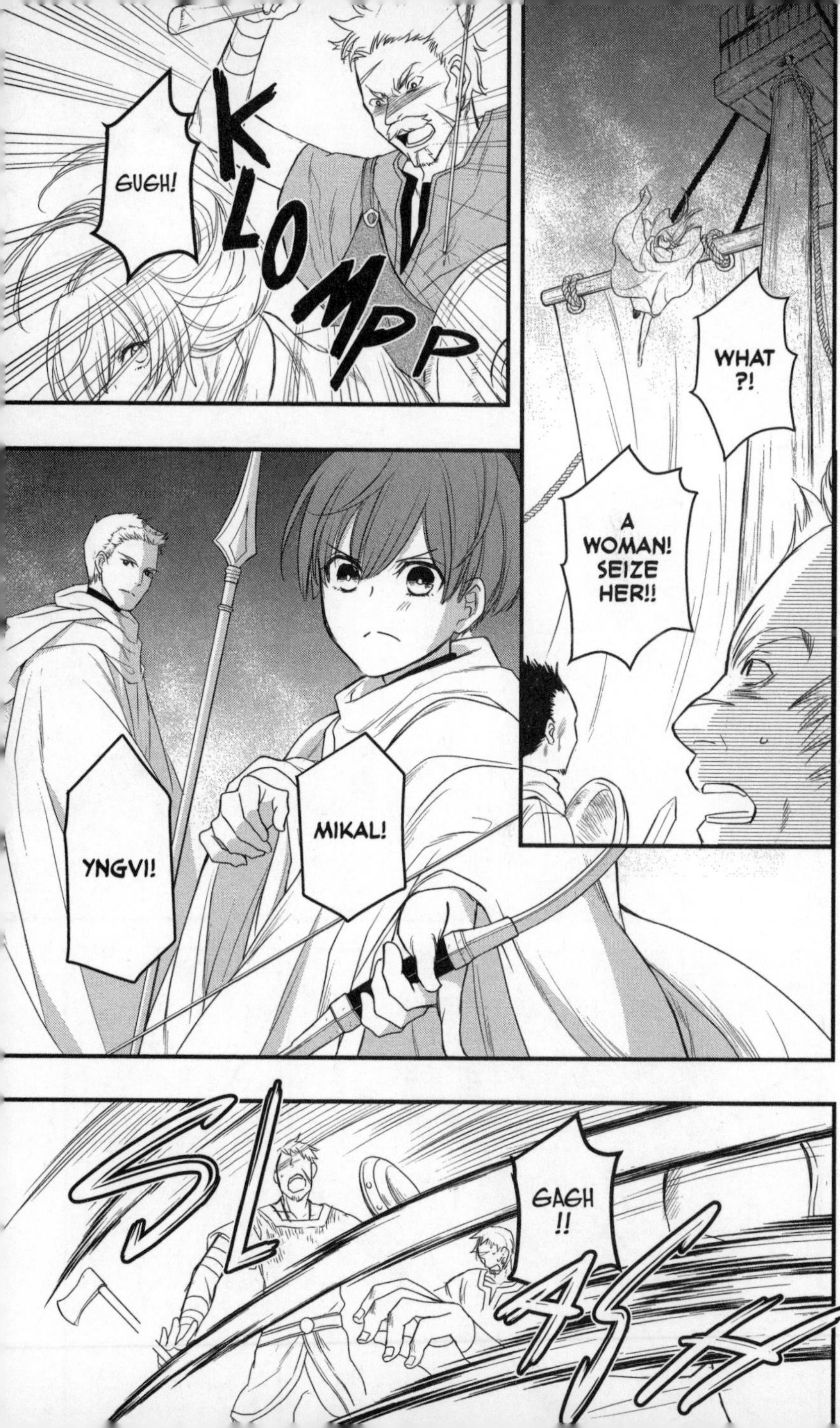
WHAT?!
A WOMAN! SEIZE HER!!
KLOMPP
GUGH!
MIKAL!
YNGVI!
GAGH!!
SLASH

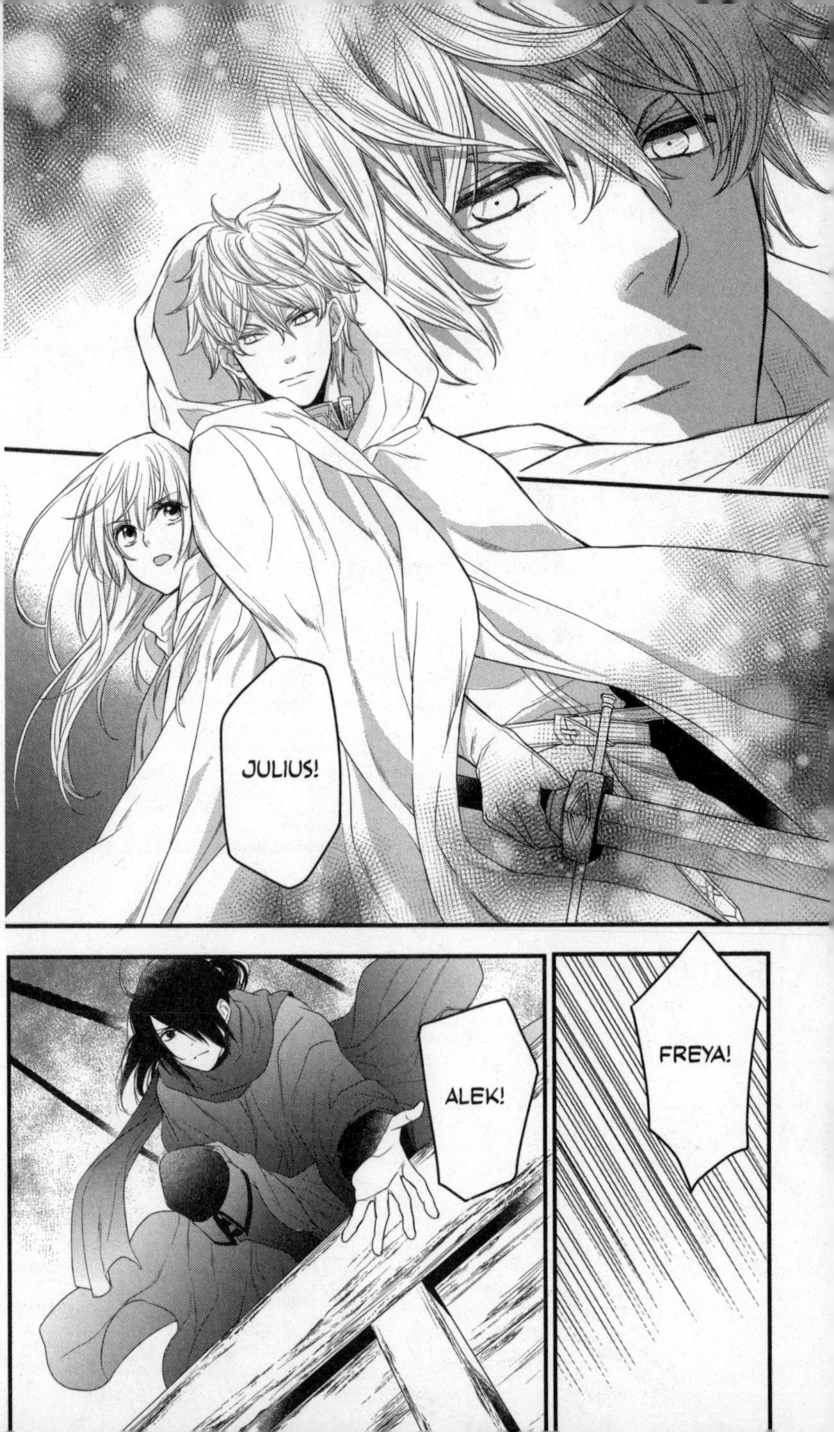
JULIUS!
FREYA!
ALEK!

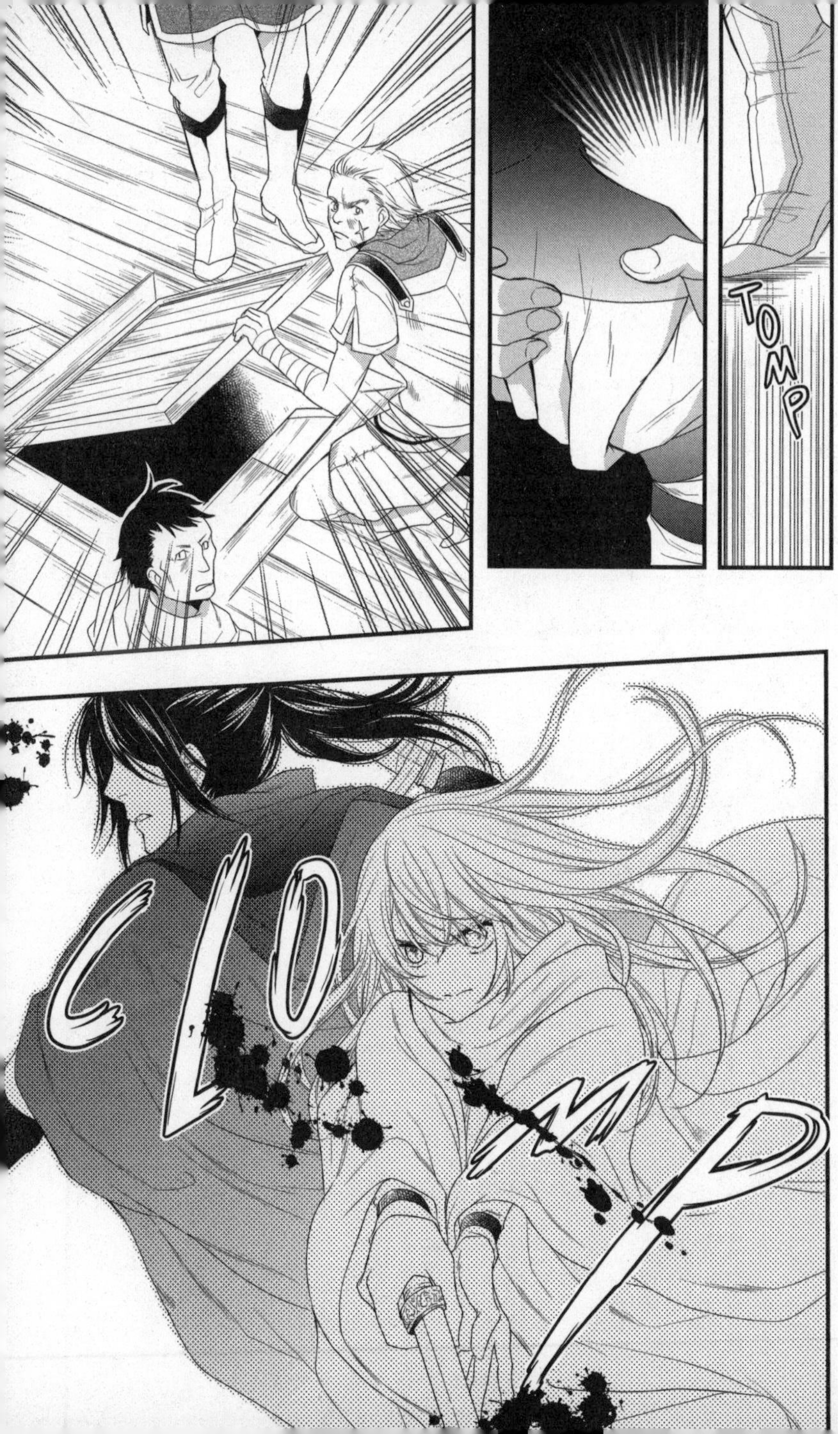
TOMP
CLOMP

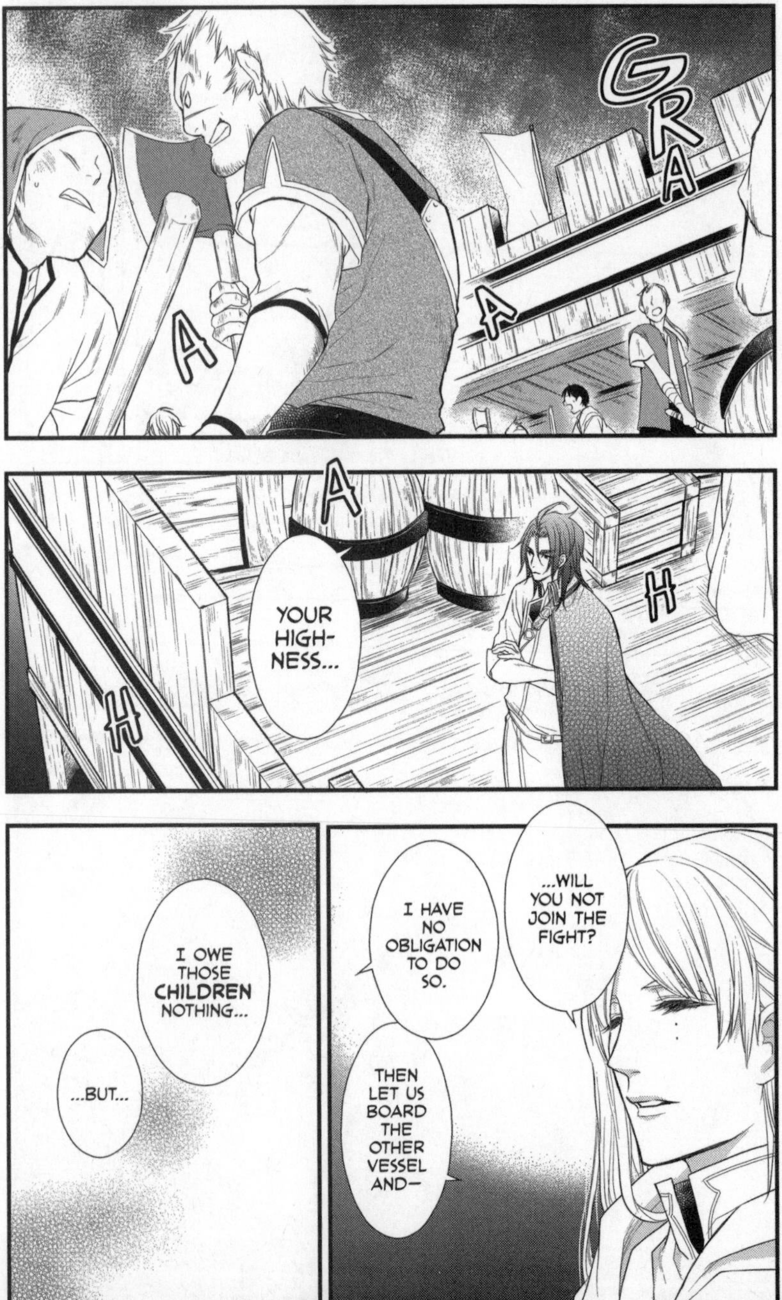
GRAAAAHH
YOUR HIGH-NESS...
...WILL YOU NOT JOIN THE FIGHT?
I HAVE NO OBLIGATION TO DO SO.
THEN LET US BOARD THE OTHER VESSEL AND—
I OWE THOSE **CHILDREN** NOTHING...
...BUT...

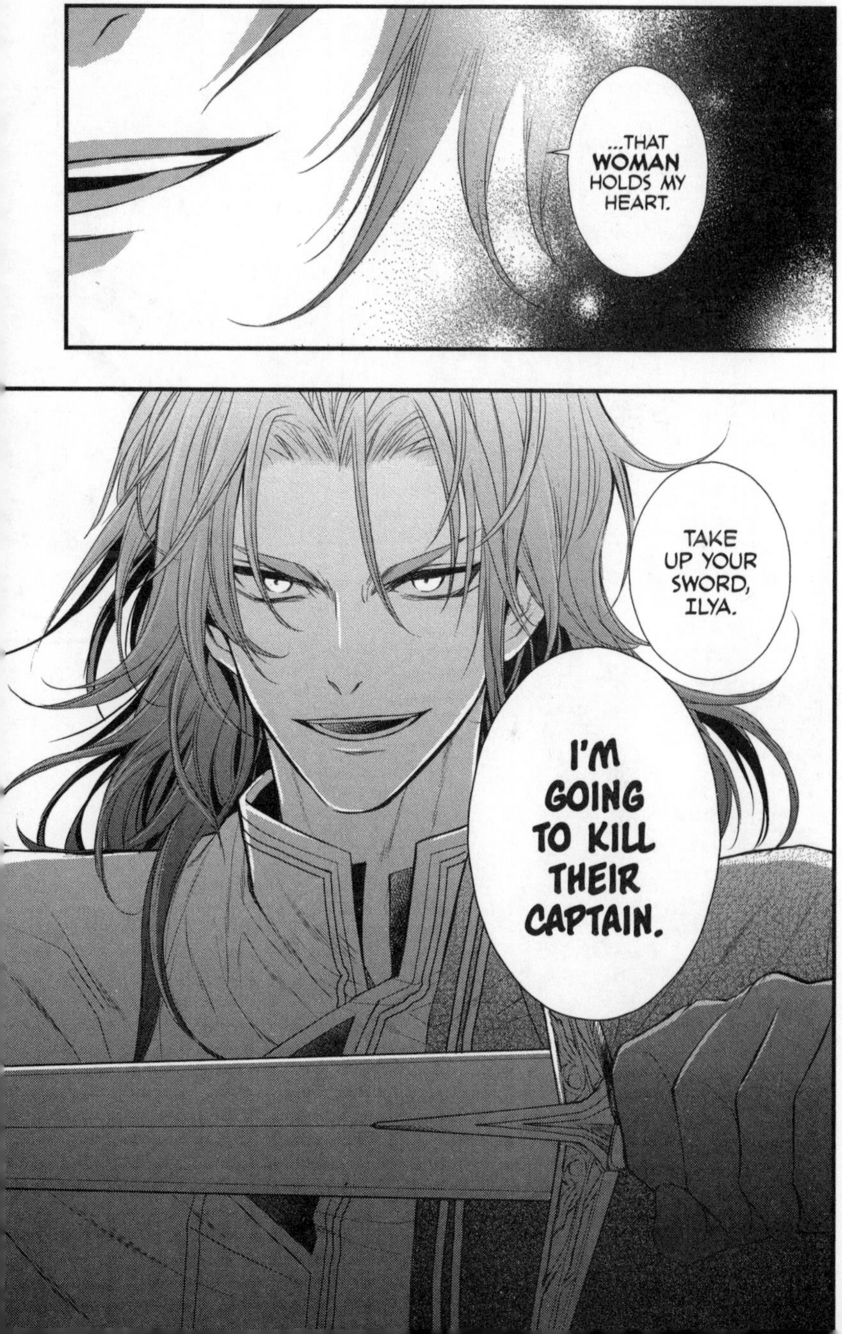
...THAT WOMAN HOLDS MY HEART.
TAKE UP YOUR SWORD, ILYA.
I'M GOING TO KILL THEIR CAPTAIN.

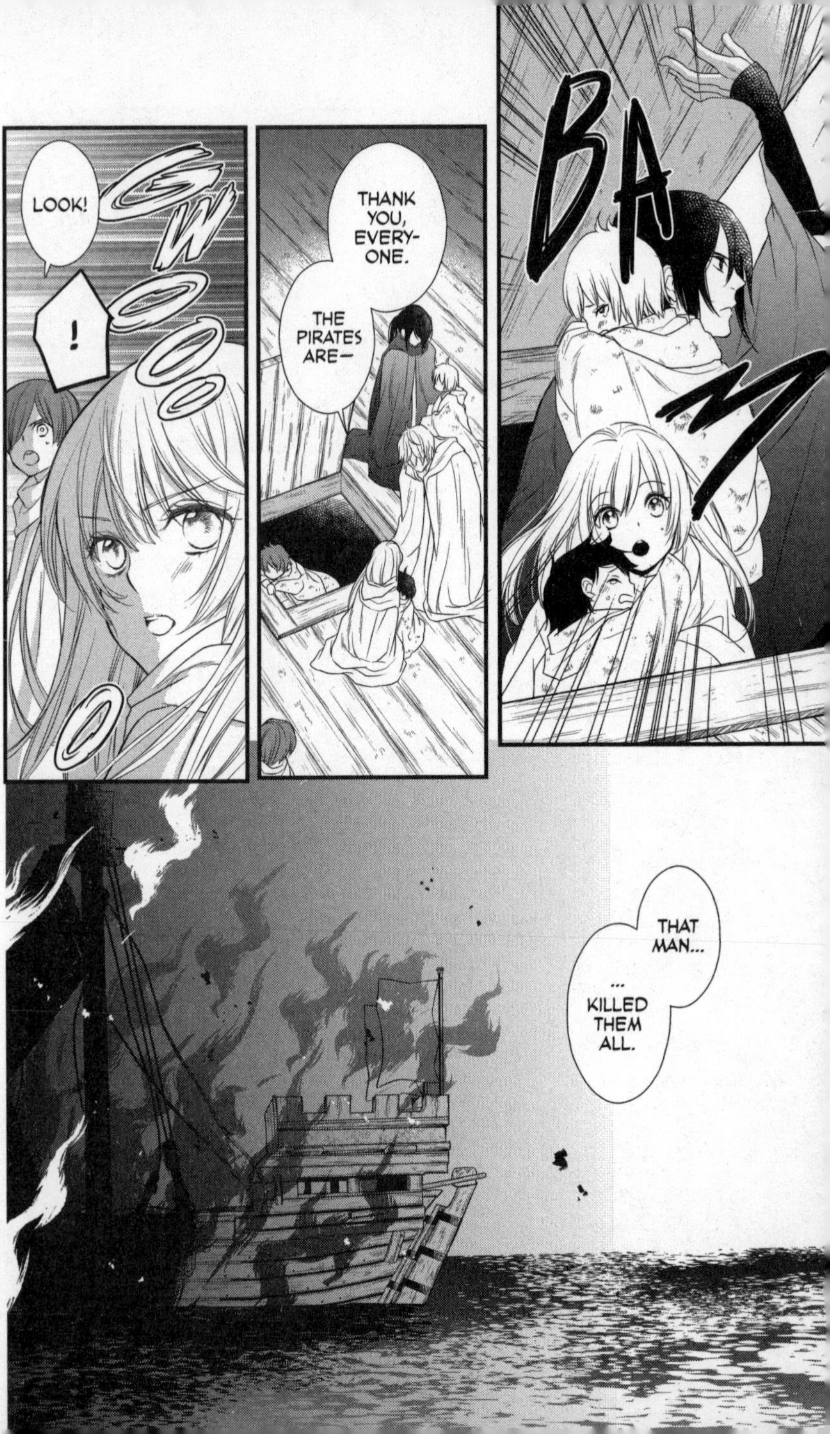
BAM
THANK YOU, EVERY-ONE.
THE PIRATES ARE—
GWOOOOO
LOOK!
!
THAT MAN...
...KILLED THEM ALL.

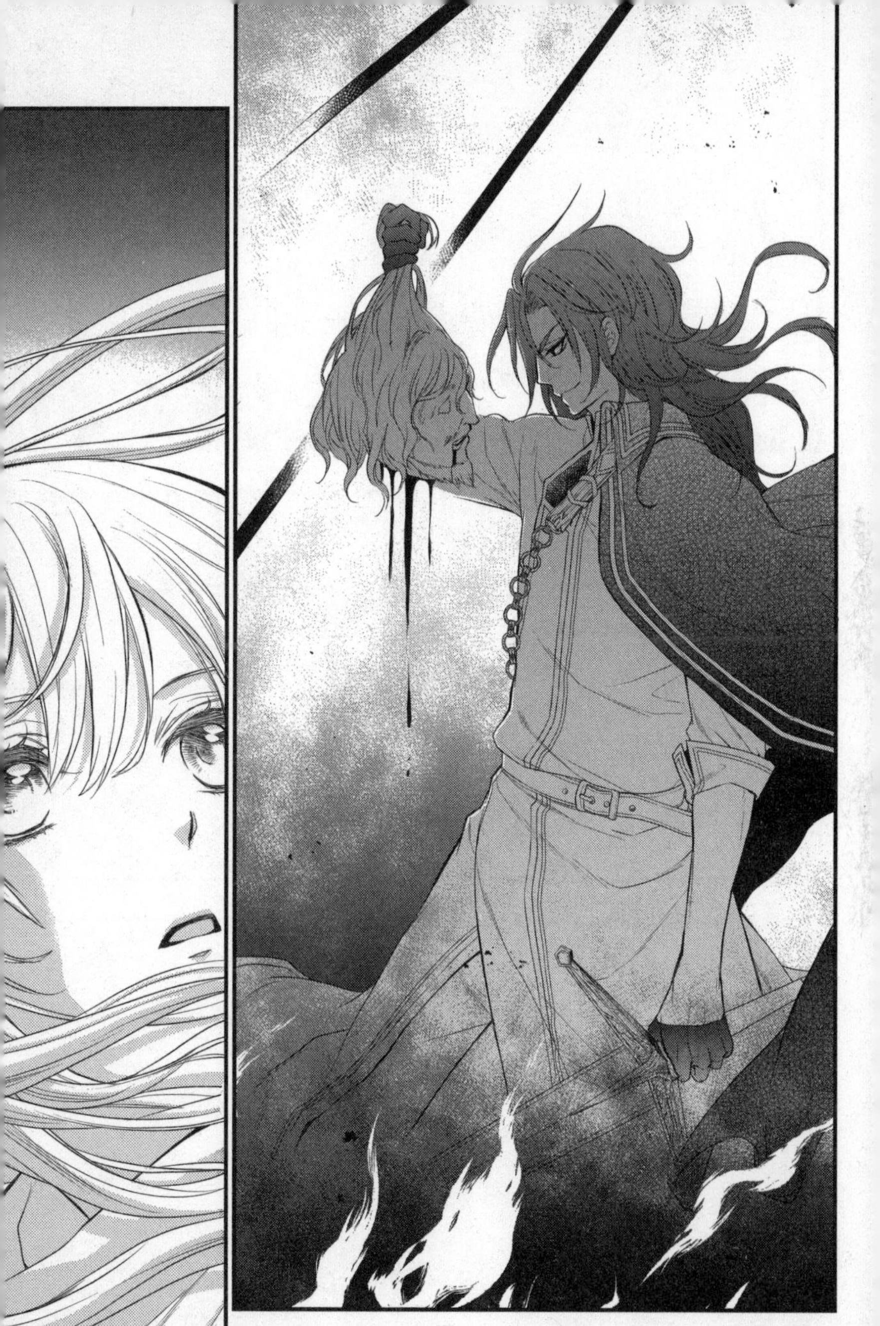

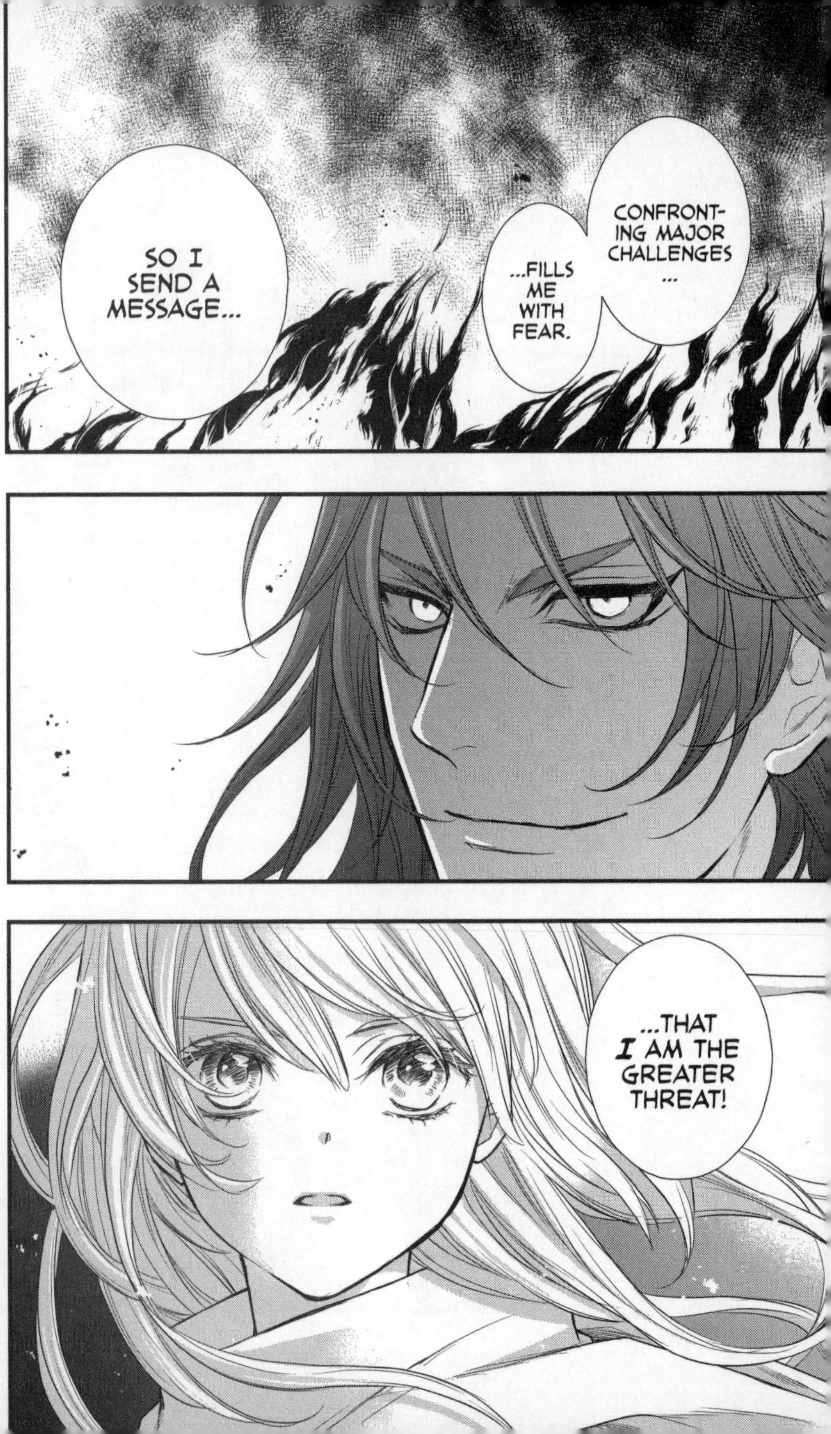
CONFRONTING MAJOR CHALLENGES...
...FILLS ME WITH FEAR.
SO I SEND A MESSAGE...
...THAT *I* AM THE GREATER THREAT!

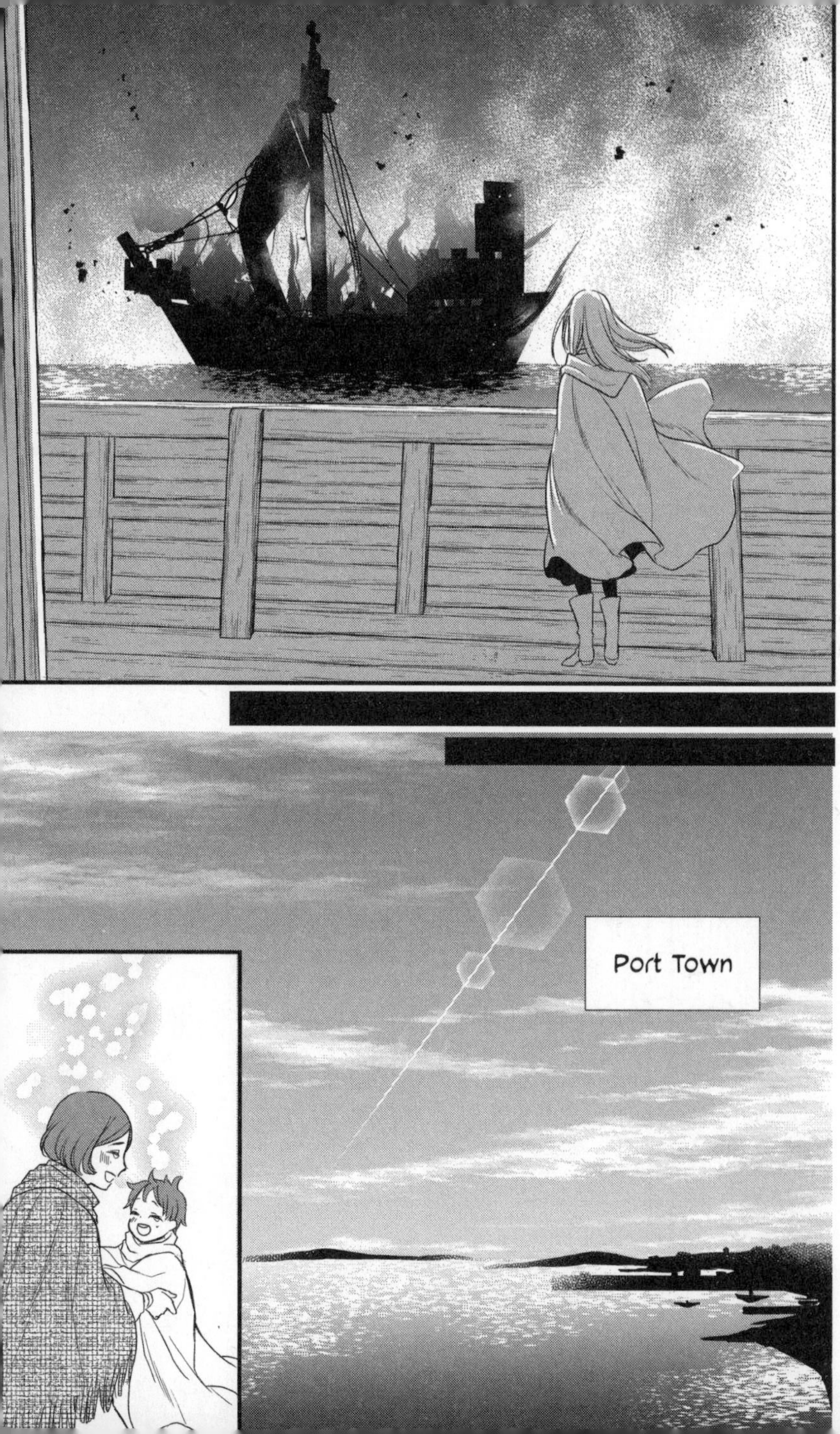
Port Town

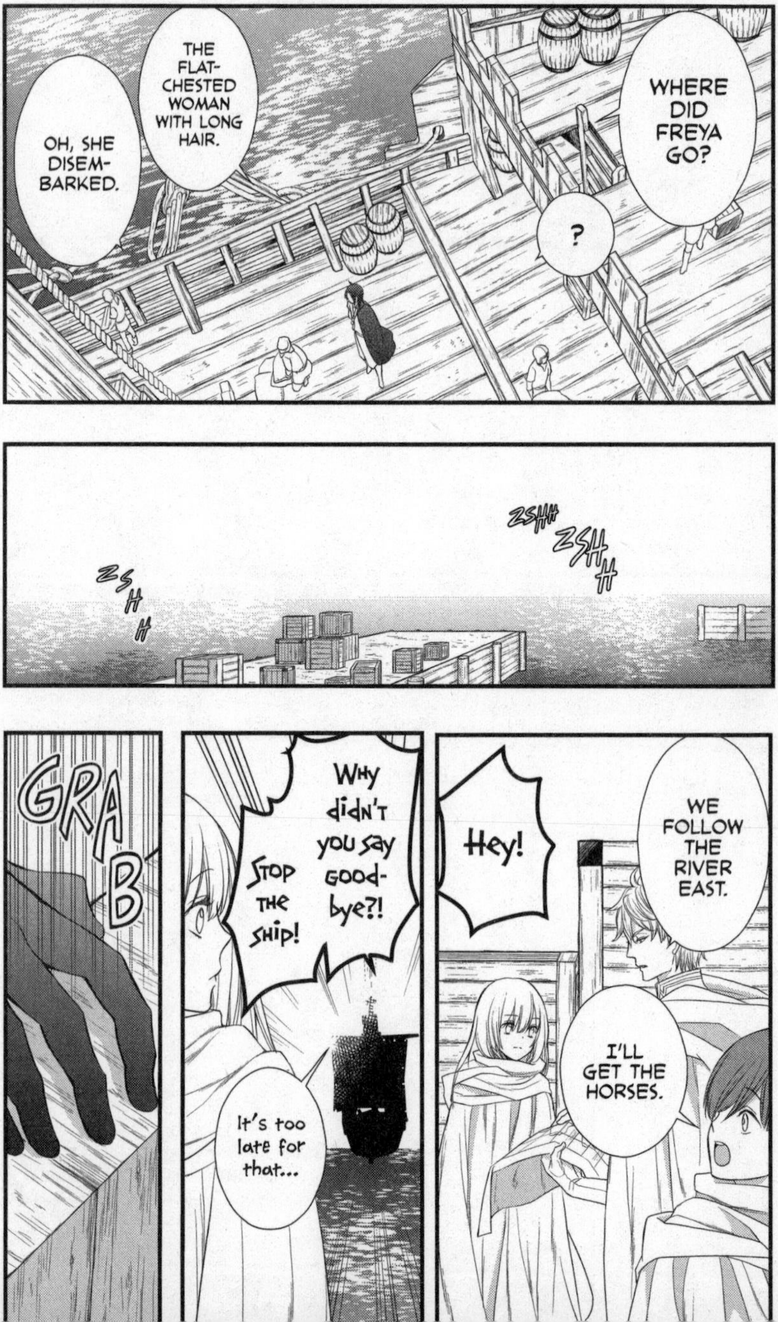
WHERE DID FREYA GO?
?
THE FLAT-CHESTED WOMAN WITH LONG HAIR.
OH, SHE DISEMBARKED.
ZSHH
ZSHH
ZSHH
WE FOLLOW THE RIVER EAST.
Hey!
I'LL GET THE HORSES.
Why didn't you say good-bye?!
Stop the ship!
It's too late for that...
GRAB

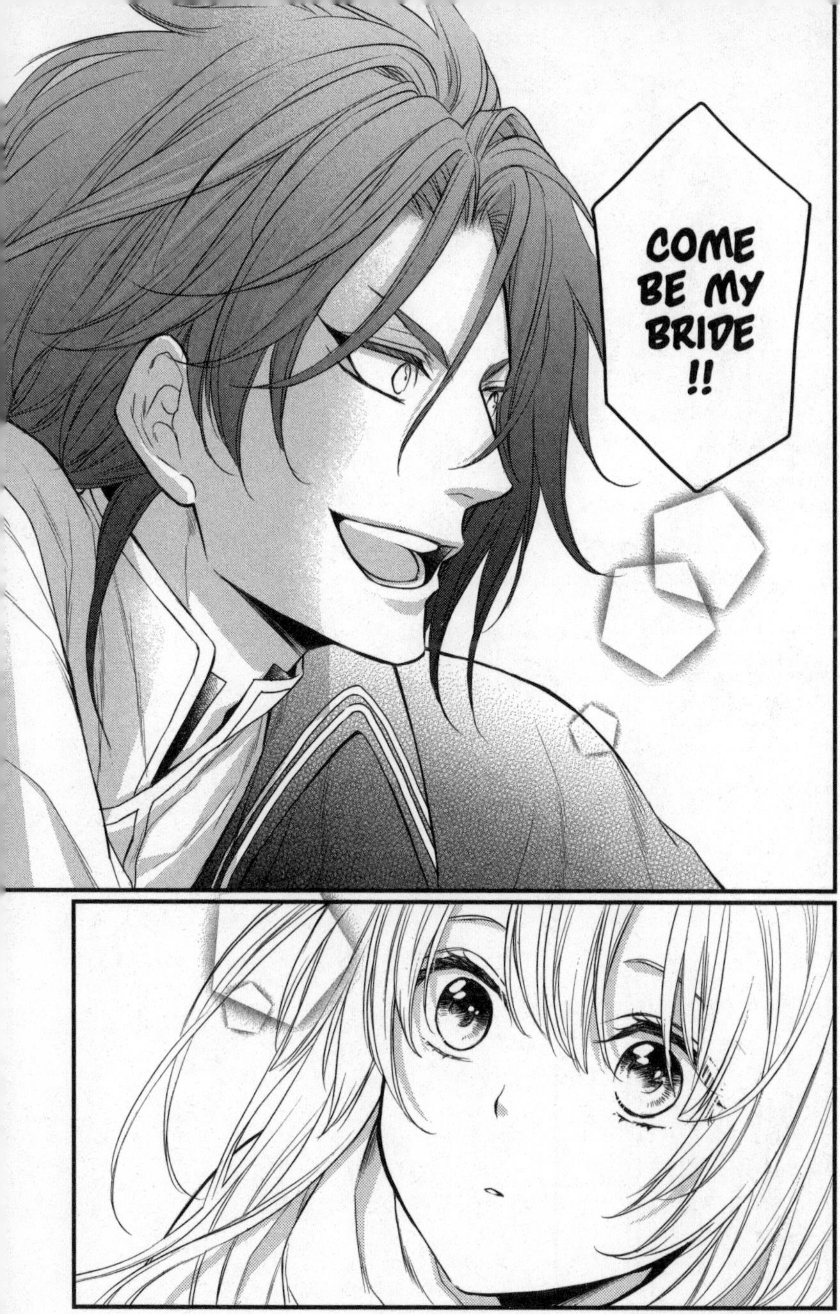
COME BE MY BRIDE !!

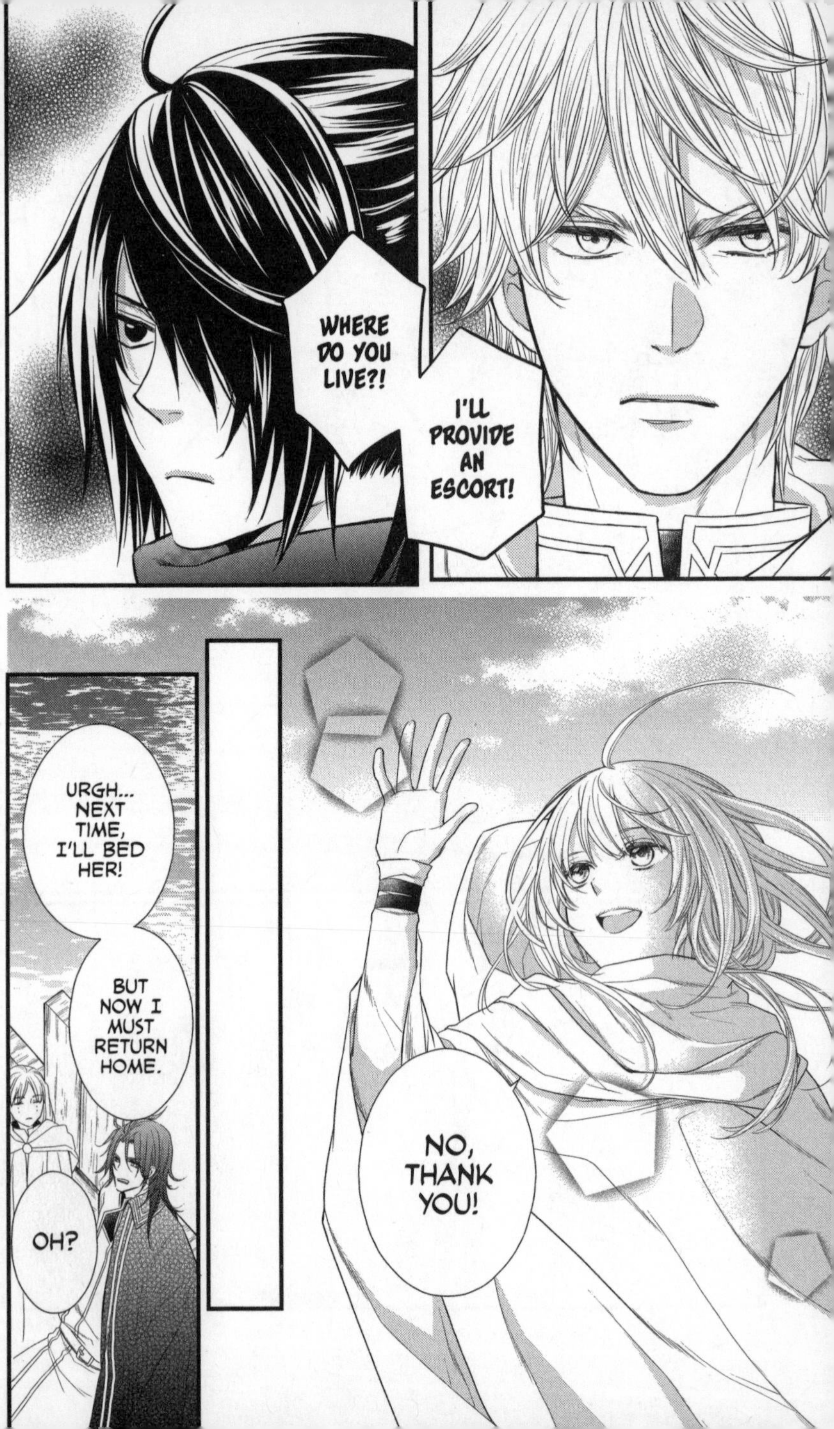
WHERE DO YOU LIVE?!
I'LL PROVIDE AN ESCORT!
NO, THANK YOU!
URGH... NEXT TIME, I'LL BED HER!
BUT NOW I MUST RETURN HOME.
OH?

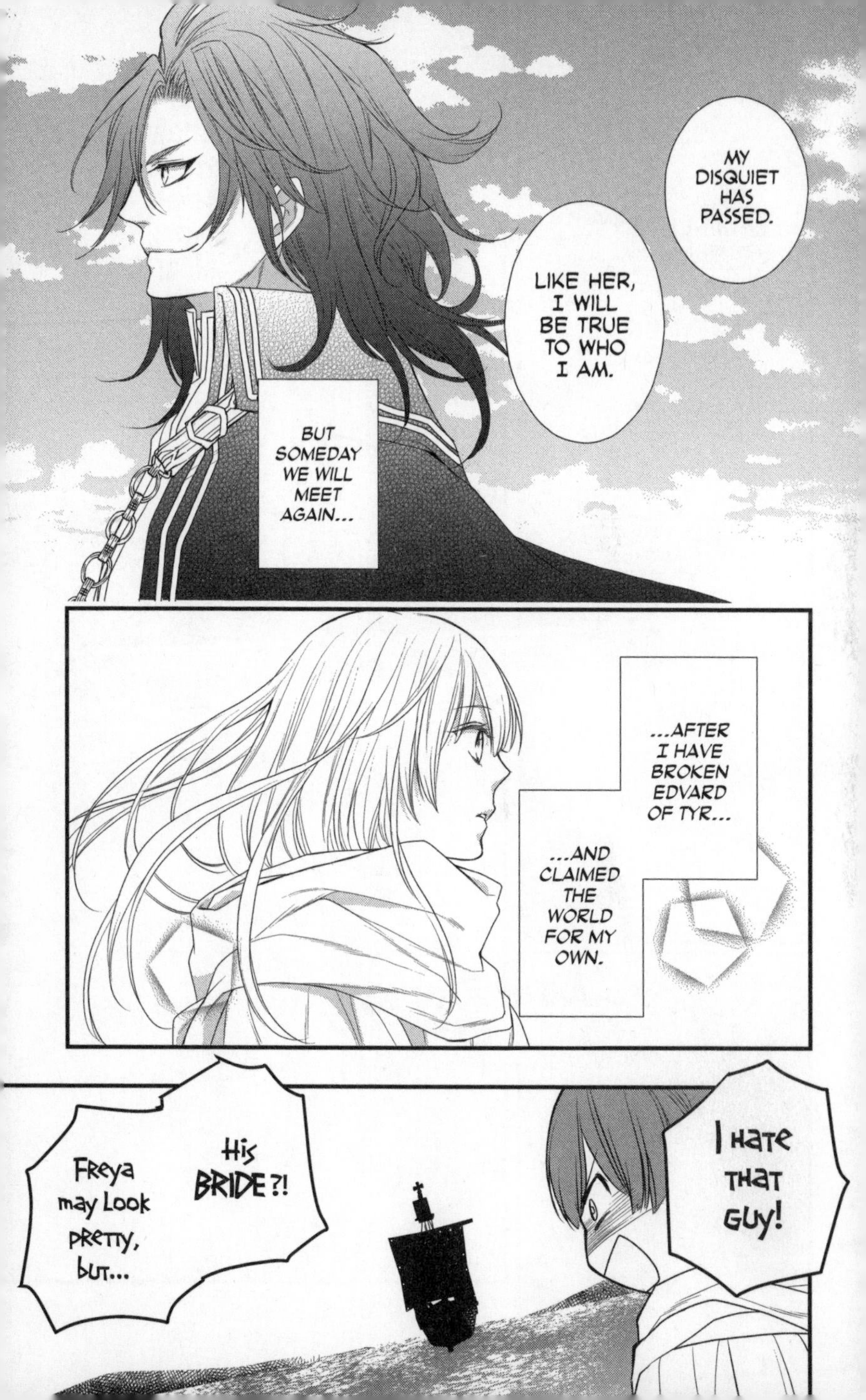
MY DISQUIET HAS PASSED.
LIKE HER, I WILL BE TRUE TO WHO I AM.
BUT SOMEDAY WE WILL MEET AGAIN...
...AFTER I HAVE BROKEN EDVARD OF TYR...
...AND CLAIMED THE WORLD FOR MY OWN.
I HATE THAT GUY!
His BRIDE?!
Freya may look pretty, but...

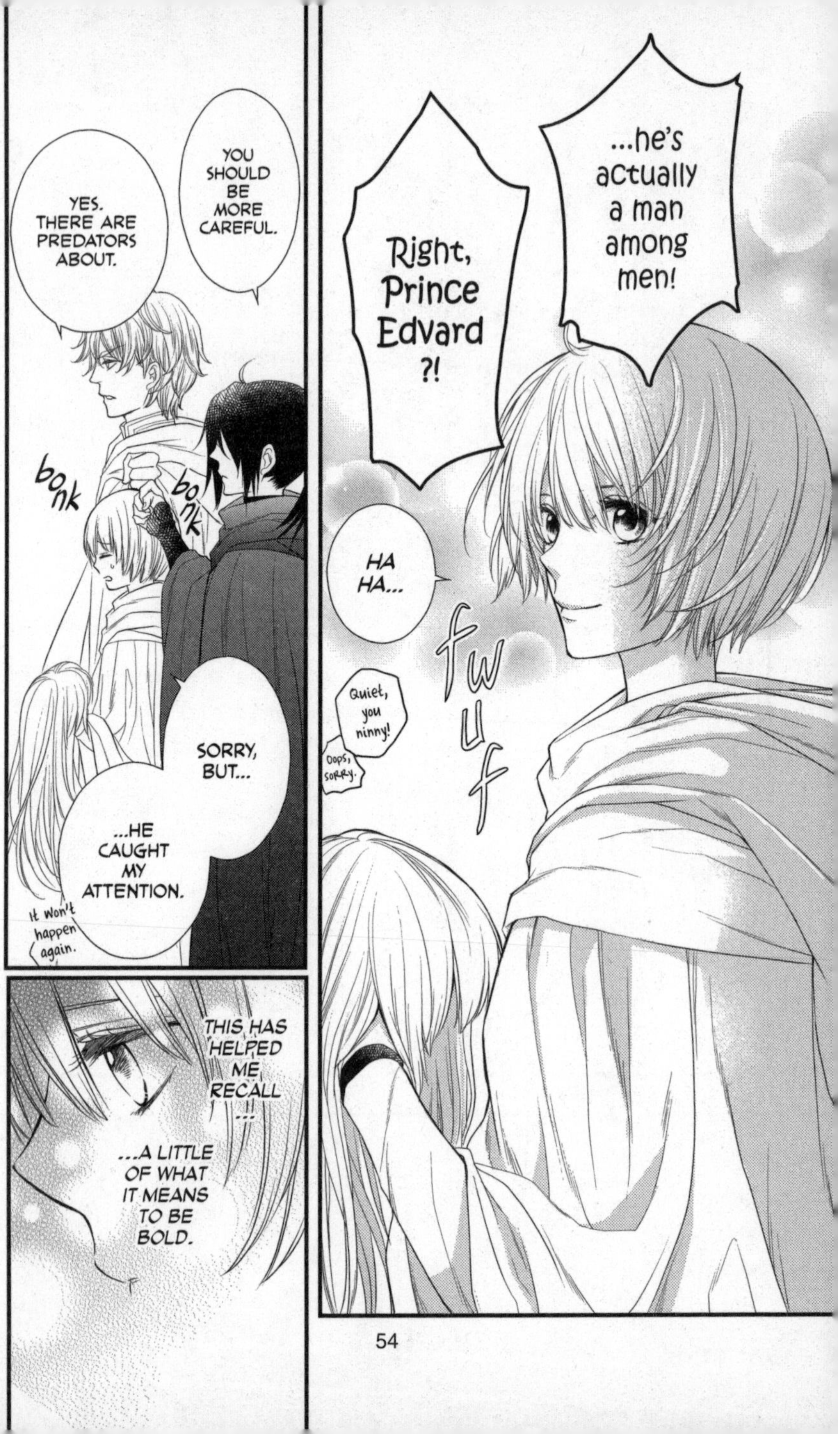
...he's actually a man among men!
Right, Prince Edvard ?!
HA HA...
fwuf
Quiet, you ninny!
Oops, sorry.
YOU SHOULD BE MORE CAREFUL.
YES. THERE ARE PREDATORS ABOUT.
bonk
bonk
SORRY, BUT...
...HE CAUGHT MY ATTENTION.
It won't happen again.
THIS HAS HELPED ME RECALL...
...A LITTLE OF WHAT IT MEANS TO BE BOLD.

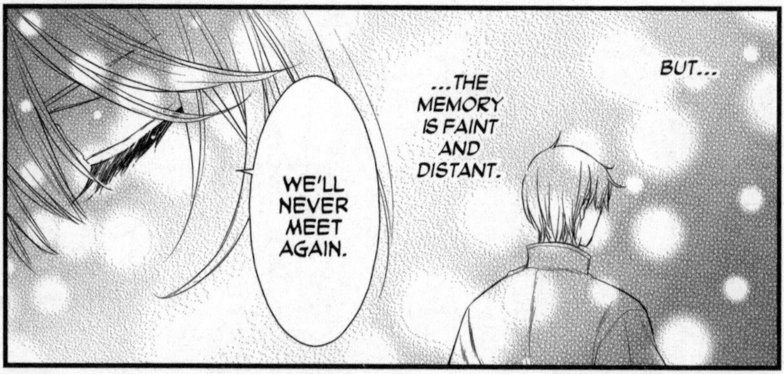
BUT...
...THE MEMORY IS FAINT AND DISTANT.
WE'LL NEVER MEET AGAIN.
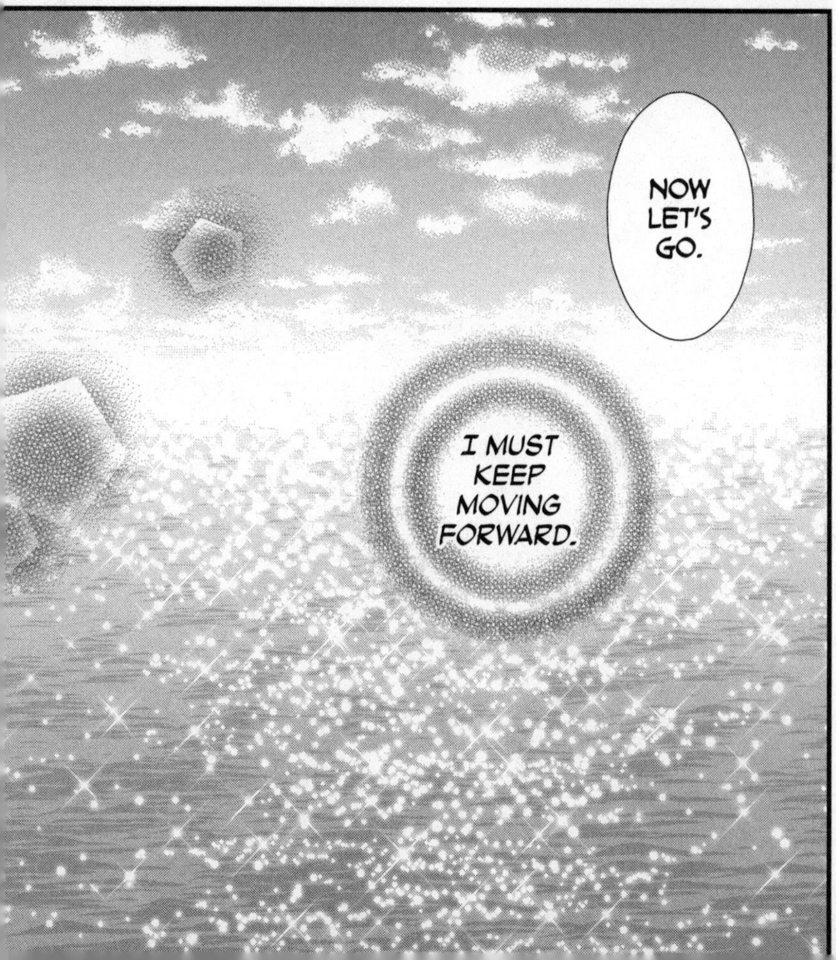
NOW LET'S GO.
I MUST KEEP MOVING FORWARD.

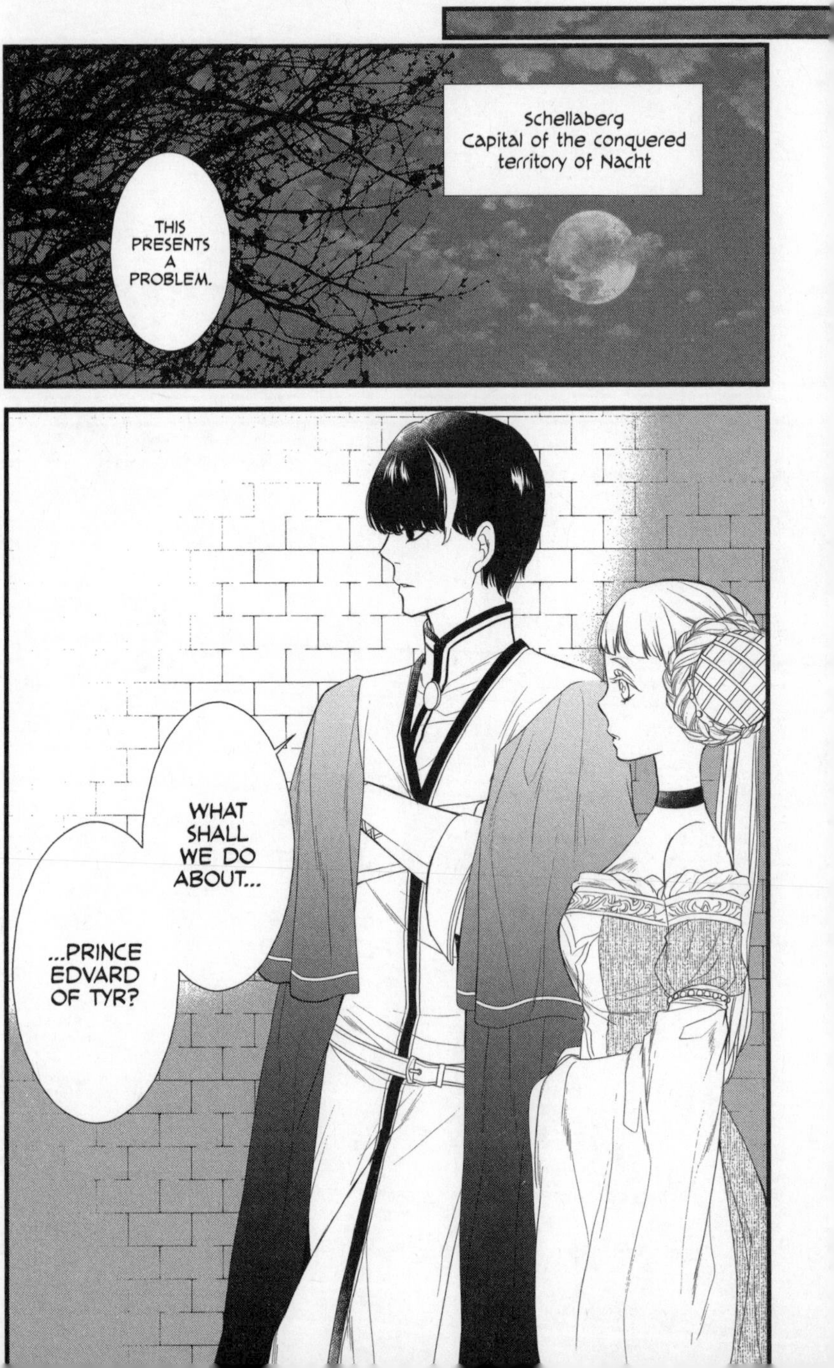
Schellaberg
Capital of the conquered territory of Nacht
THIS PRESENTS A PROBLEM.
WHAT SHALL WE DO ABOUT...
...PRINCE EDVARD OF TYR?

Chapter 14: Nacht, Land of Silver and Night

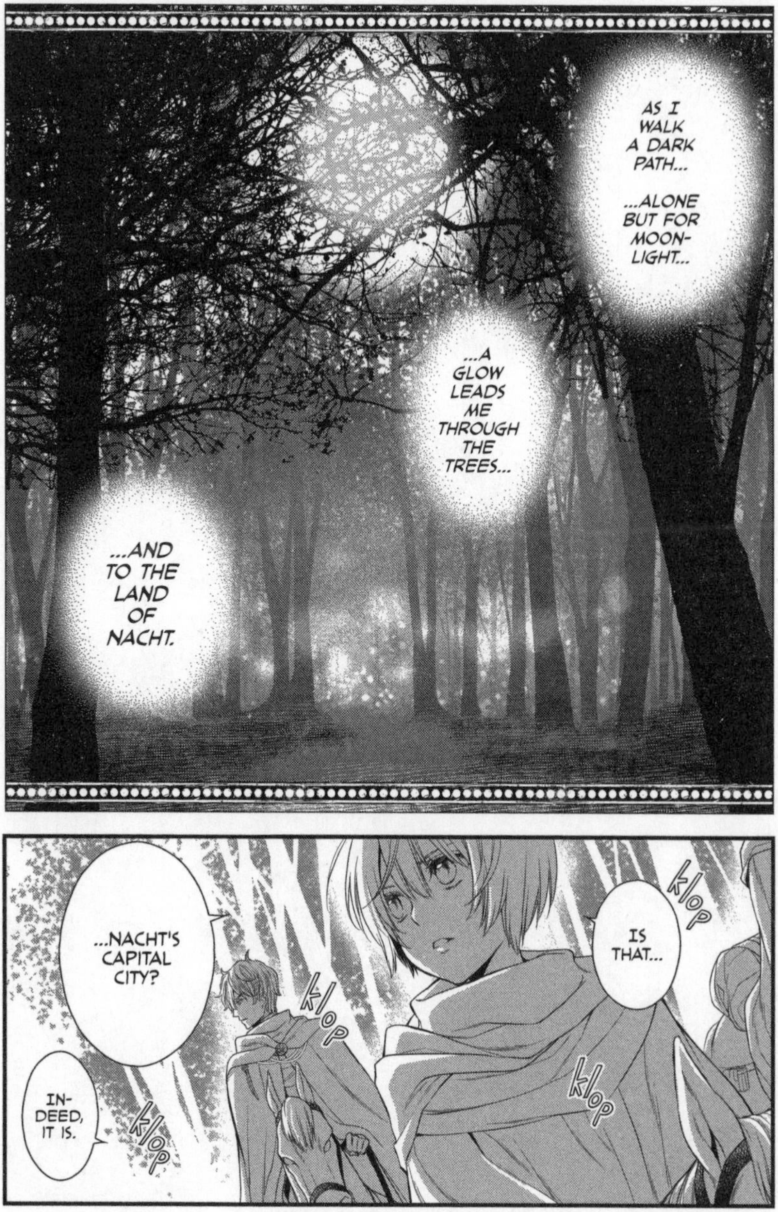
AS I WALK A DARK PATH...
...ALONE BUT FOR MOON-LIGHT...
...A GLOW LEADS ME THROUGH THE TREES...
...AND TO THE LAND OF NACHT.
klop
IS THAT...
...NACHT'S CAPITAL CITY?
klop
klop
IN-DEED, IT IS.
klop

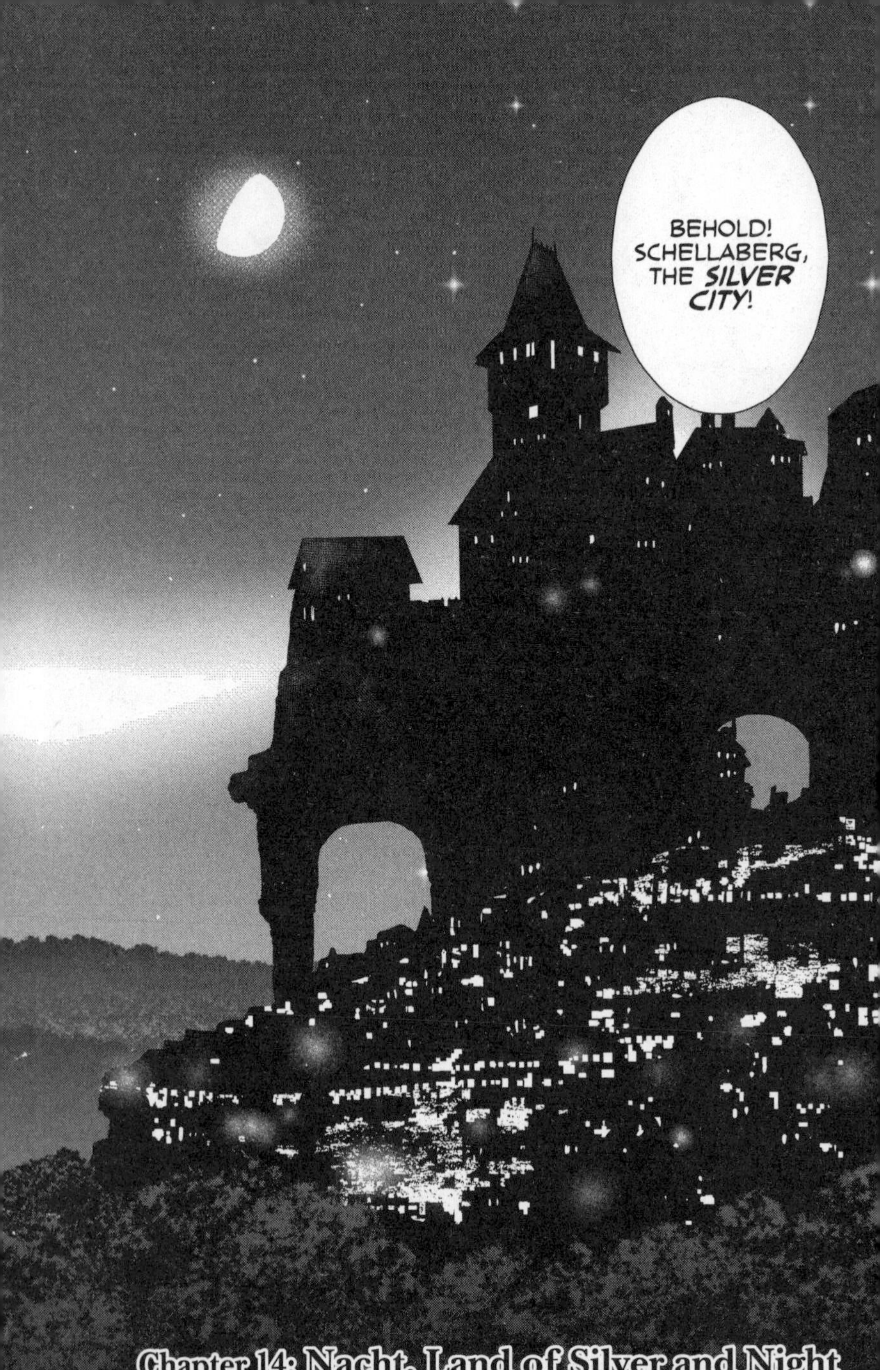
BEHOLD! SCHELLABERG, THE SILVER CITY!

Chapter 14: Nacht, Land of Silver and Night

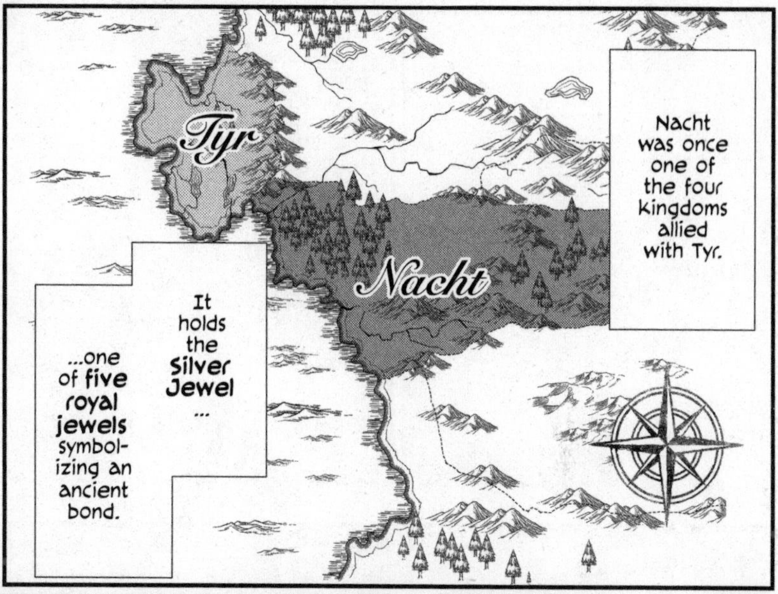
Nacht was once one of the four kingdoms allied with Tyr.
Tyr
Nacht
It holds the Silver Jewel ...
...one of five royal jewels symbolizing an ancient bond.

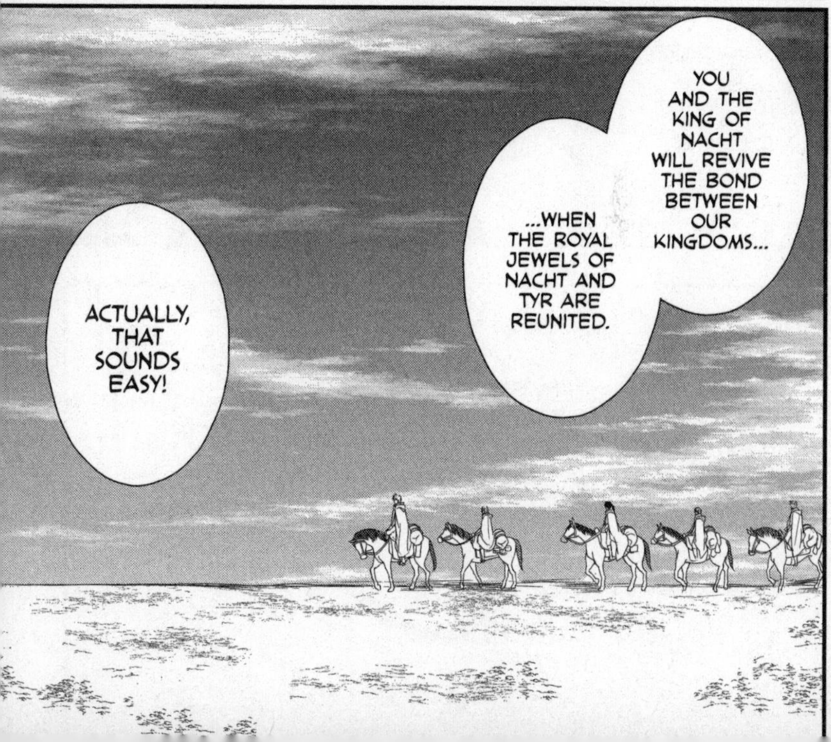
YOU AND THE KING OF NACHT WILL REVIVE THE BOND BETWEEN OUR KINGDOMS...
...WHEN THE ROYAL JEWELS OF NACHT AND TYR ARE REUNITED.
ACTUALLY, THAT SOUNDS EASY!

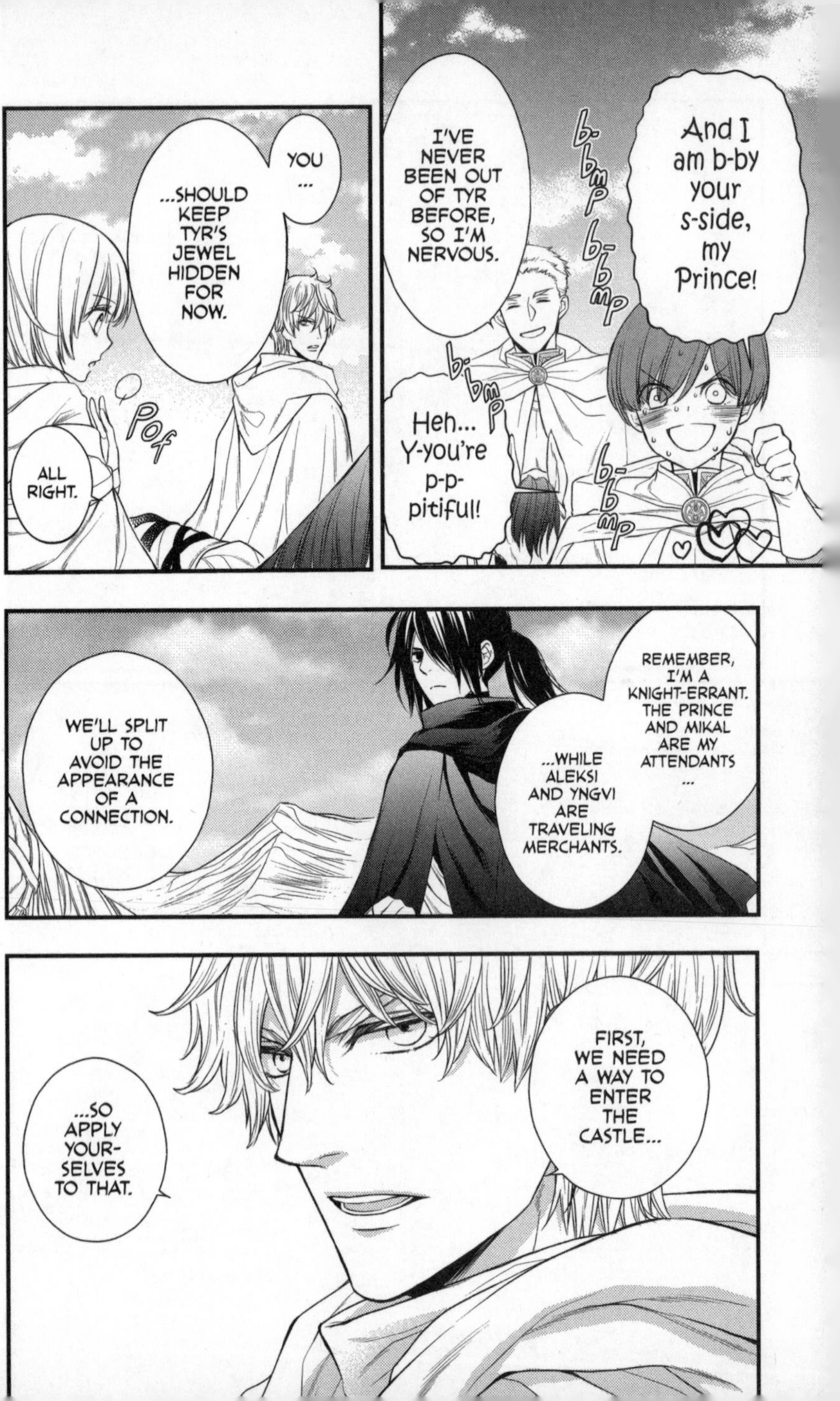
I'VE NEVER BEEN OUT OF TYR BEFORE, SO I'M NERVOUS.
And I am b-by your s-side, my Prince!
b-bmp b-bmp
b-bmp b-bmp
Heh... Y-you're p-p-pitiful!
YOU...
...SHOULD KEEP TYR'S JEWEL HIDDEN FOR NOW.
Pof
ALL RIGHT.
REMEMBER, I'M A KNIGHT-ERRANT. THE PRINCE AND MIKAL ARE MY ATTENDANTS...
...WHILE ALEKSI AND YNGVI ARE TRAVELING MERCHANTS.
WE'LL SPLIT UP TO AVOID THE APPEARANCE OF A CONNECTION.
FIRST, WE NEED A WAY TO ENTER THE CASTLE...
...SO APPLY YOUR-SELVES TO THAT.

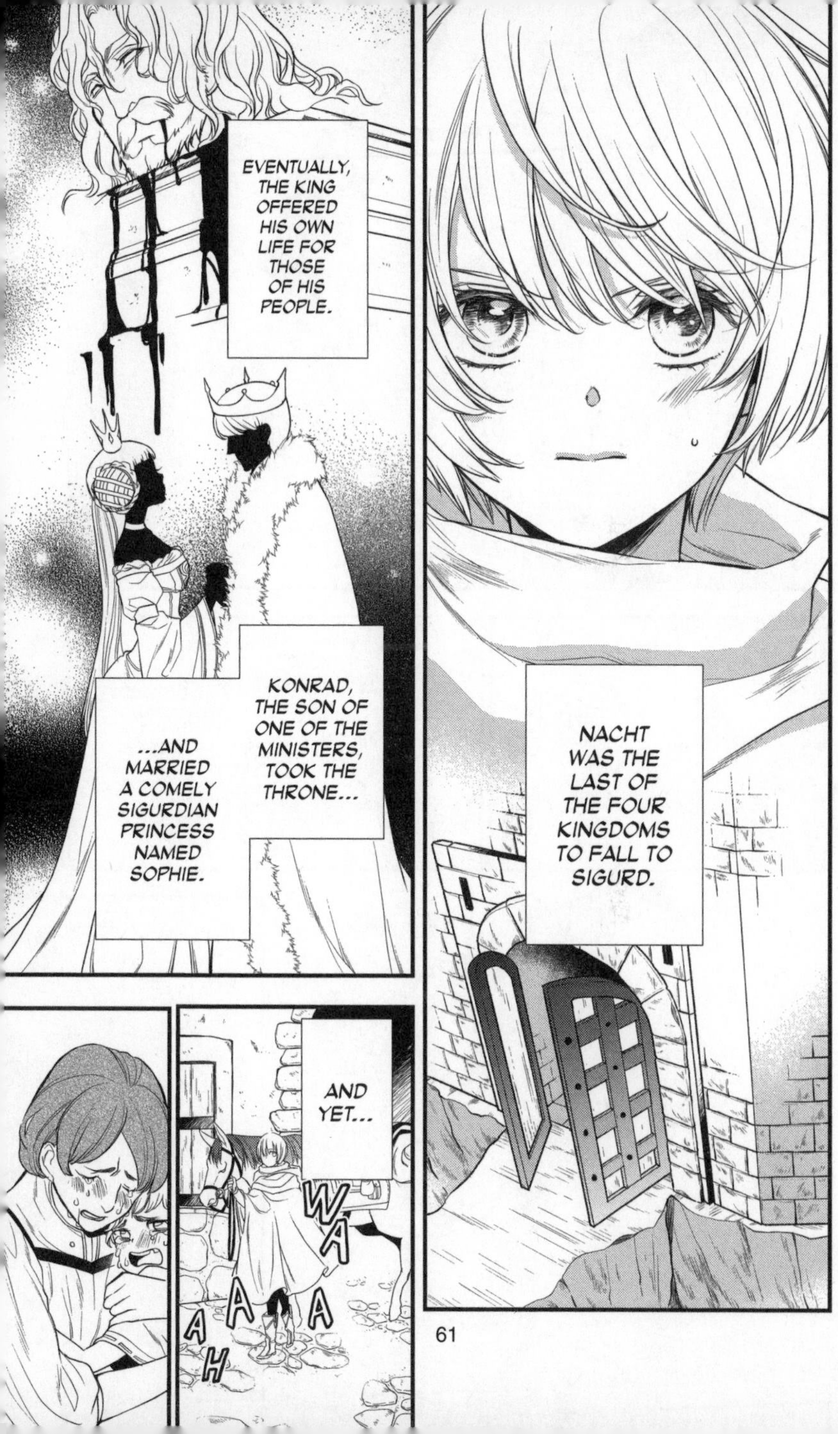
NACHT WAS THE LAST OF THE FOUR KINGDOMS TO FALL TO SIGURD.
EVENTUALLY, THE KING OFFERED HIS OWN LIFE FOR THOSE OF HIS PEOPLE.
KONRAD, THE SON OF ONE OF THE MINISTERS, TOOK THE THRONE...
...AND MARRIED A COMELY SIGURDIAN PRINCESS NAMED SOPHIE.
AND YET...
WAAAAAH

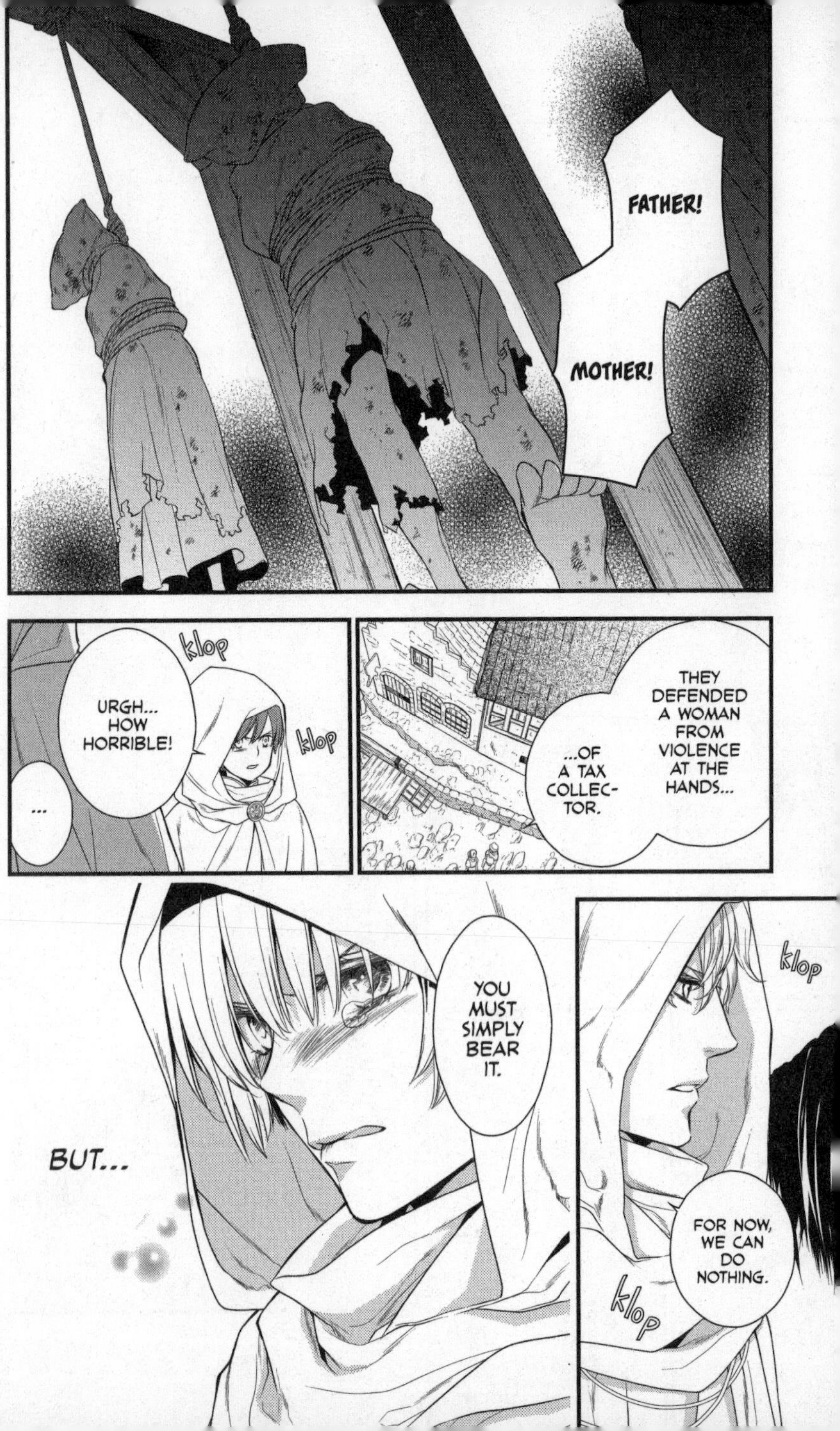
FATHER!
MOTHER!
THEY DEFENDED A WOMAN FROM VIOLENCE AT THE HANDS...
...OF A TAX COLLECTOR.
klop
URGH... HOW HORRIBLE!
klop
...
klop
FOR NOW, WE CAN DO NOTHING.
klop
YOU MUST SIMPLY BEAR IT.
BUT...

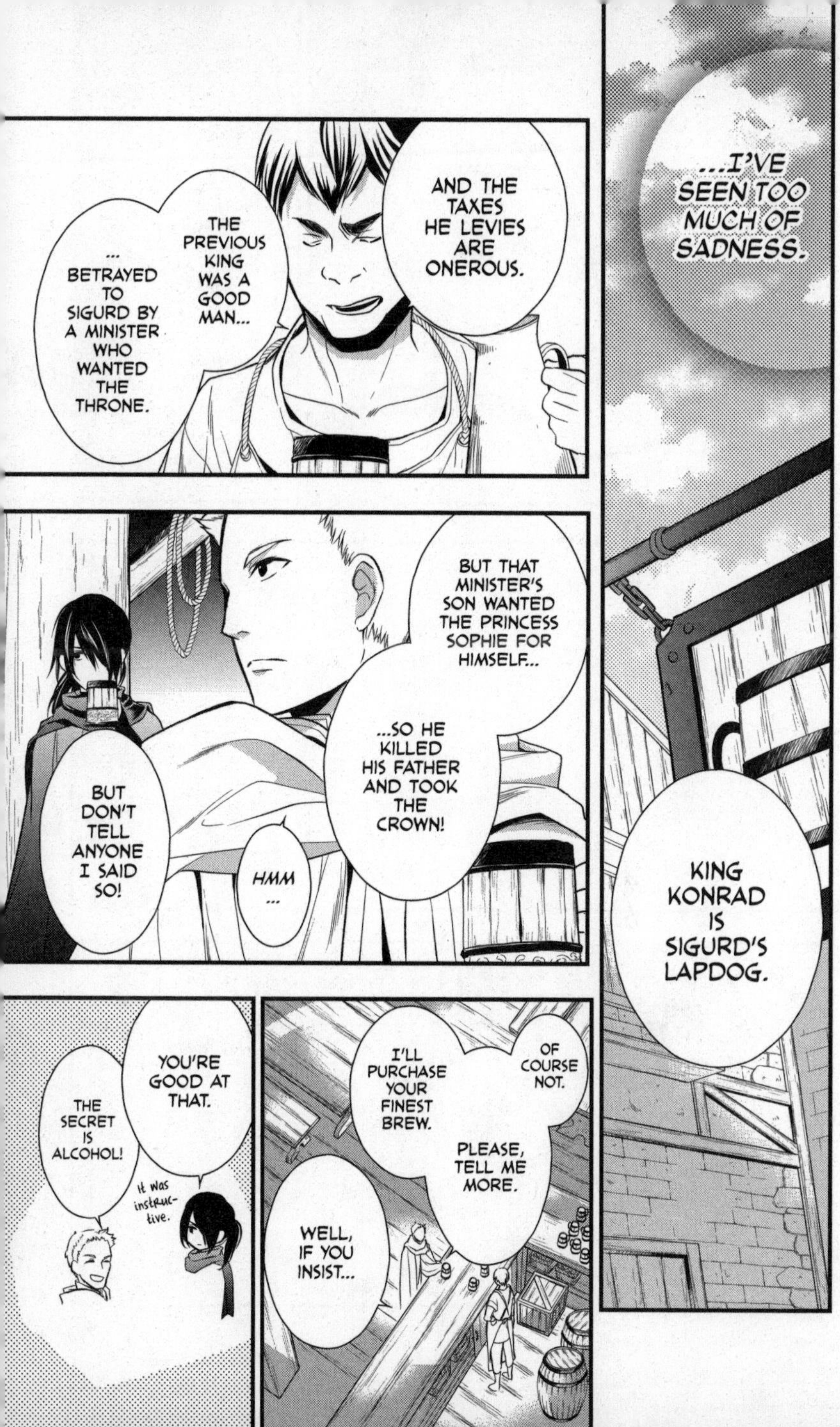
...I'VE SEEN TOO MUCH OF SADNESS.
KING KONRAD IS SIGURD'S LAPDOG.
AND THE TAXES HE LEVIES ARE ONEROUS.
THE PREVIOUS KING WAS A GOOD MAN...
...BETRAYED TO SIGURD BY A MINISTER WHO WANTED THE THRONE.
BUT THAT MINISTER'S SON WANTED THE PRINCESS SOPHIE FOR HIMSELF...
...SO HE KILLED HIS FATHER AND TOOK THE CROWN!
HMM...
BUT DON'T TELL ANYONE I SAID SO!
OF COURSE NOT.
I'LL PURCHASE YOUR FINEST BREW.
PLEASE, TELL ME MORE.
WELL, IF YOU INSIST...
YOU'RE GOOD AT THAT.
THE SECRET IS ALCOHOL!
It was instructive.

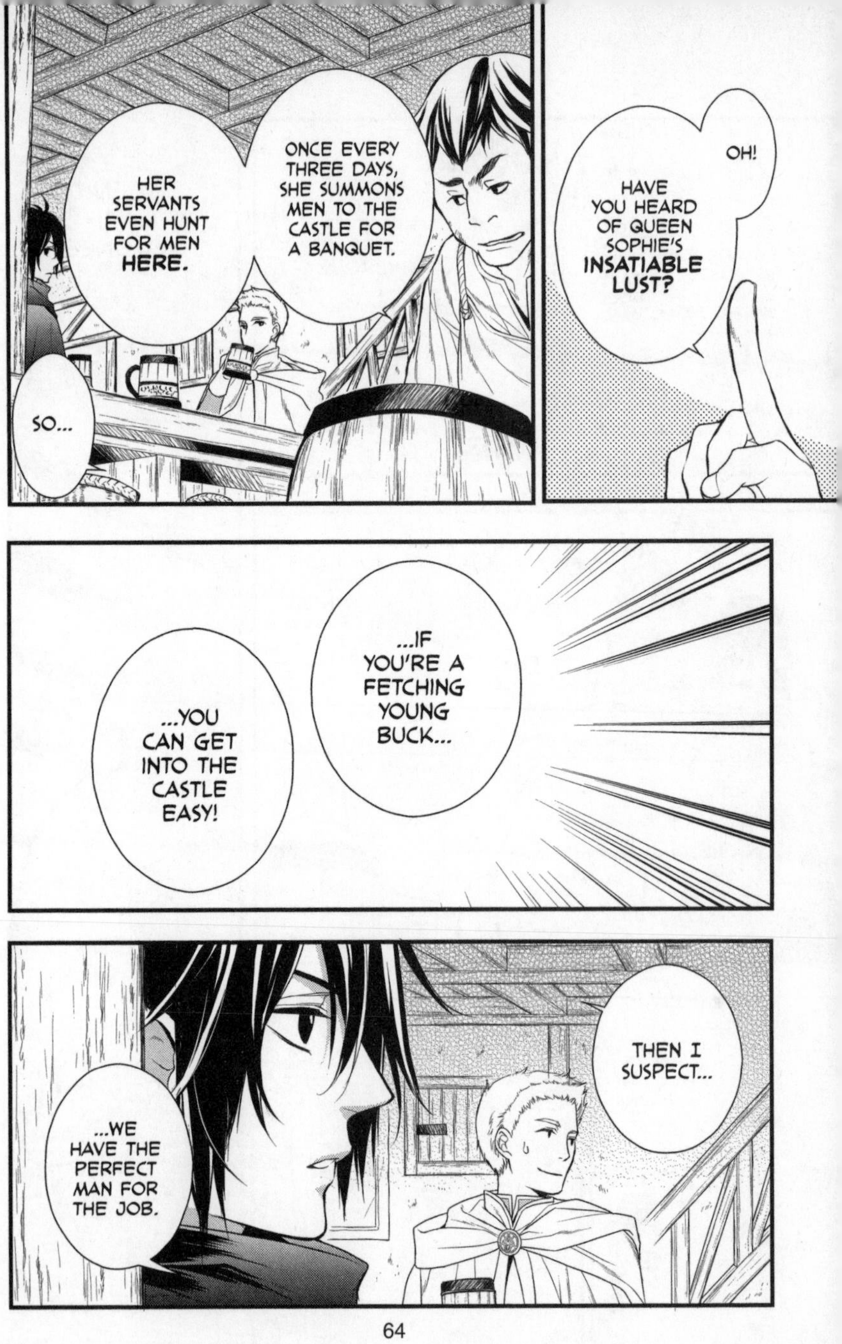
OH!
HAVE YOU HEARD OF QUEEN SOPHIE'S INSATIABLE LUST?
ONCE EVERY THREE DAYS, SHE SUMMONS MEN TO THE CASTLE FOR A BANQUET.
HER SERVANTS EVEN HUNT FOR MEN HERE.
SO...
...IF YOU'RE A FETCHING YOUNG BUCK...
...YOU CAN GET INTO THE CASTLE EASY!
THEN I SUSPECT...
...WE HAVE THE PERFECT MAN FOR THE JOB.

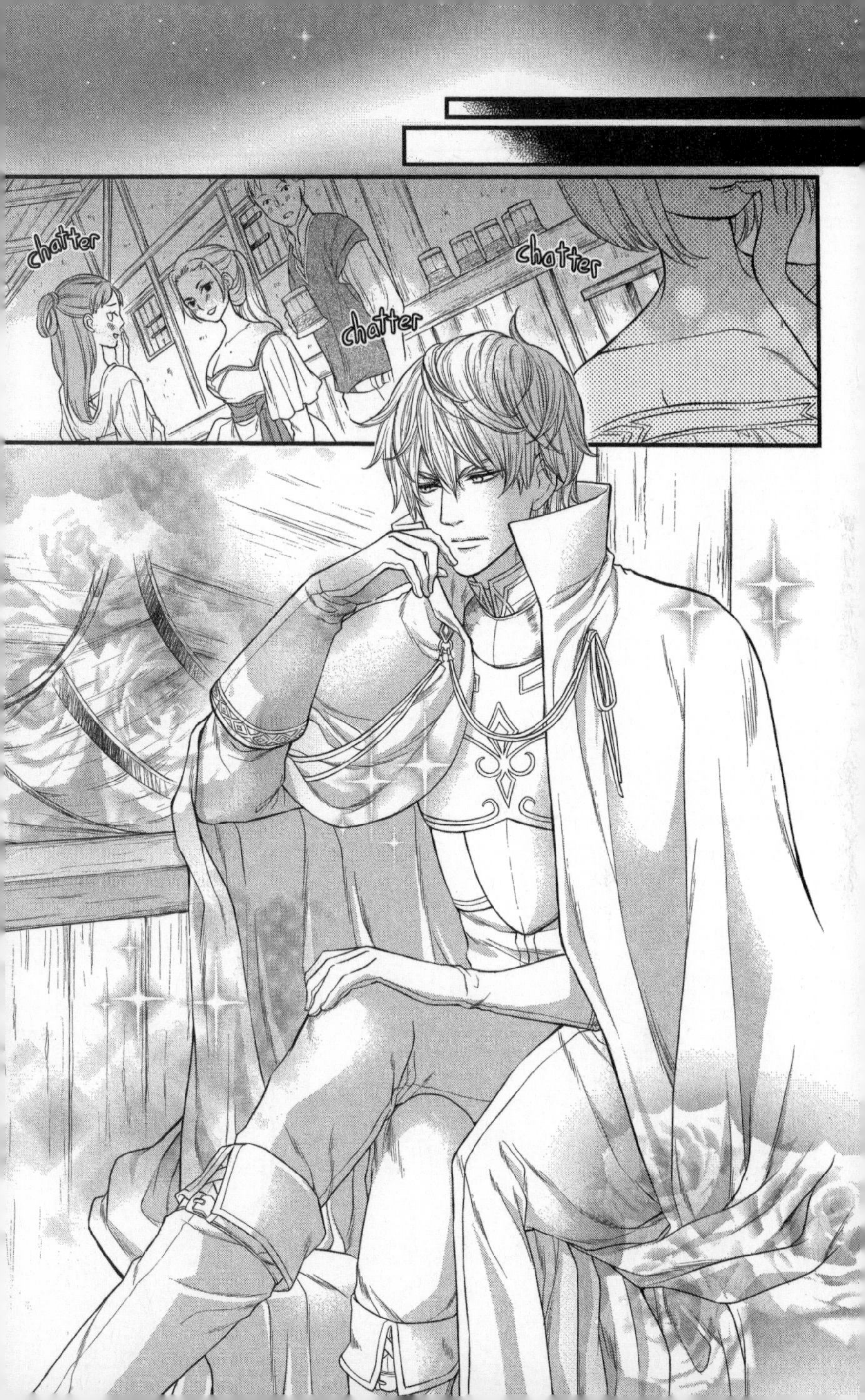
chatter
chatter
chatter

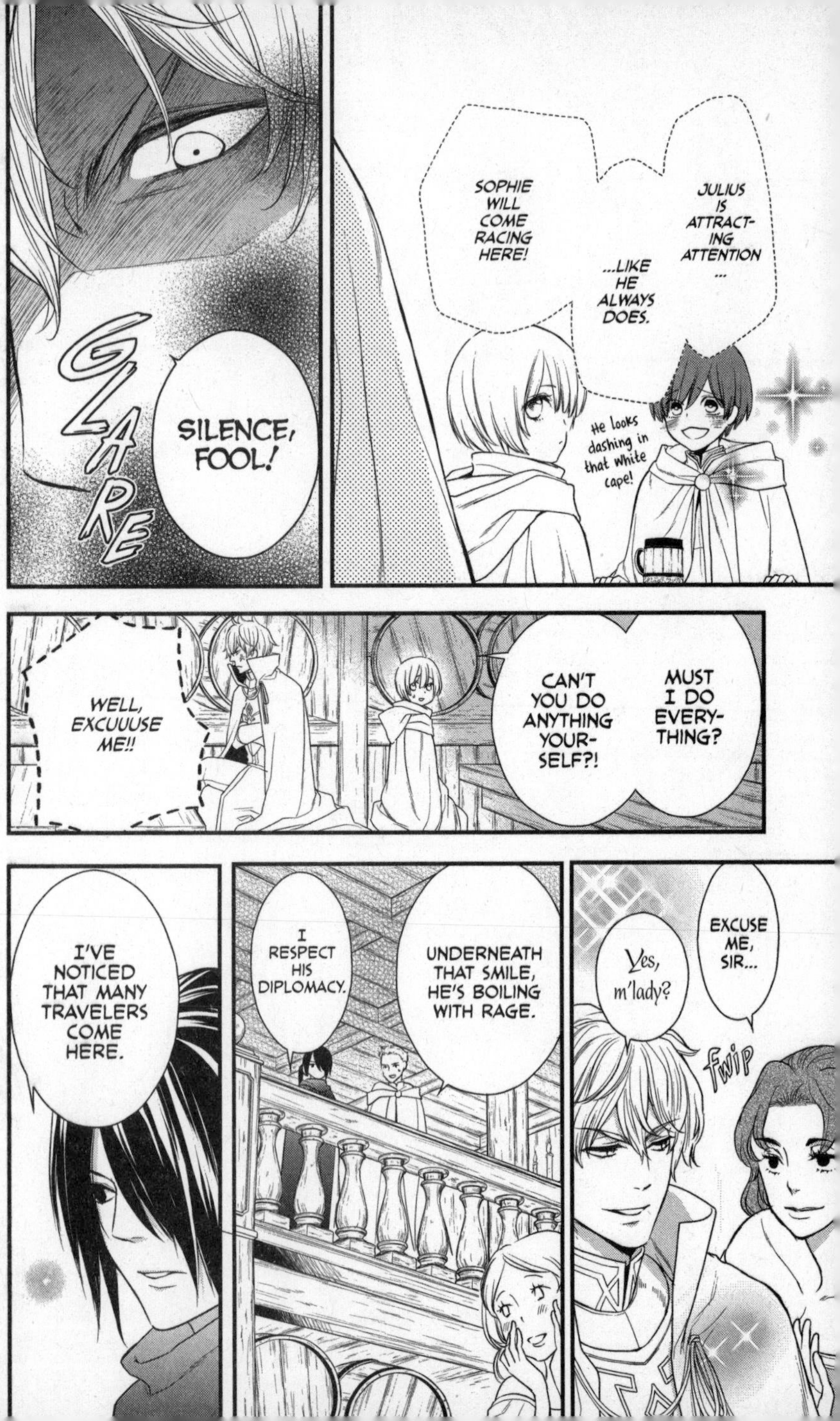
JULIUS IS ATTRACT-ING ATTENTION...
...LIKE HE ALWAYS DOES.
SOPHIE WILL COME RACING HERE!
He looks dashing in that white cape!
GLARE
SILENCE, FOOL!
MUST I DO EVERY-THING?
CAN'T YOU DO ANYTHING YOUR-SELF?!
WELL, EXCUUUSE ME!!
EXCUSE ME, SIR...
Yes, m'lady?
fwip
UNDERNEATH THAT SMILE, HE'S BOILING WITH RAGE.
I RESPECT HIS DIPLOMACY.
I'VE NOTICED THAT MANY TRAVELERS COME HERE.

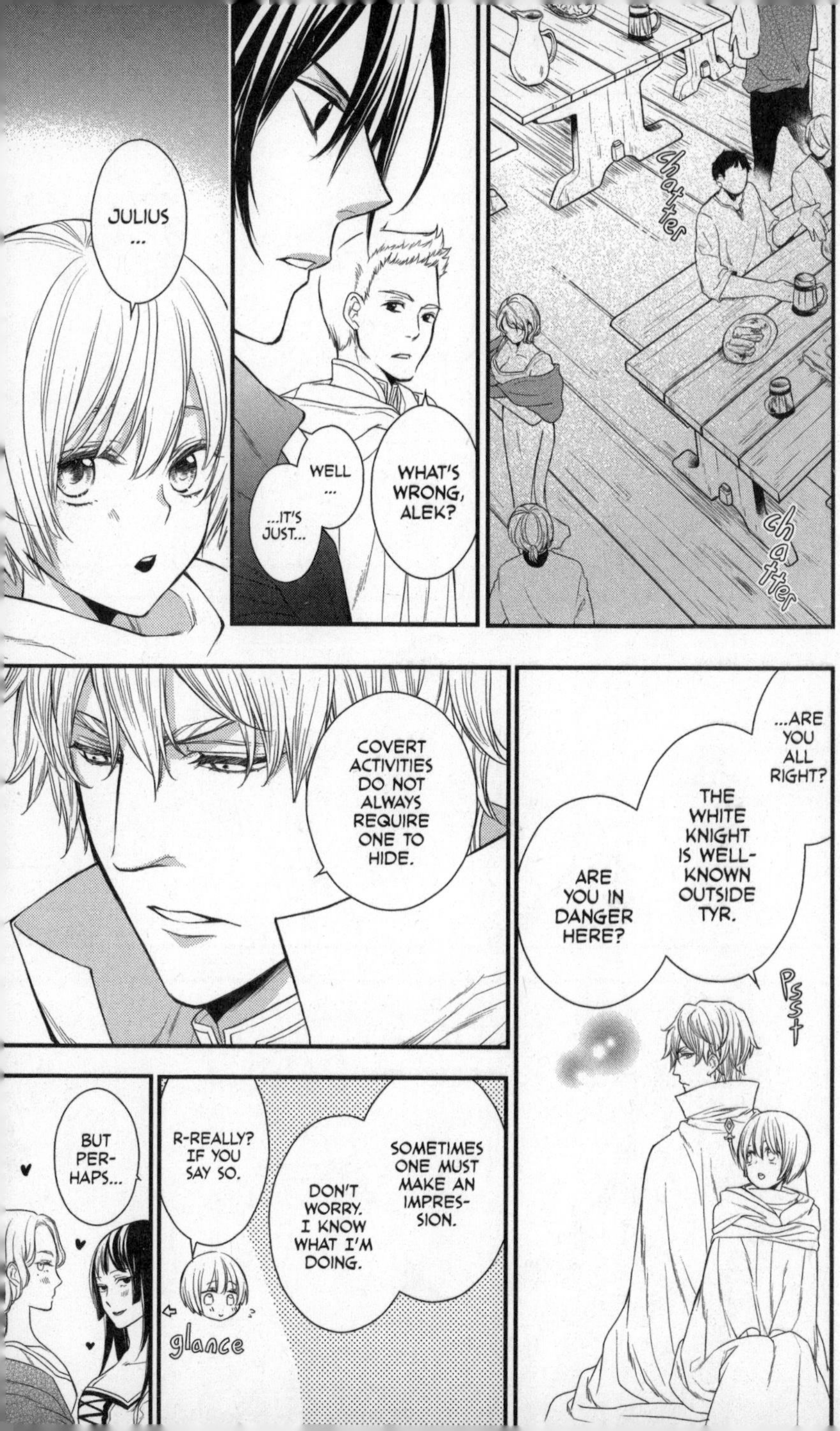
chatter
chatter
WHAT'S WRONG, ALEK?
WELL...
...IT'S JUST...
JULIUS...
...ARE YOU ALL RIGHT?
THE WHITE KNIGHT IS WELL-KNOWN OUTSIDE TYR.
ARE YOU IN DANGER HERE?
Psst
COVERT ACTIVITIES DO NOT ALWAYS REQUIRE ONE TO HIDE.
SOMETIMES ONE MUST MAKE AN IMPRESSION.
DON'T WORRY. I KNOW WHAT I'M DOING.
R-REALLY? IF YOU SAY SO.
glance
BUT PERHAPS...

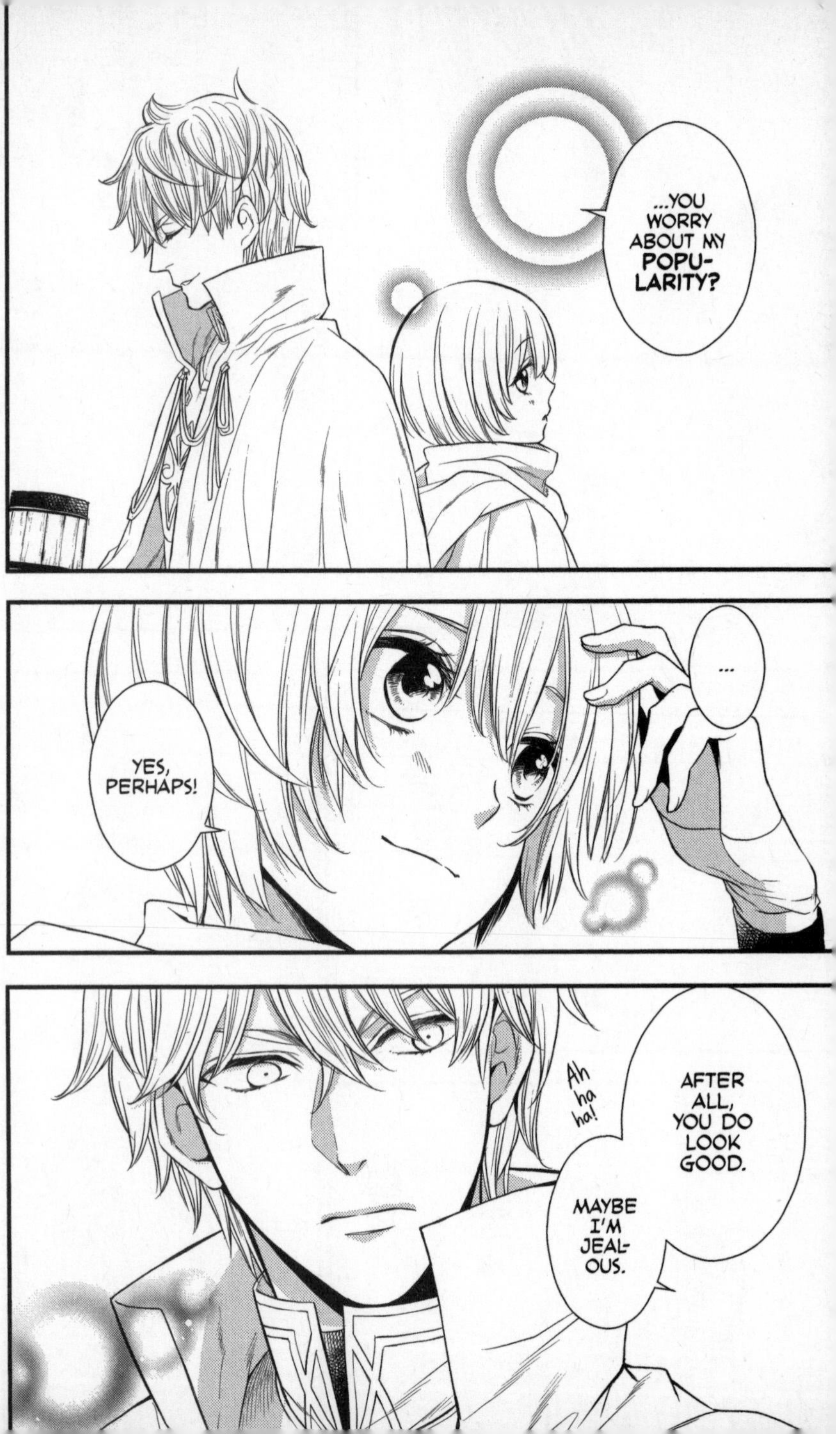
...YOU WORRY ABOUT MY POPULARITY?
...
YES, PERHAPS!
AFTER ALL, YOU DO LOOK GOOD.
Ah ha ha!
MAYBE I'M JEALOUS.

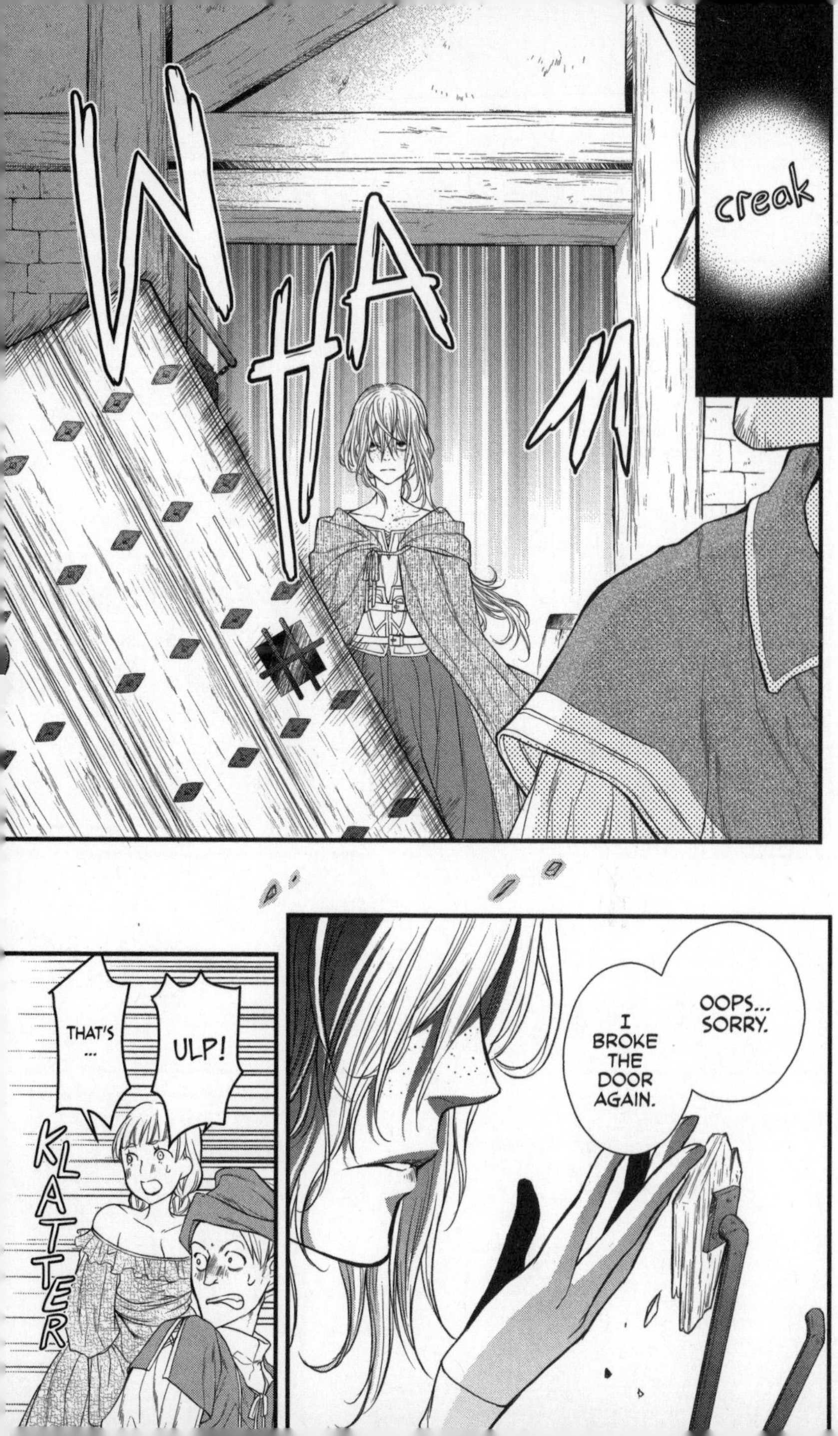
creak
WHAM
OOPS... SORRY.
I BROKE THE DOOR AGAIN.
ULP!
THAT'S ...
KLATTER

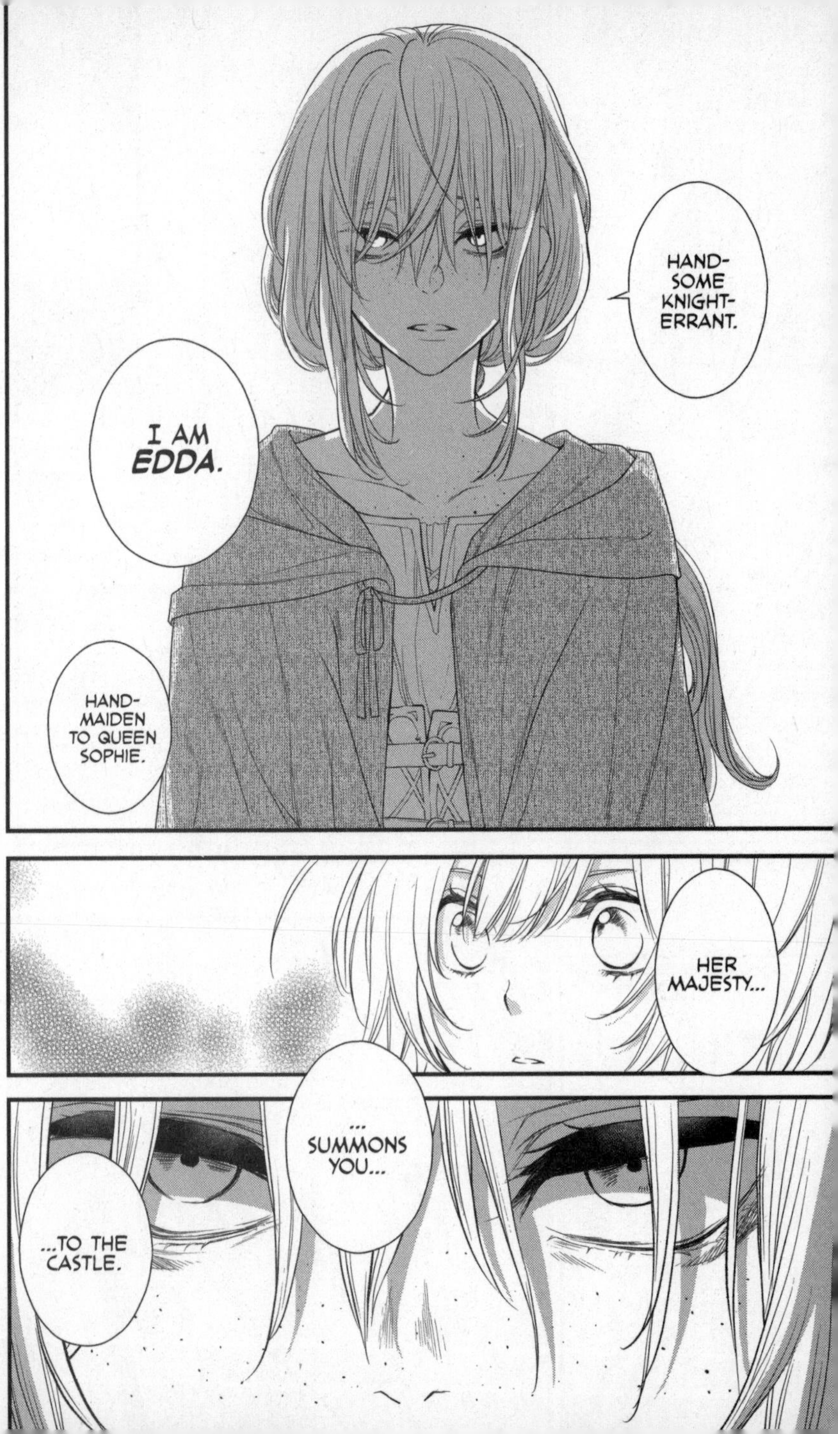
HAND-SOME KNIGHT-ERRANT.
I AM EDDA.
HAND-MAIDEN TO QUEEN SOPHIE.
HER MAJESTY...
... SUMMONS YOU...
...TO THE CASTLE.

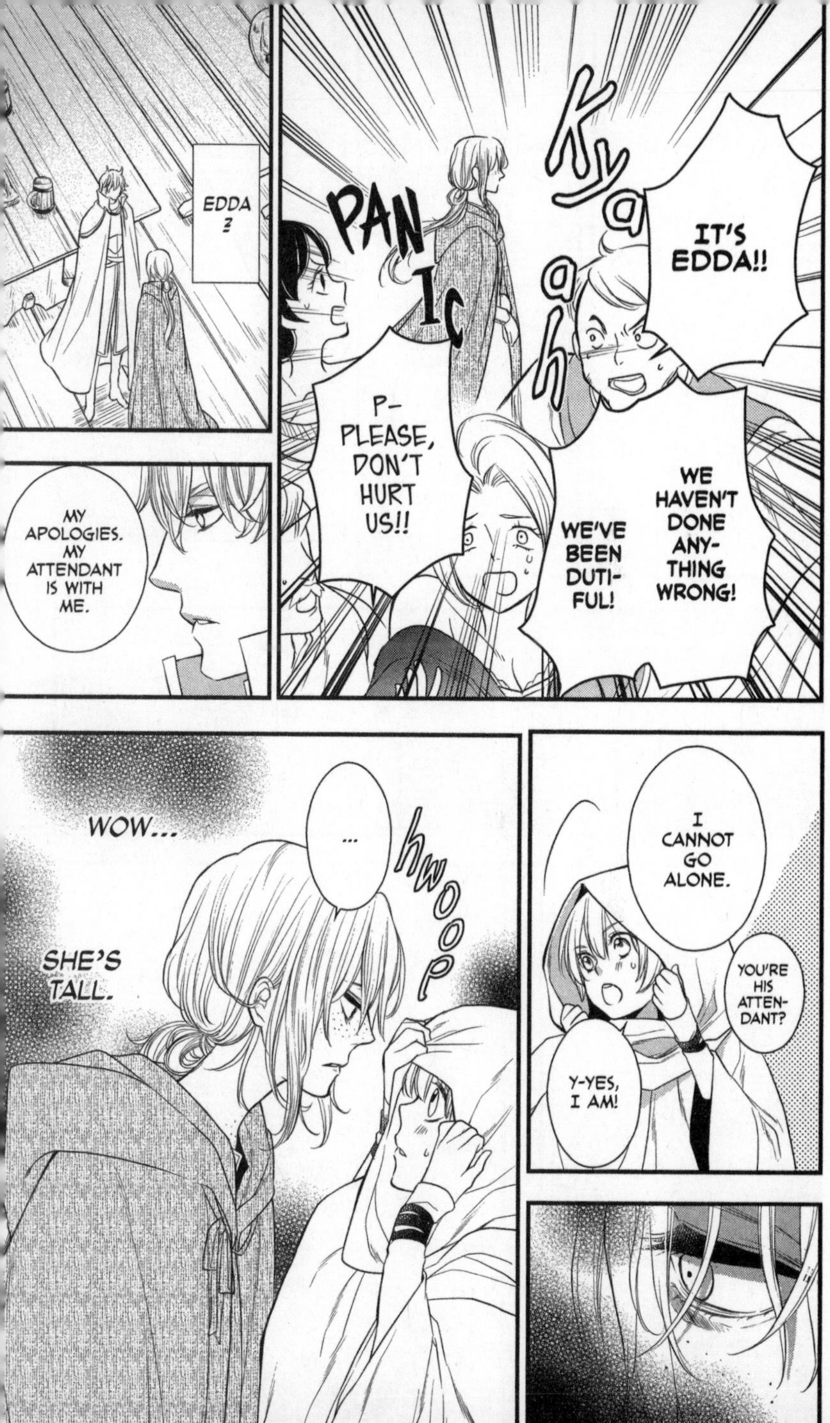

Kyaah
IT'S EDDA!!
PANIC
P-PLEASE, DON'T HURT US!!
WE HAVEN'T DONE ANYTHING WRONG!
WE'VE BEEN DUTIFUL!
EDDA?
MY APOLOGIES. MY ATTENDANT IS WITH ME.
I CANNOT GO ALONE.
YOU'RE HIS ATTENDANT?
Y-YES, I AM!
...
hwoop
WOW...
SHE'S TALL.

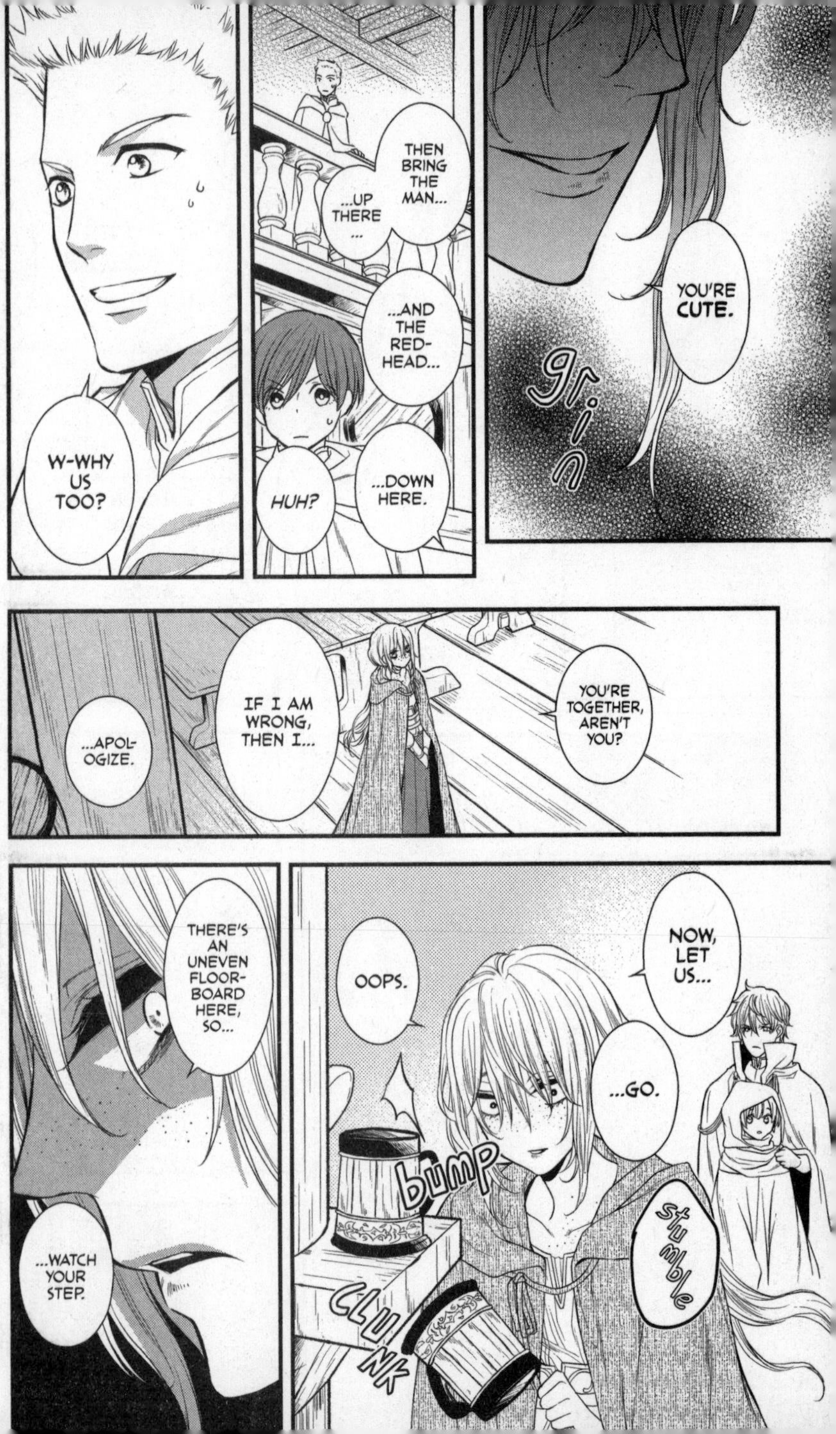
YOU'RE CUTE.
grin
THEN BRING THE MAN...
...UP THERE...
...AND THE RED-HEAD...
...DOWN HERE.
HUH?
W-WHY US TOO?
YOU'RE TOGETHER, AREN'T YOU?
IF I AM WRONG, THEN I...
...APOL-OGIZE.
NOW, LET US...
...GO.
stumble
OOPS.
bump
CLUNK
THERE'S AN UNEVEN FLOOR-BOARD HERE, SO...
...WATCH YOUR STEP.

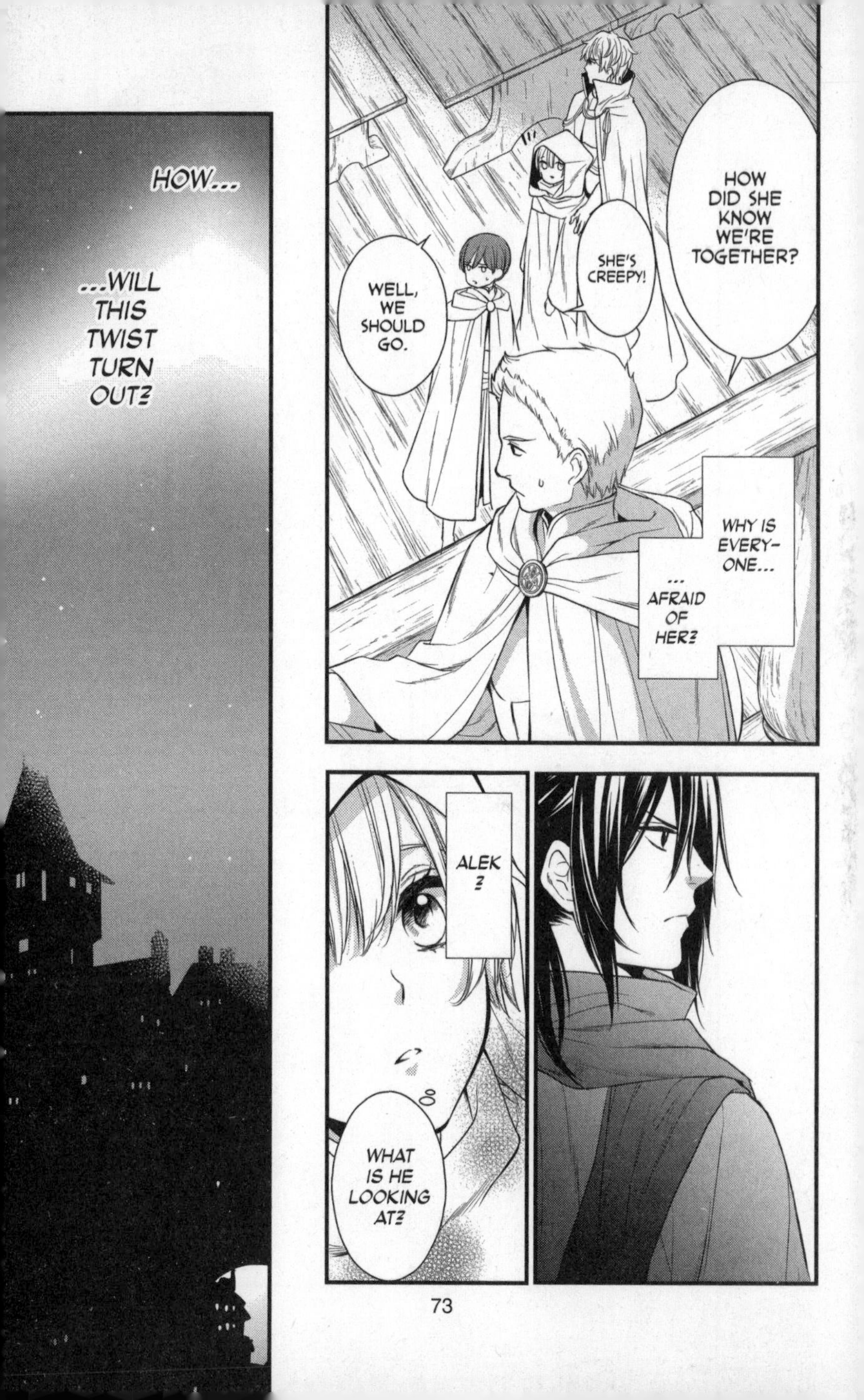
HOW DID SHE KNOW WE'RE TOGETHER?
SHE'S CREEPY!
WELL, WE SHOULD GO.
WHY IS EVERYONE...
...AFRAID OF HER?
ALEK?
WHAT IS HE LOOKING AT?
HOW...
...WILL THIS TWIST TURN OUT?

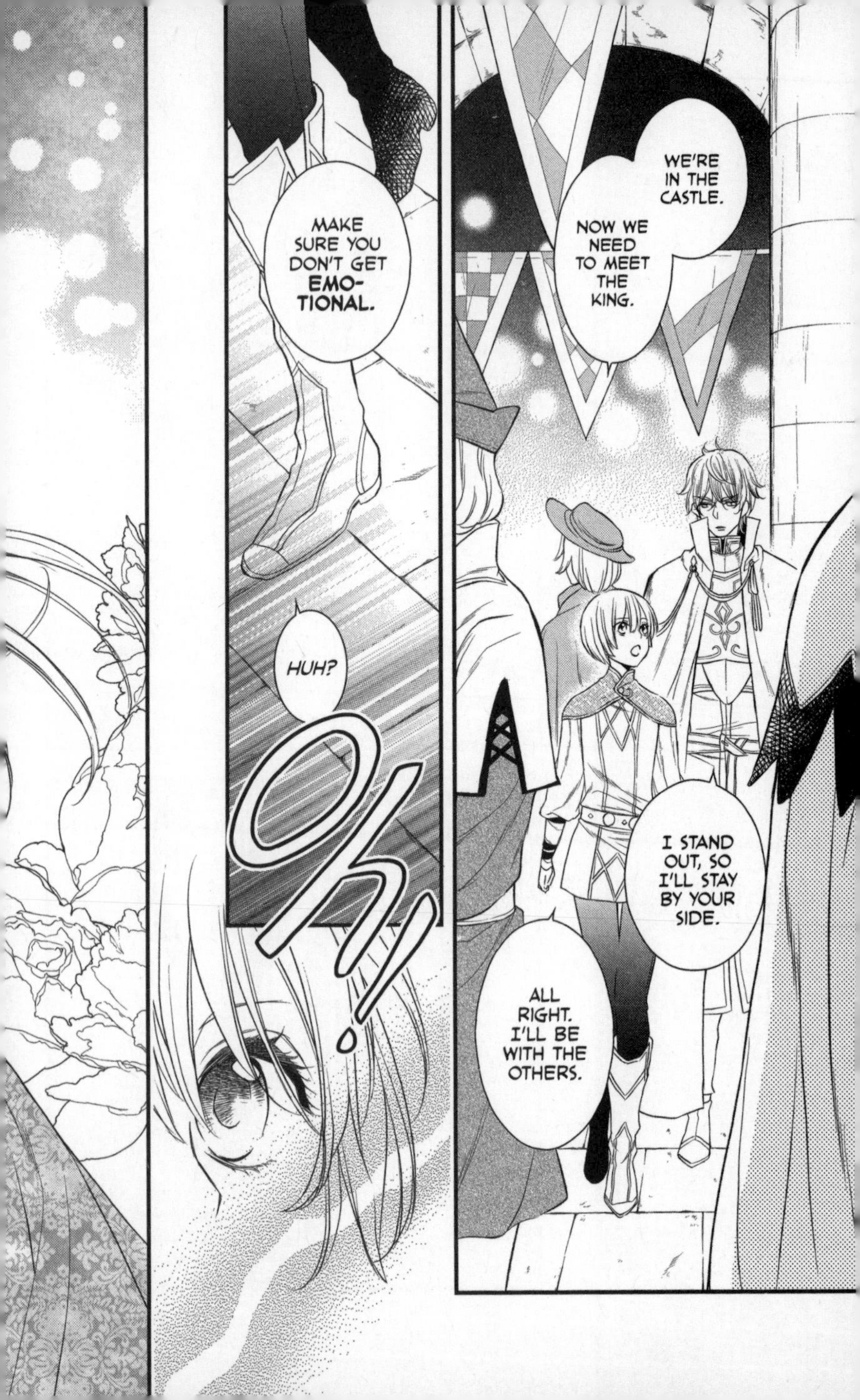
WE'RE IN THE CASTLE. NOW WE NEED TO MEET THE KING.
I STAND OUT, SO I'LL STAY BY YOUR SIDE.
ALL RIGHT. I'LL BE WITH THE OTHERS.
MAKE SURE YOU DON'T GET EMO-TIONAL.
HUH?
OH!

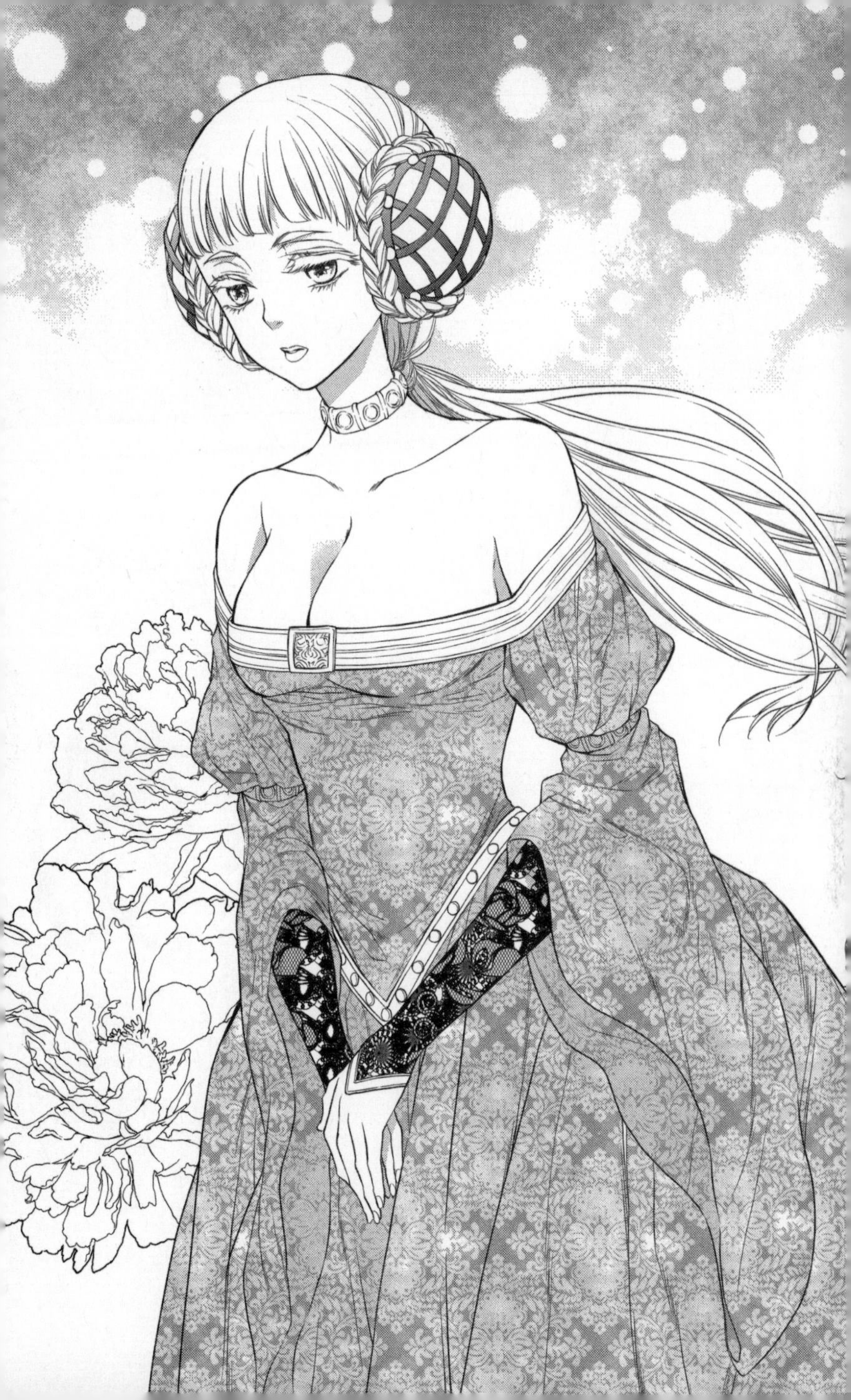

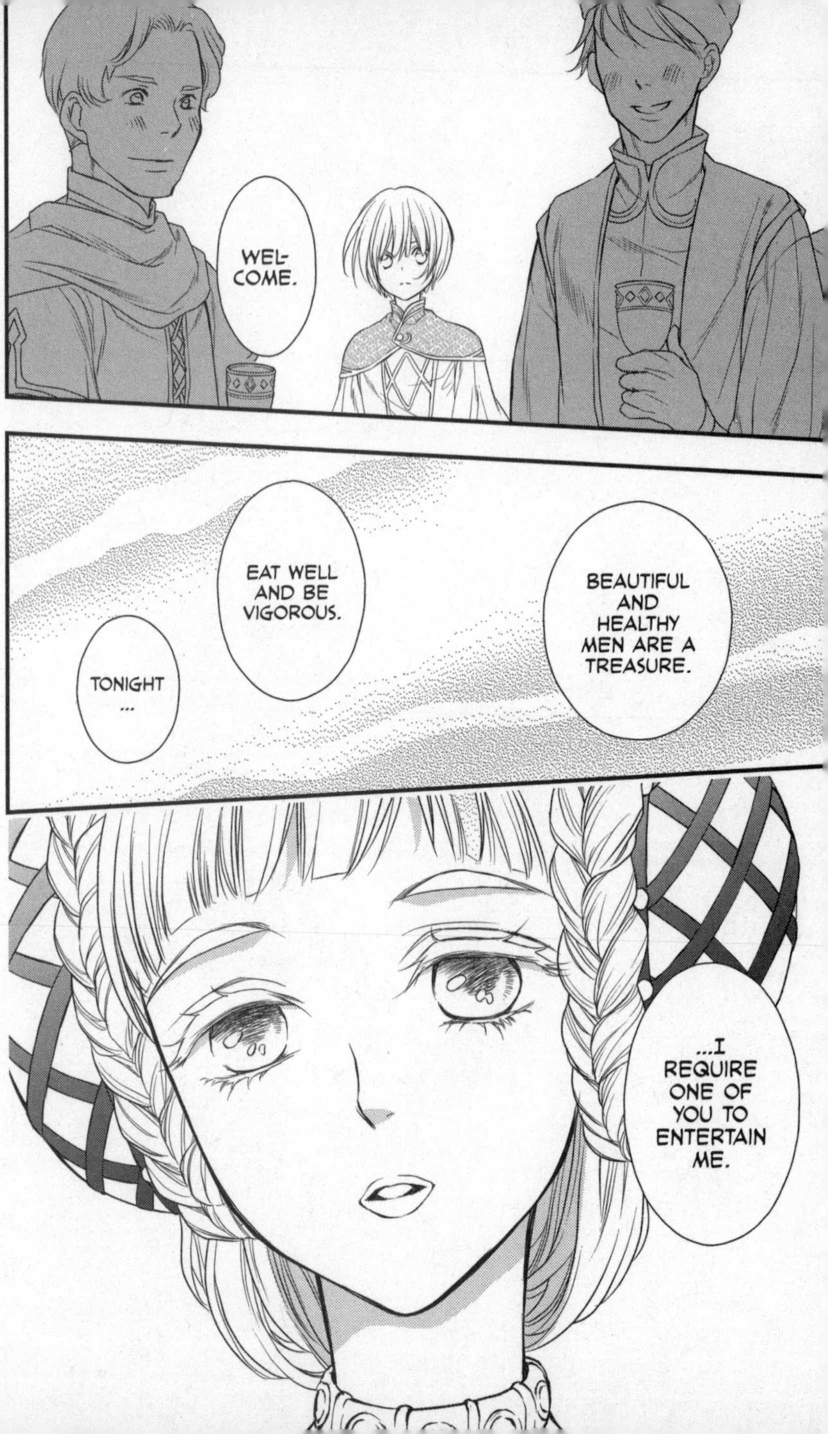
WEL-COME.
BEAUTIFUL AND HEALTHY MEN ARE A TREASURE.
EAT WELL AND BE VIGOROUS.
TONIGHT...
...I REQUIRE ONE OF YOU TO ENTERTAIN ME.

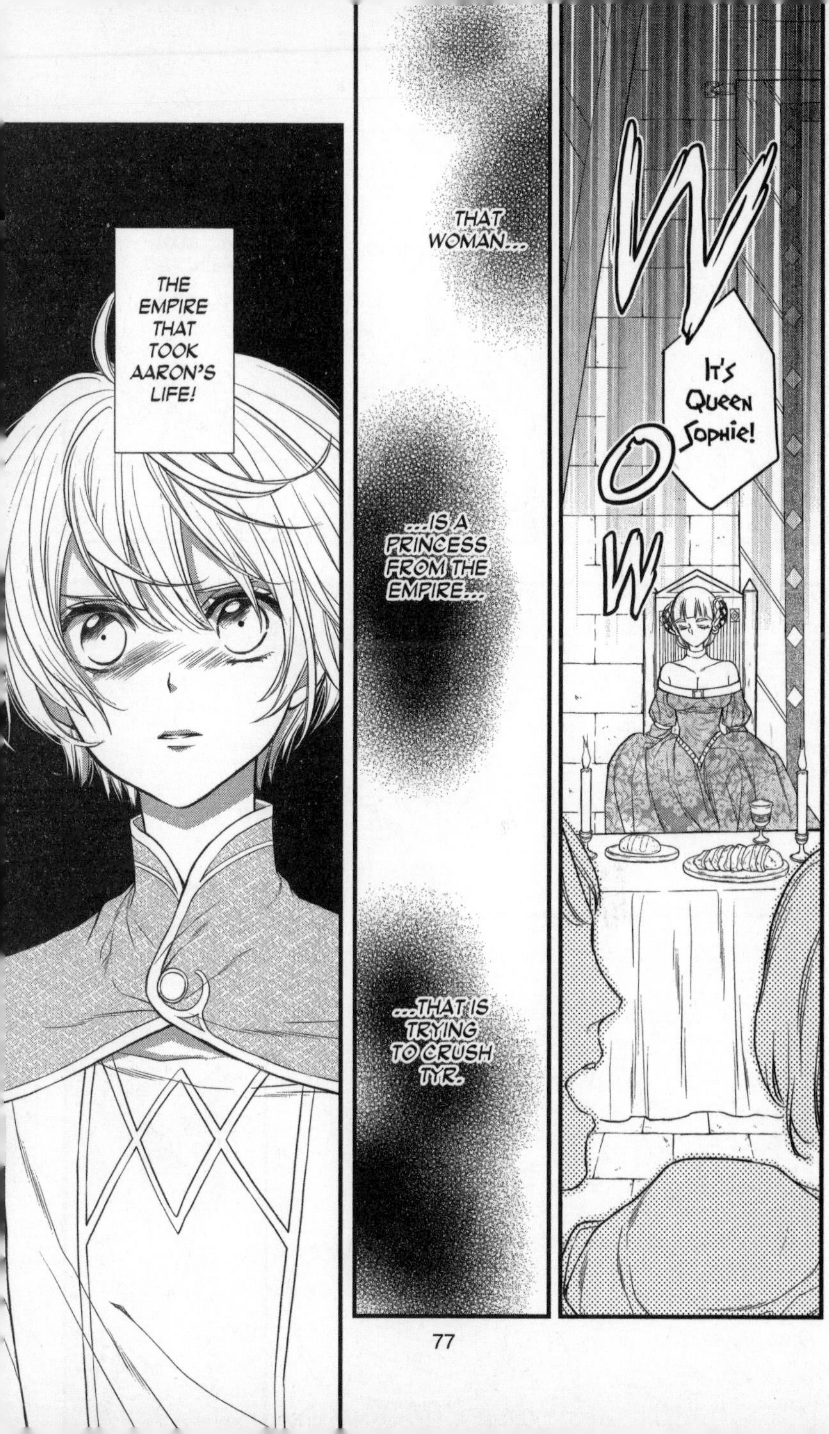
WOW
It's Queen Sophie!
THAT WOMAN...
...IS A PRINCESS FROM THE EMPIRE...
...THAT IS TRYING TO CRUSH TYR.
THE EMPIRE THAT TOOK AARON'S LIFE!

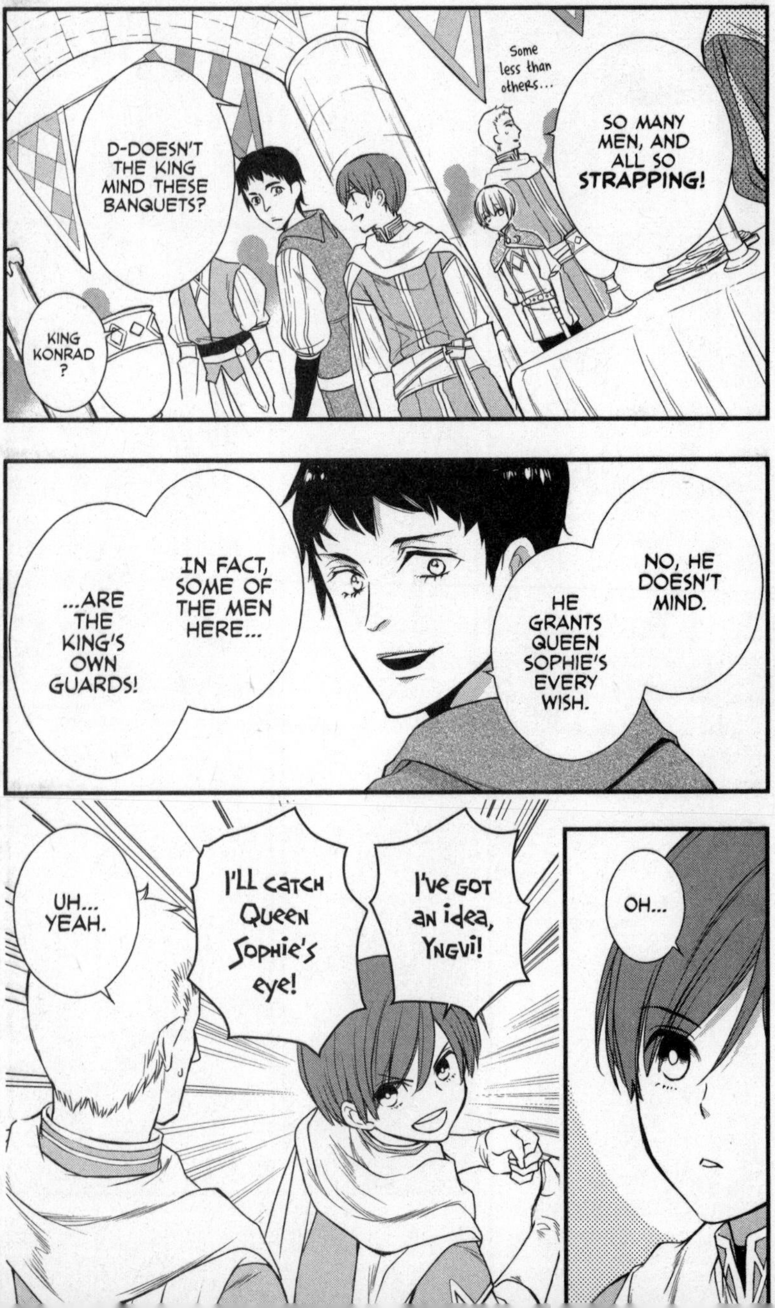
SO MANY MEN, AND ALL SO STRAPPING!
Some less than others...
D-DOESN'T THE KING MIND THESE BANQUETS?
KING KONRAD?
NO, HE DOESN'T MIND.
HE GRANTS QUEEN SOPHIE'S EVERY WISH.
IN FACT, SOME OF THE MEN HERE...
...ARE THE KING'S OWN GUARDS!
OH...
I've got an idea, Yngvi!
I'll catch Queen Sophie's eye!
UH... YEAH.

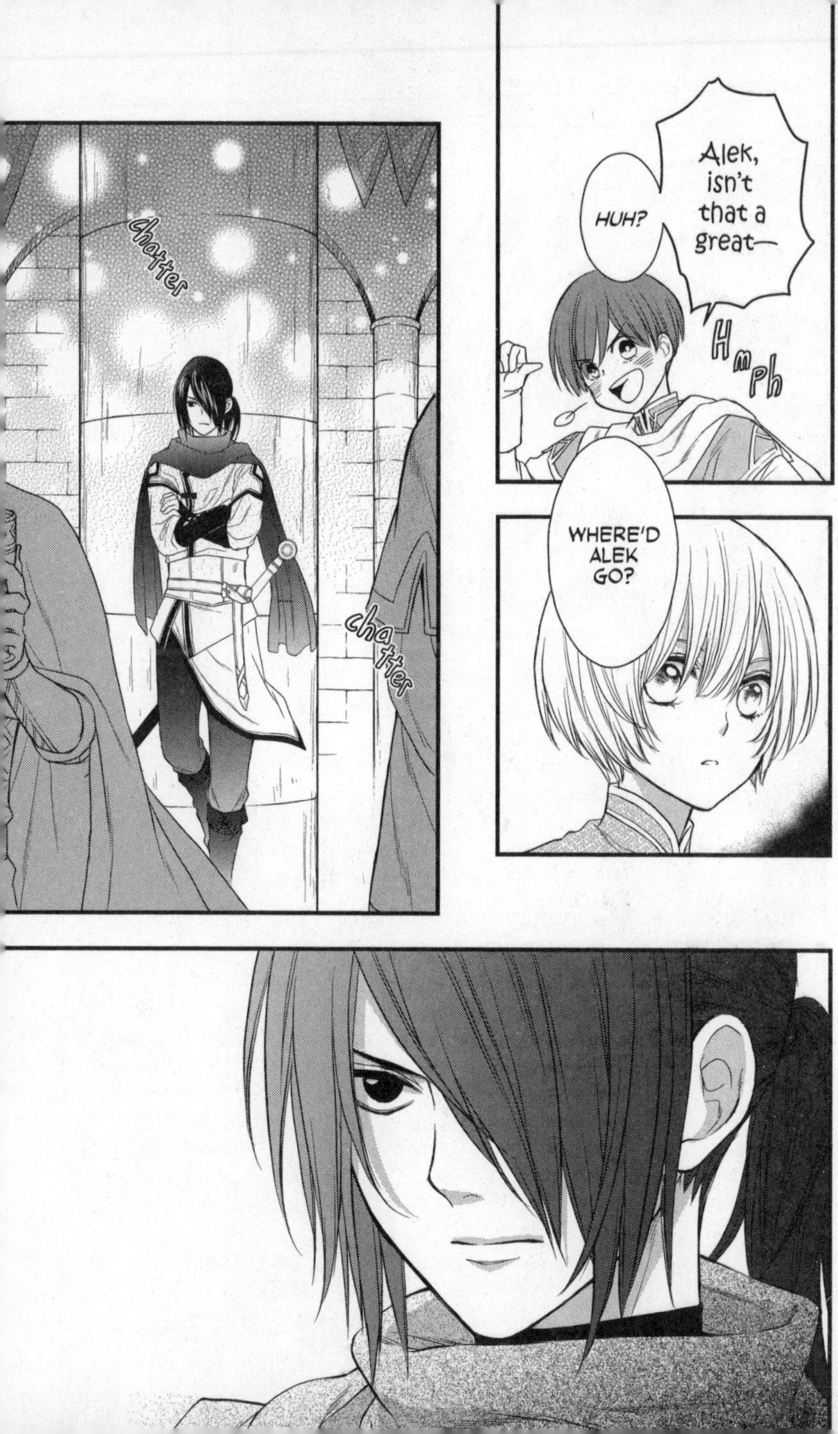
Alek, isn't that a great—
HUH?
Hmph
WHERE'D ALEK GO?
chatter
chatter

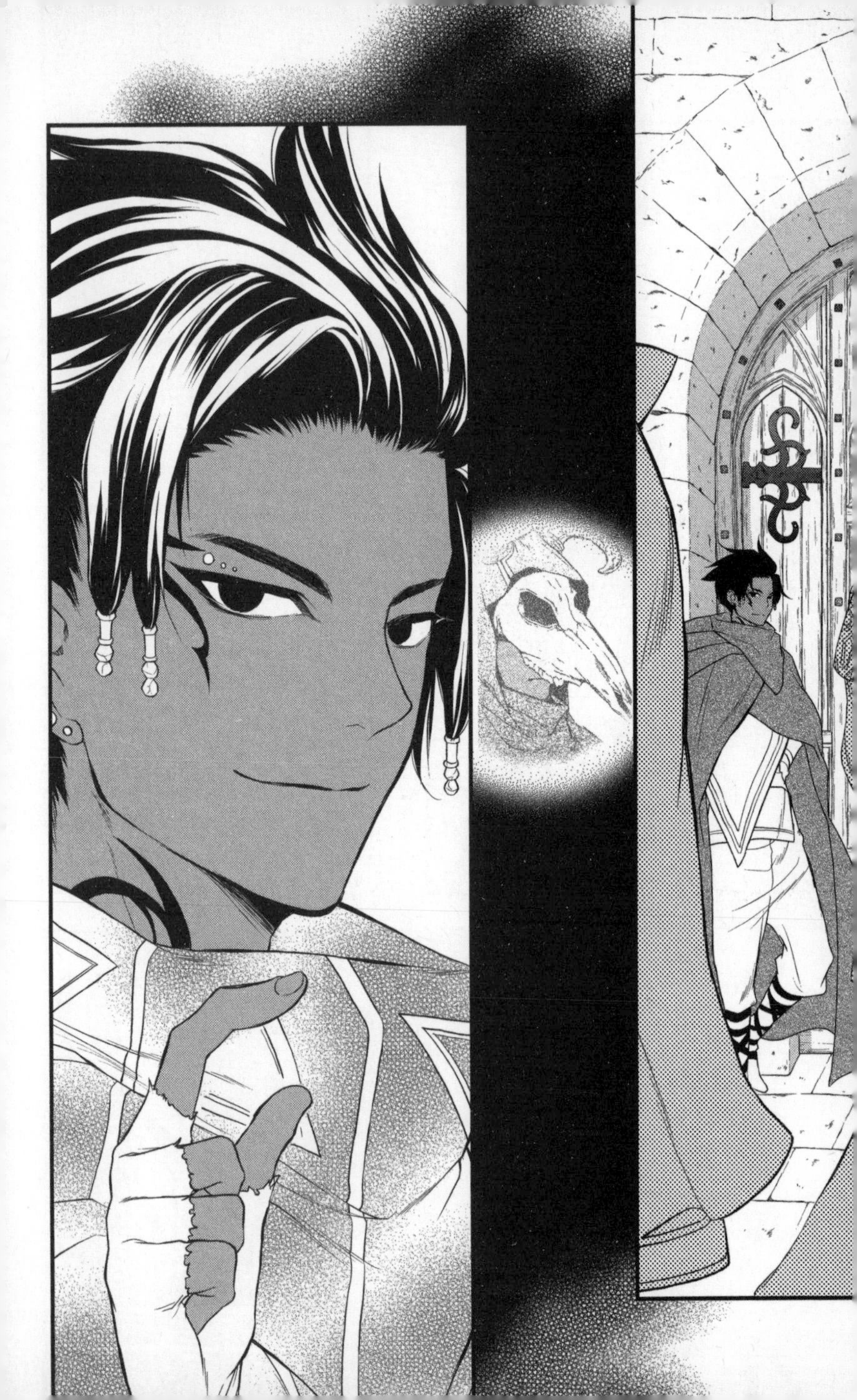

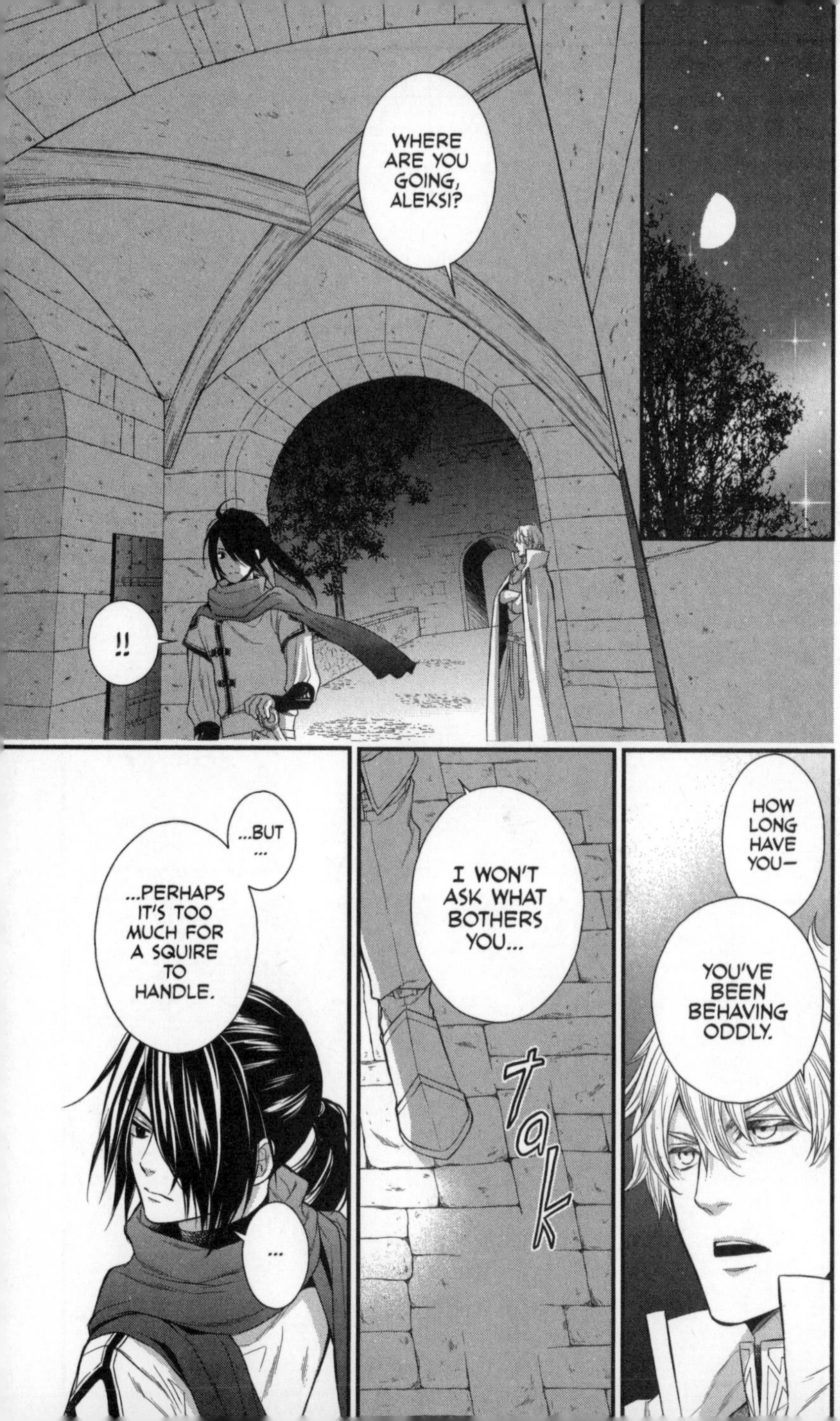
WHERE ARE YOU GOING, ALEKSI?
!!
HOW LONG HAVE YOU—
YOU'VE BEEN BEHAVING ODDLY.
I WON'T ASK WHAT BOTHERS YOU...
tak
...BUT ...
...PERHAPS IT'S TOO MUCH FOR A SQUIRE TO HANDLE.
...

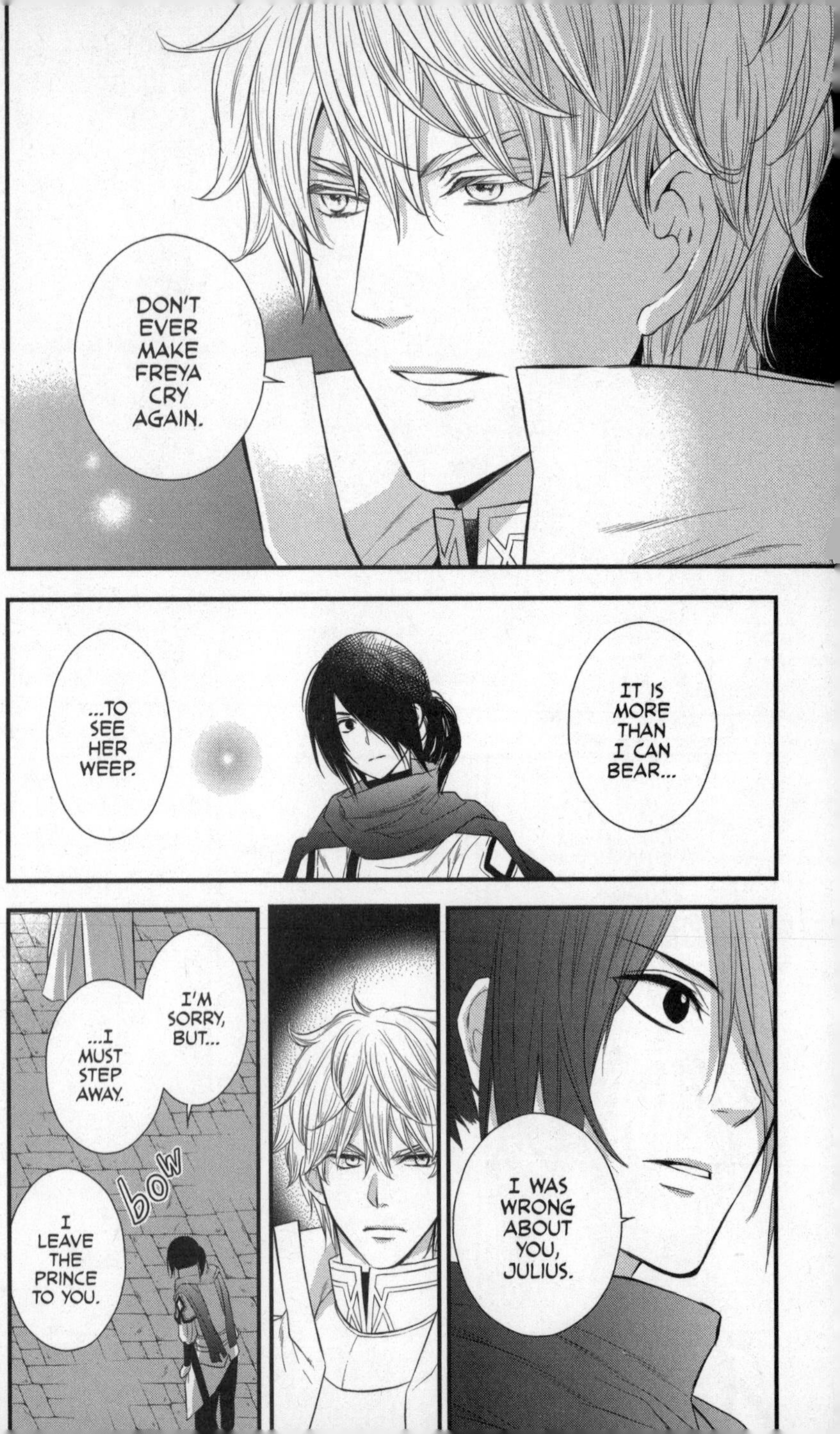
DON'T EVER MAKE FREYA CRY AGAIN.
IT IS MORE THAN I CAN BEAR...
...TO SEE HER WEEP.
I WAS WRONG ABOUT YOU, JULIUS.
I'M SORRY, BUT...
...I MUST STEP AWAY.
bow
I LEAVE THE PRINCE TO YOU.

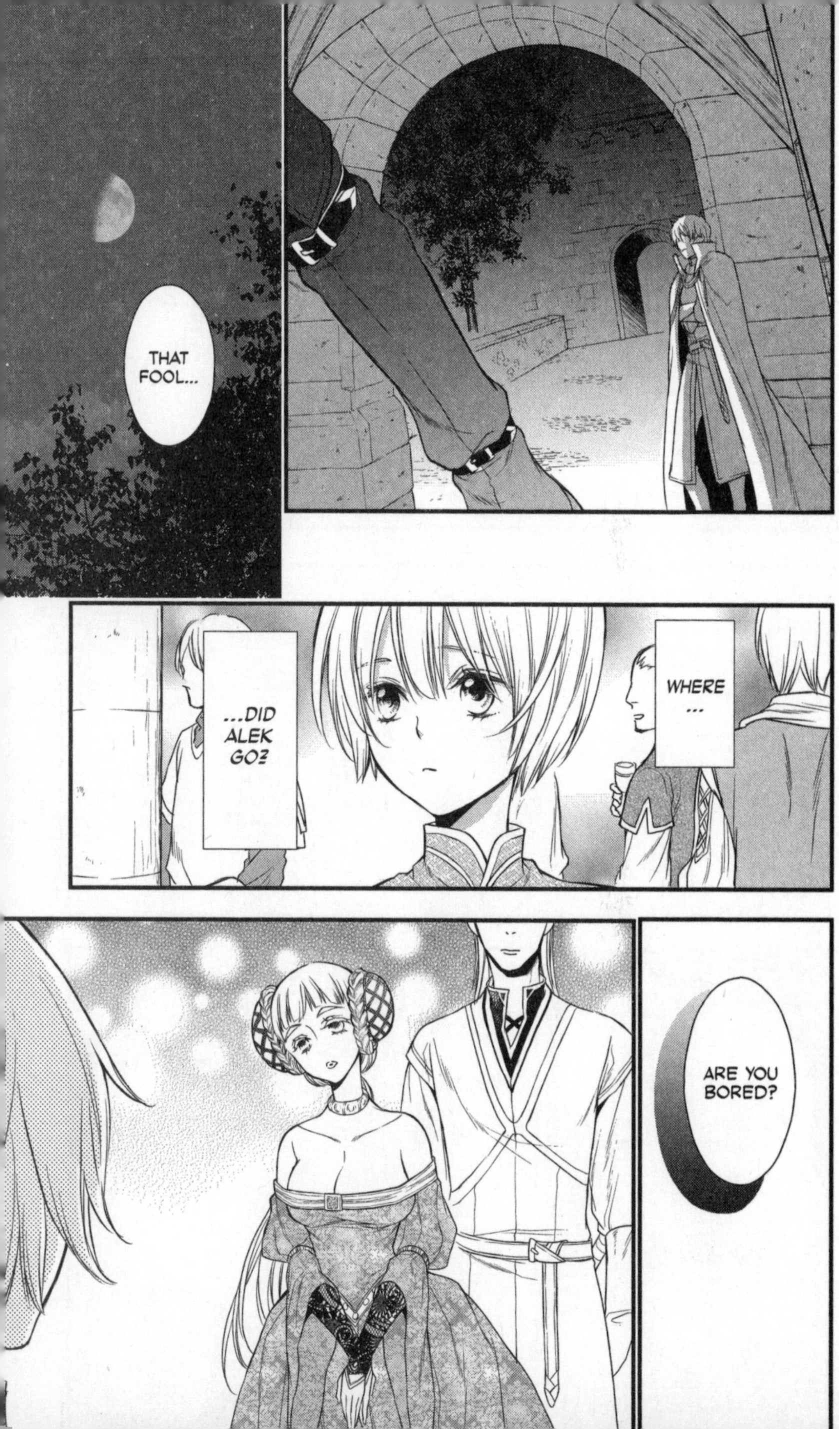
THAT FOOL...
WHERE ...
...DID ALEK GO?
ARE YOU BORED?

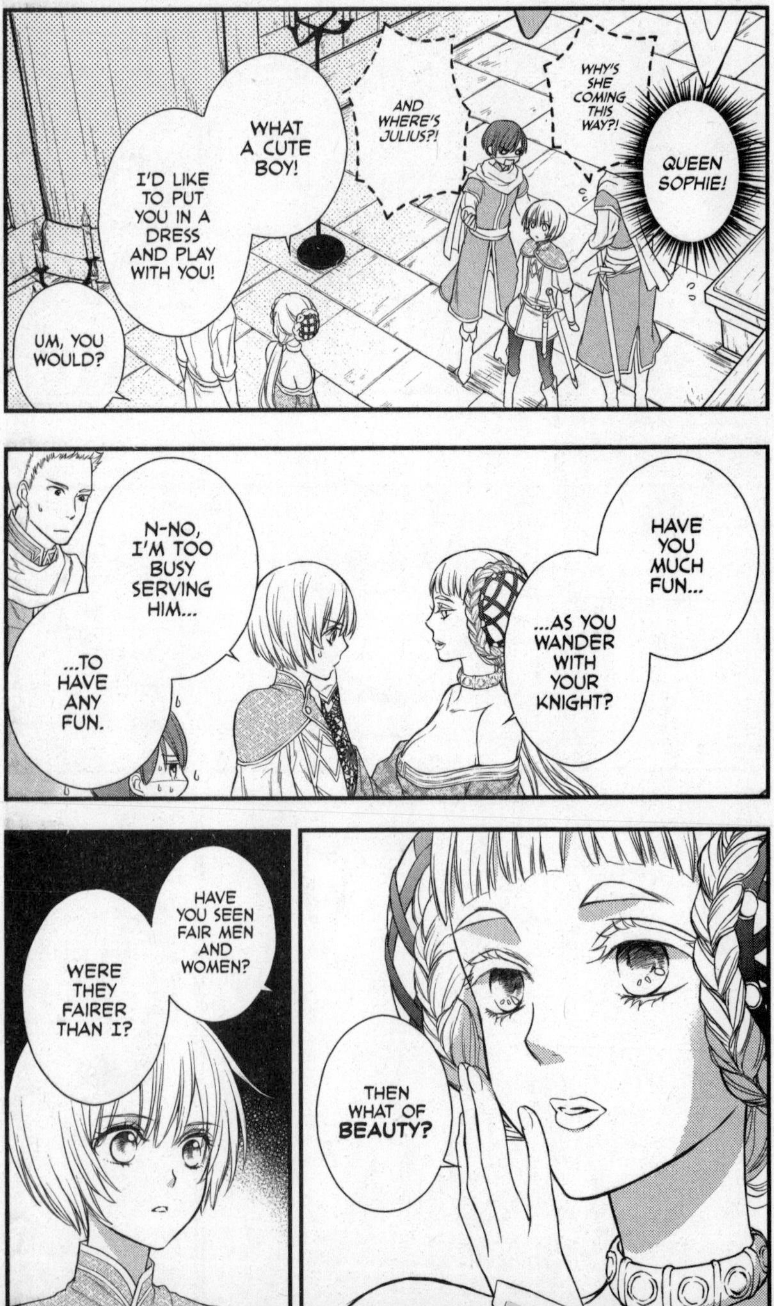
QUEEN SOPHIE!
WHY'S SHE COMING THIS WAY?!
AND WHERE'S JULIUS?!
WHAT A CUTE BOY!
I'D LIKE TO PUT YOU IN A DRESS AND PLAY WITH YOU!
UM, YOU WOULD?
HAVE YOU MUCH FUN...
...AS YOU WANDER WITH YOUR KNIGHT?
N-NO, I'M TOO BUSY SERVING HIM...
...TO HAVE ANY FUN.
THEN WHAT OF BEAUTY?
HAVE YOU SEEN FAIR MEN AND WOMEN?
WERE THEY FAIRER THAN I?

DOESN'T SHE KNOW...

gwup

...WHAT HAPPENS BEYOND THE CASTLE WALLS?

PEOPLE DON'T HAVE TIME FOR BEAUTY OUT THERE.

THEY ARE STRUGGLING TO SURVIVE.

THEY FALL AND SUFFER...

...YET THEY CONTINUE TO STRIVE, COVERED IN MUD AND BLOOD!

WHY DOESN'T SHE CARE?

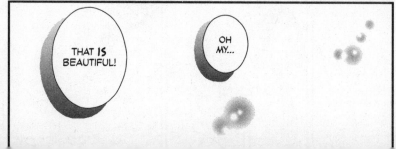

THAT IS BEAUTIFUL!

OH MY...

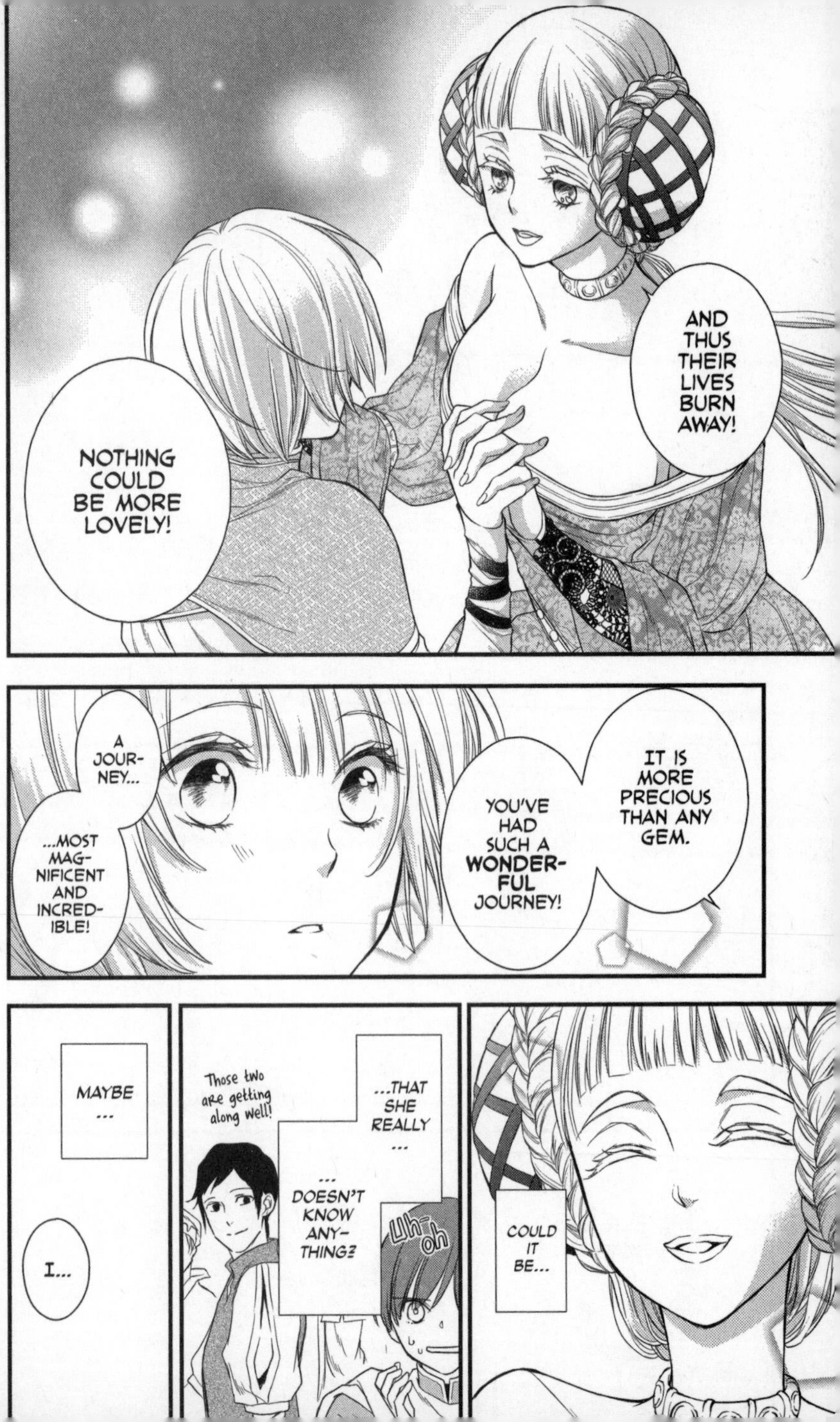
AND THUS THEIR LIVES BURN AWAY!
NOTHING COULD BE MORE LOVELY!
IT IS MORE PRECIOUS THAN ANY GEM.
YOU'VE HAD SUCH A **WONDERFUL** JOURNEY!
A JOURNEY...
...MOST MAGNIFICENT AND INCREDIBLE!
COULD IT BE...
...THAT SHE REALLY...
Those two are getting along well!
...DOESN'T KNOW ANYTHING?
Uh-oh
MAYBE...
I...

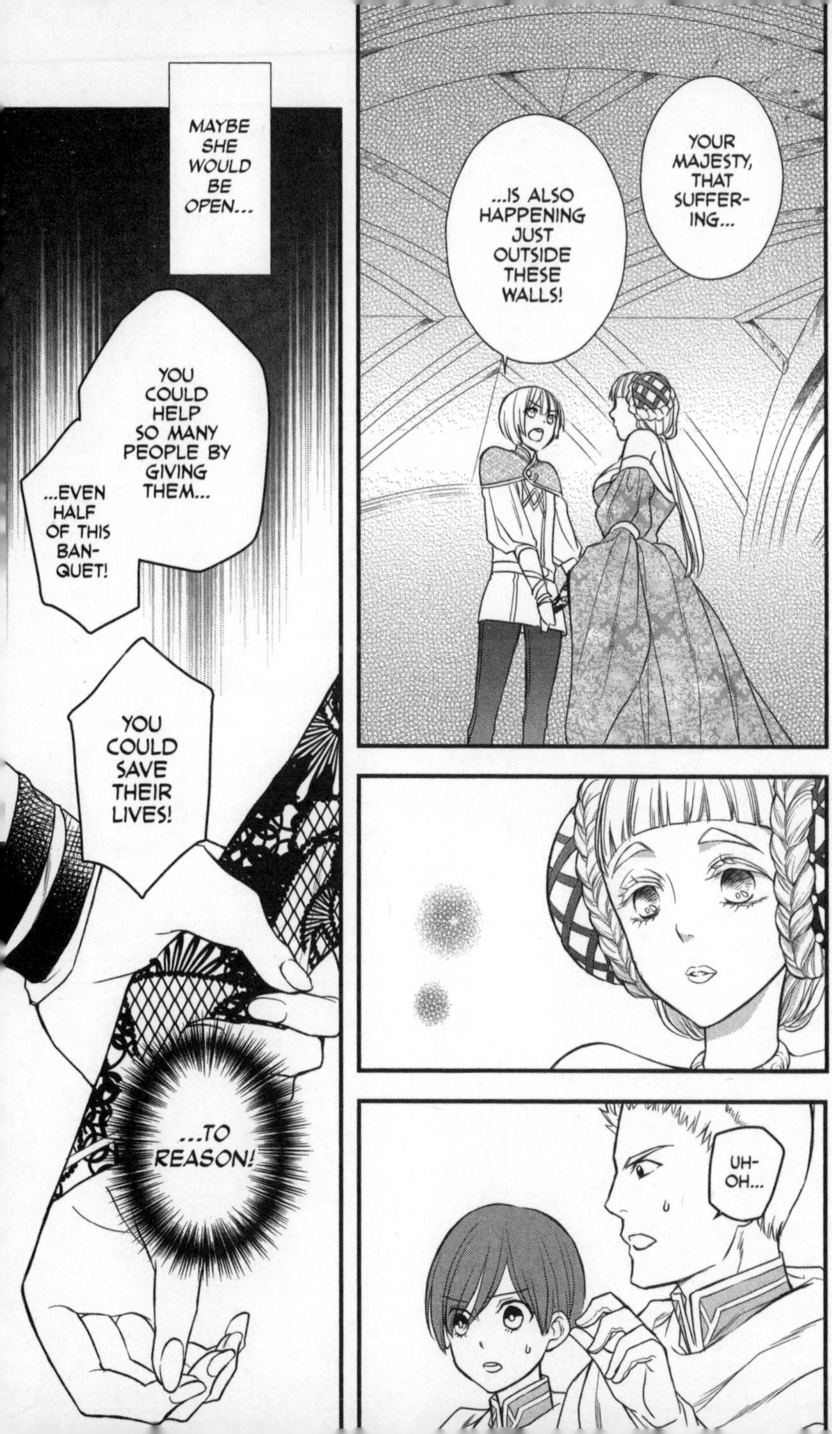
YOUR MAJESTY, THAT SUFFERING...
...IS ALSO HAPPENING JUST OUTSIDE THESE WALLS!
UH-OH...
MAYBE SHE WOULD BE OPEN...
YOU COULD HELP SO MANY PEOPLE BY GIVING THEM...
...EVEN HALF OF THIS BANQUET!
YOU COULD SAVE THEIR LIVES!
...TO REASON!

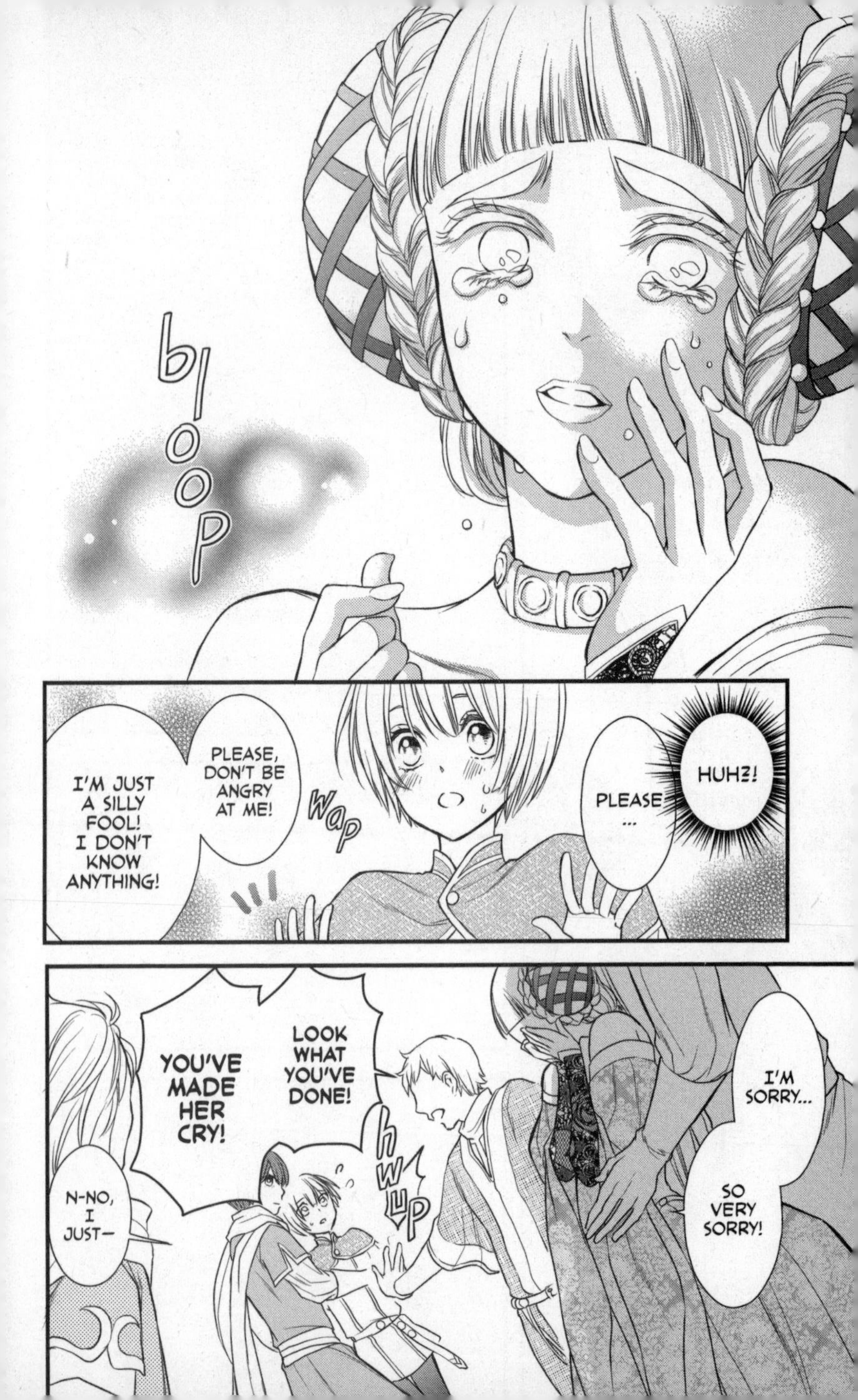
bloop
HUH?!
PLEASE...
PLEASE, DON'T BE ANGRY AT ME!
wap
I'M JUST A SILLY FOOL! I DON'T KNOW ANYTHING!
I'M SORRY...
SO VERY SORRY!
LOOK WHAT YOU'VE DONE!
hwup
YOU'VE MADE HER CRY!
N-NO, I JUST—

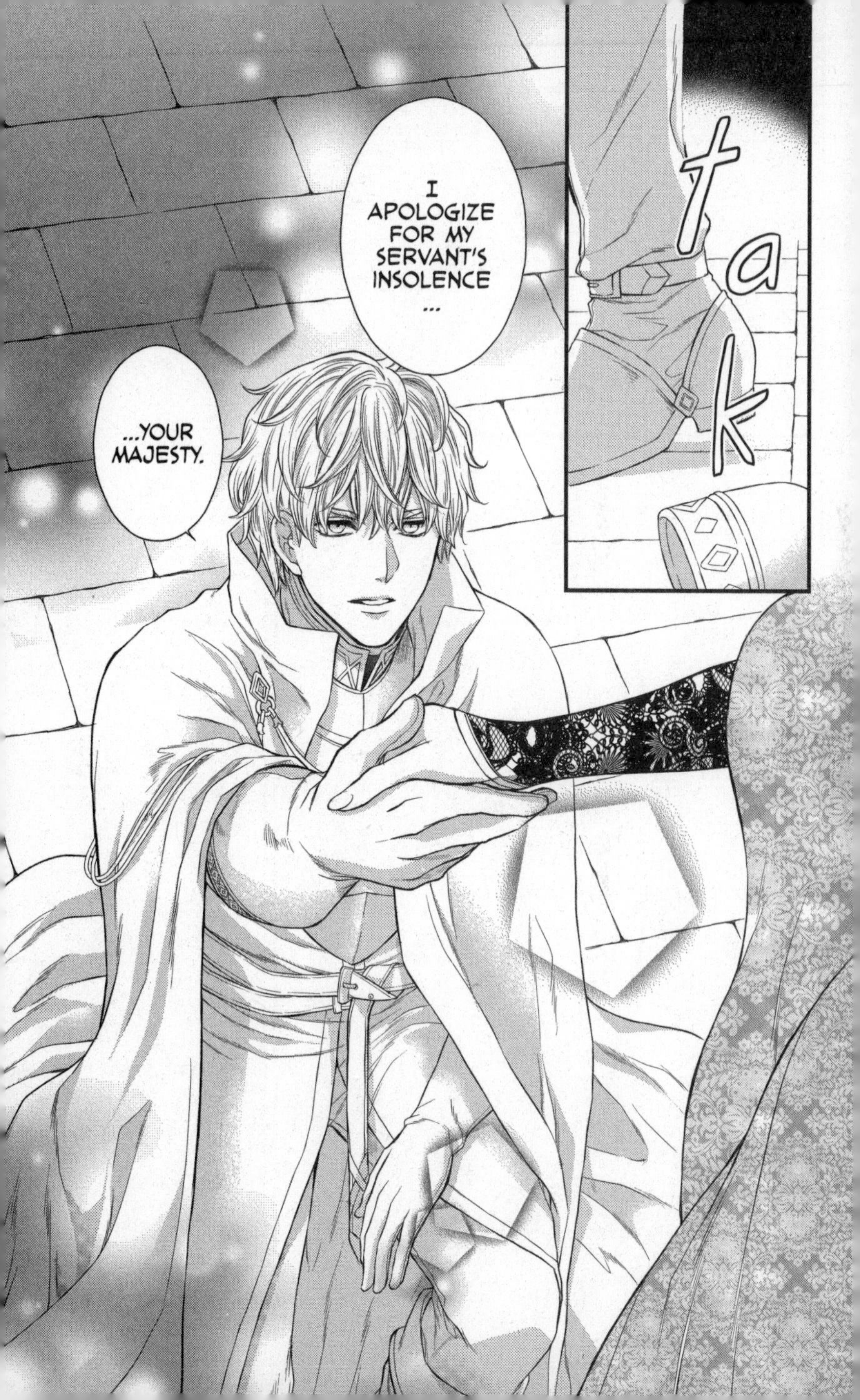
tak
I APOLOGIZE FOR MY SERVANT'S INSOLENCE ...
...YOUR MAJESTY.

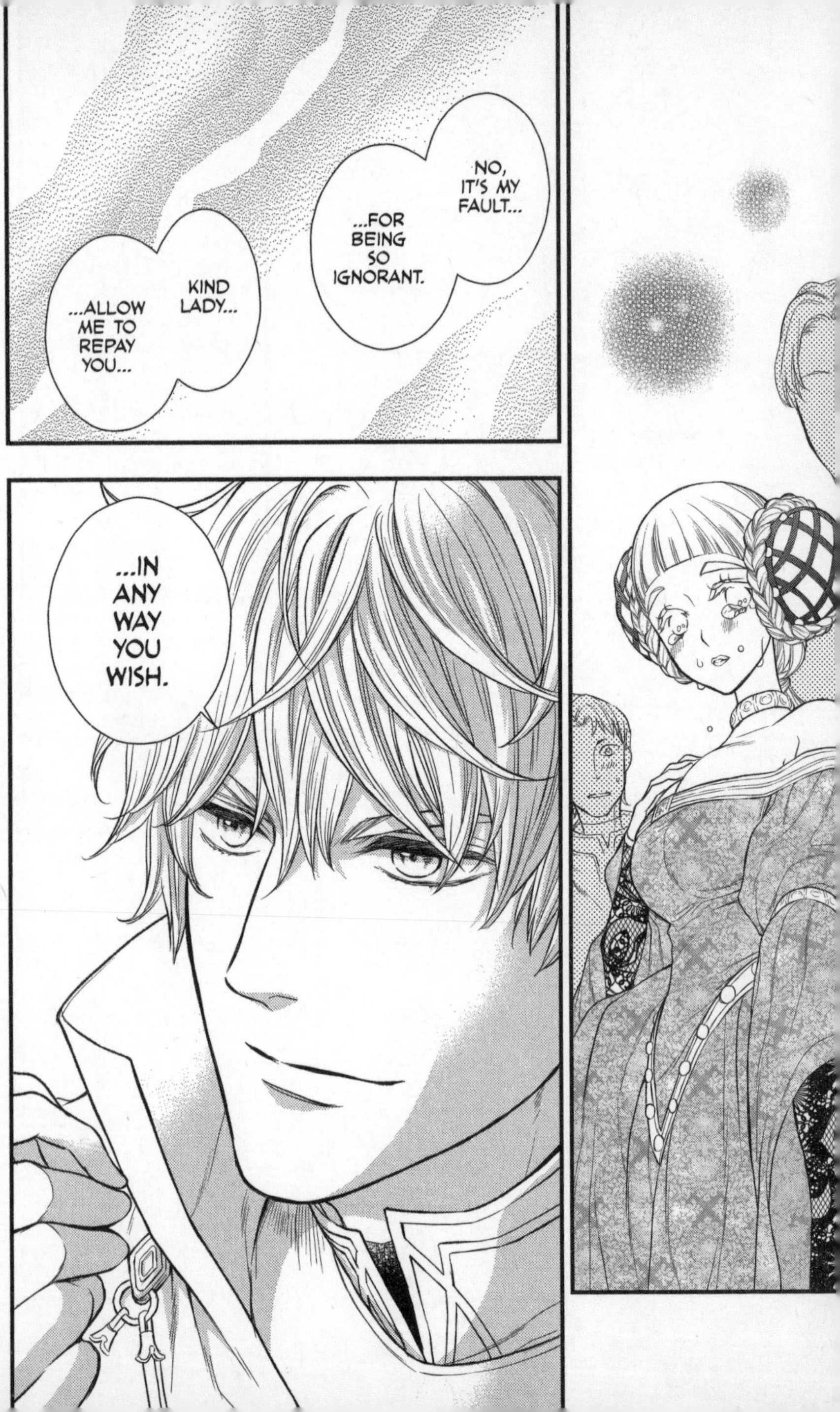
NO, IT'S MY FAULT...
...FOR BEING SO IGNORANT.
KIND LADY...
...ALLOW ME TO REPAY YOU...
...IN ANY WAY YOU WISH.

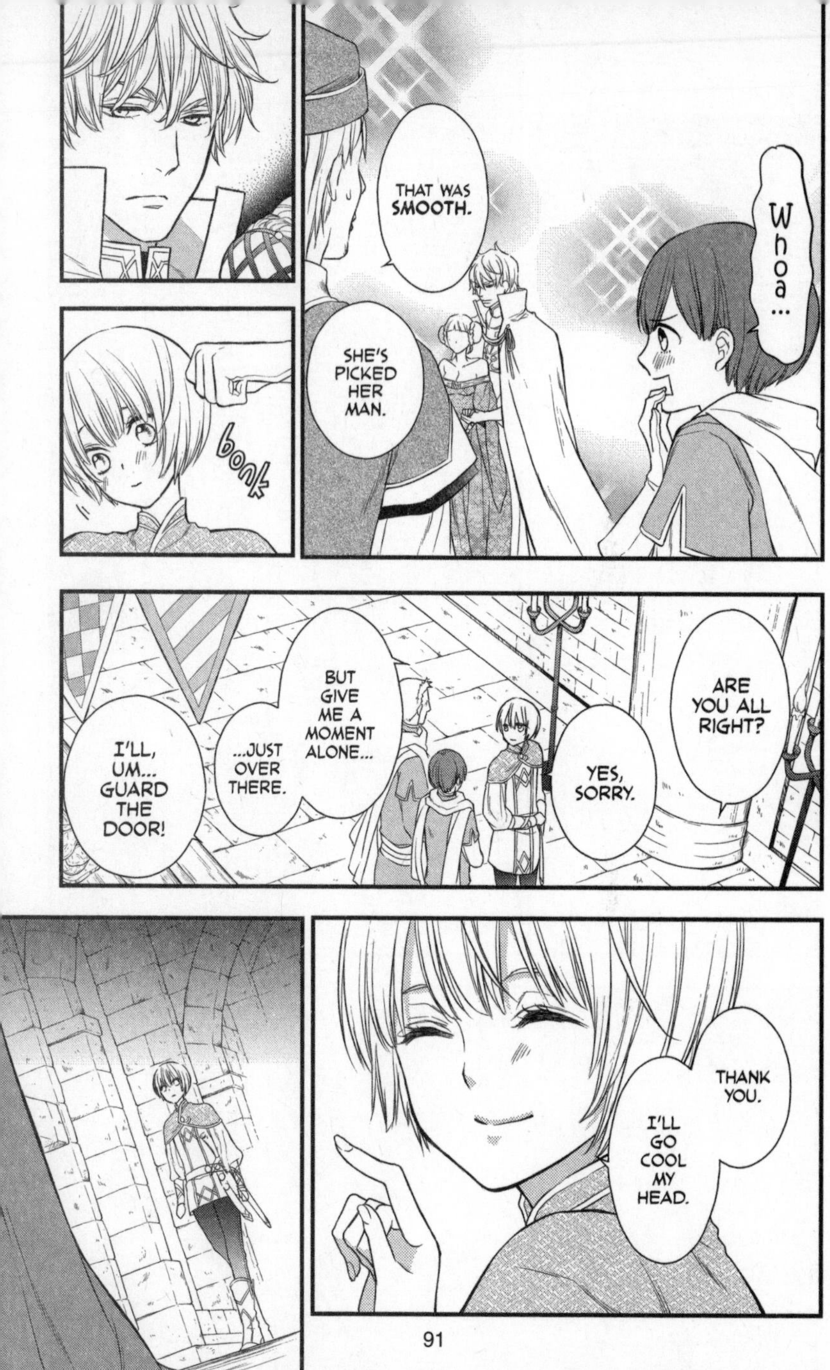
Whoa...
THAT WAS SMOOTH.
SHE'S PICKED HER MAN.
bonk
ARE YOU ALL RIGHT?
YES, SORRY.
BUT GIVE ME A MOMENT ALONE...
...JUST OVER THERE.
I'LL, UM... GUARD THE DOOR!
THANK YOU.
I'LL GO COOL MY HEAD.

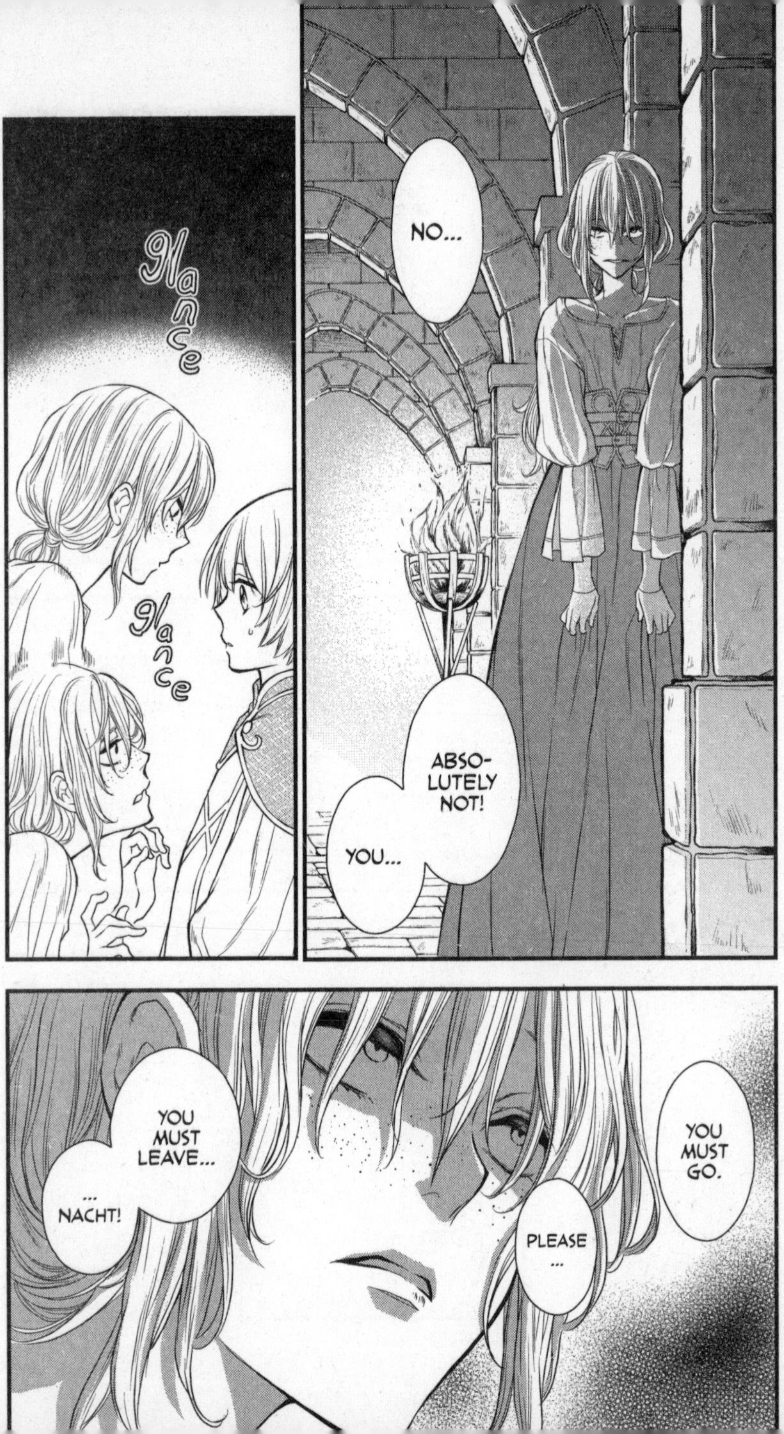
NO...
ABSO-LUTELY NOT!
YOU...
glance
glance
YOU MUST GO.
PLEASE ...
YOU MUST LEAVE...
... NACHT!

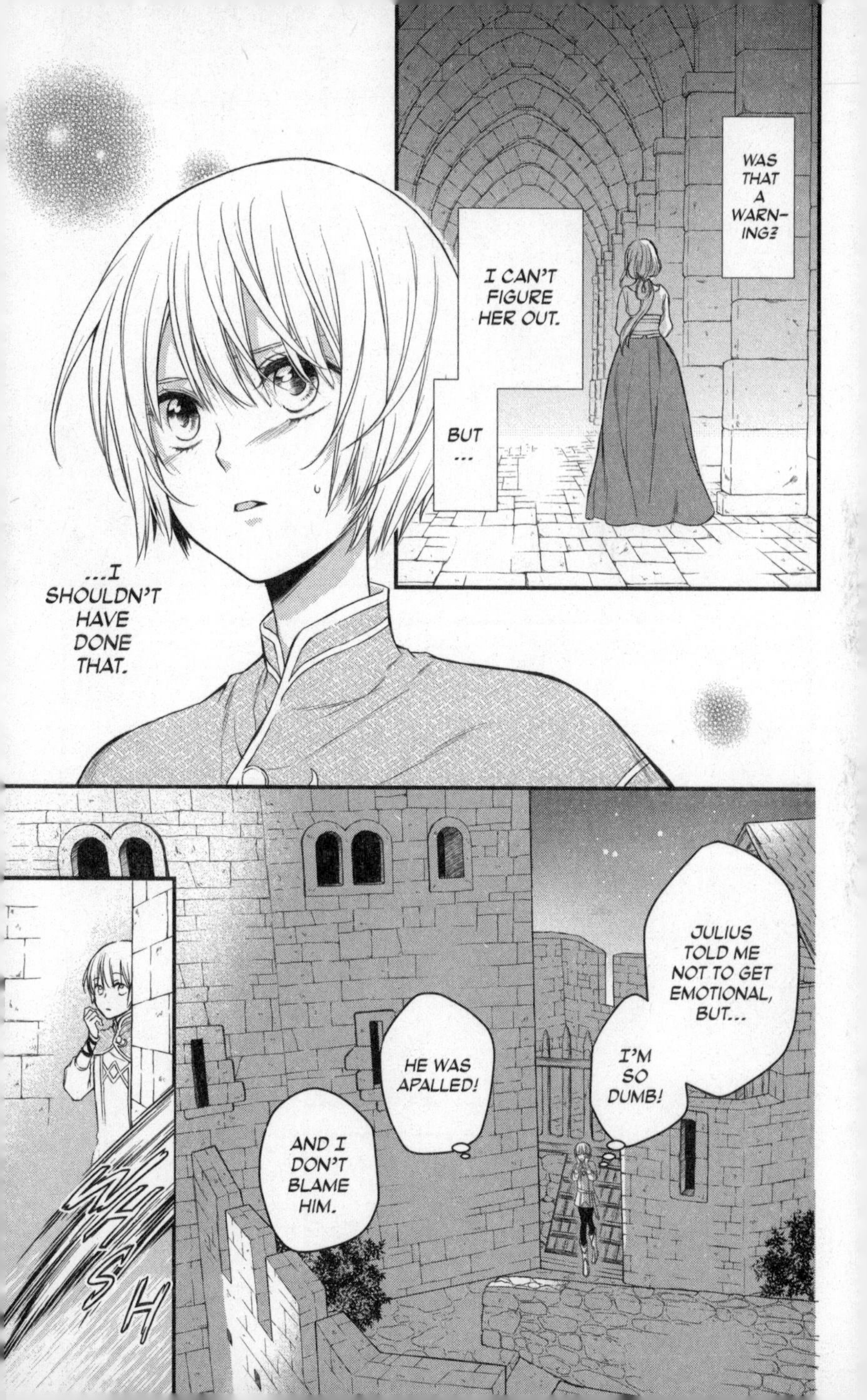
WAS THAT A WARNING?
I CAN'T FIGURE HER OUT.
BUT...
...I SHOULDN'T HAVE DONE THAT.
JULIUS TOLD ME NOT TO GET EMOTIONAL, BUT...
I'M SO DUMB!
HE WAS APALLED!
AND I DON'T BLAME HIM.

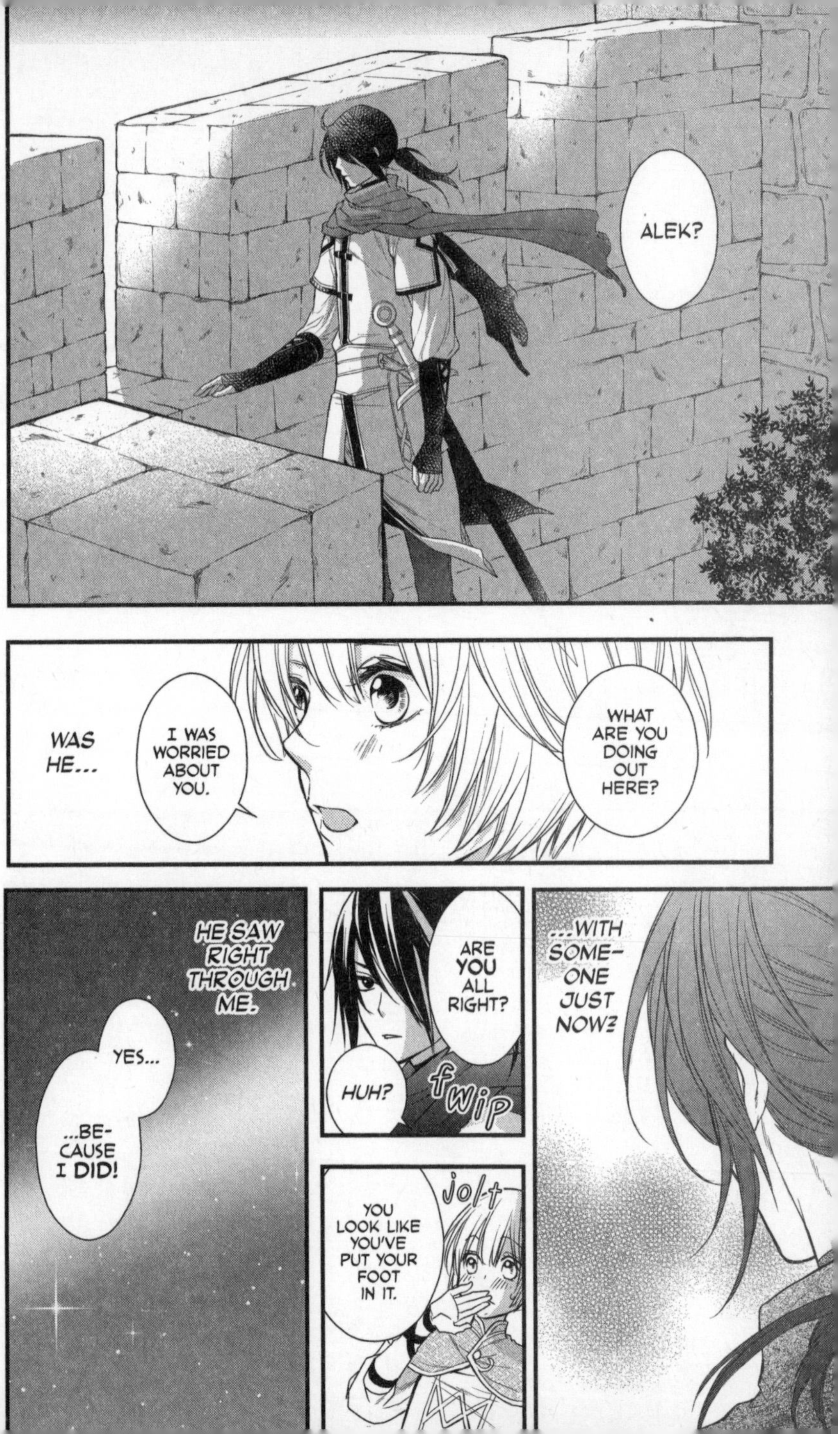
ALEK?
WHAT ARE YOU DOING OUT HERE?
I WAS WORRIED ABOUT YOU.
WAS HE...
...WITH SOME-ONE JUST NOW?
ARE YOU ALL RIGHT?
HUH?
fwip
jolt
YOU LOOK LIKE YOU'VE PUT YOUR FOOT IN IT.
HE SAW RIGHT THROUGH ME.
YES...
...BE-CAUSE I DID!

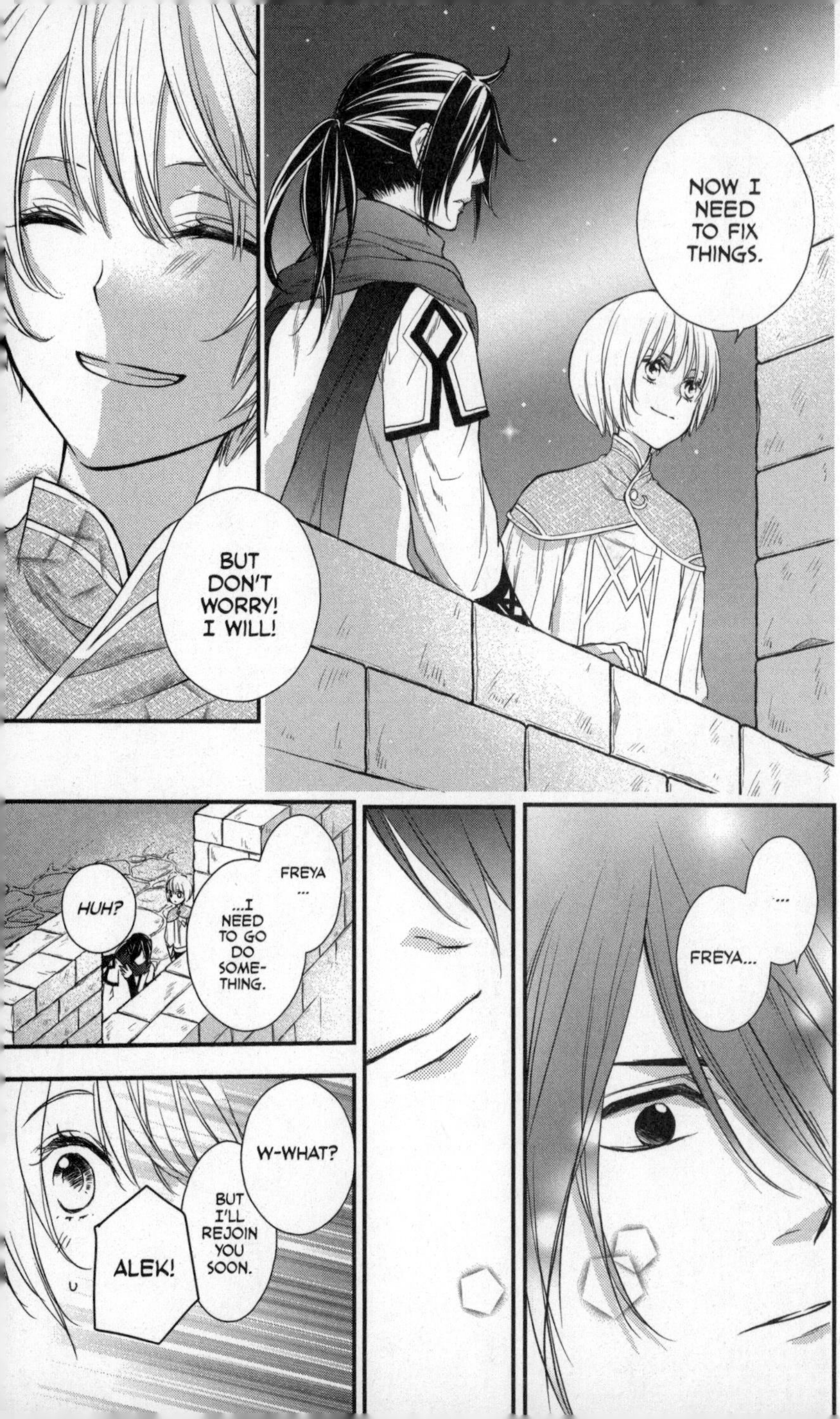
NOW I NEED TO FIX THINGS.
BUT DON'T WORRY! I WILL!
...
FREYA...
FREYA ...
...I NEED TO GO DO SOME-THING.
HUH?
W-WHAT?
BUT I'LL REJOIN YOU SOON.
ALEK!

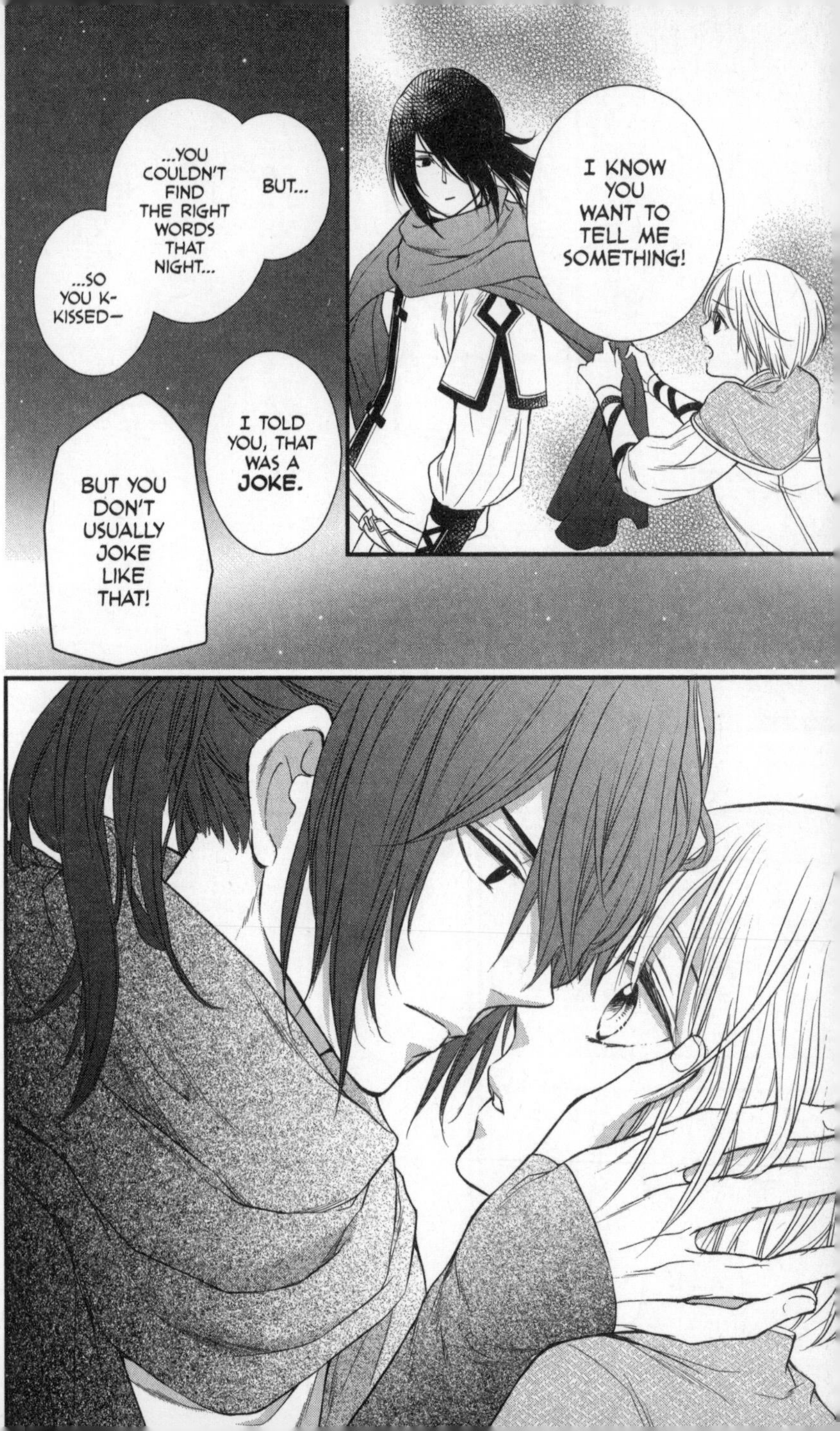
I KNOW YOU WANT TO TELL ME SOMETHING!
BUT...
...YOU COULDN'T FIND THE RIGHT WORDS THAT NIGHT...
...SO YOU K-KISSED—
I TOLD YOU, THAT WAS A **JOKE.**
BUT YOU DON'T USUALLY JOKE LIKE THAT!

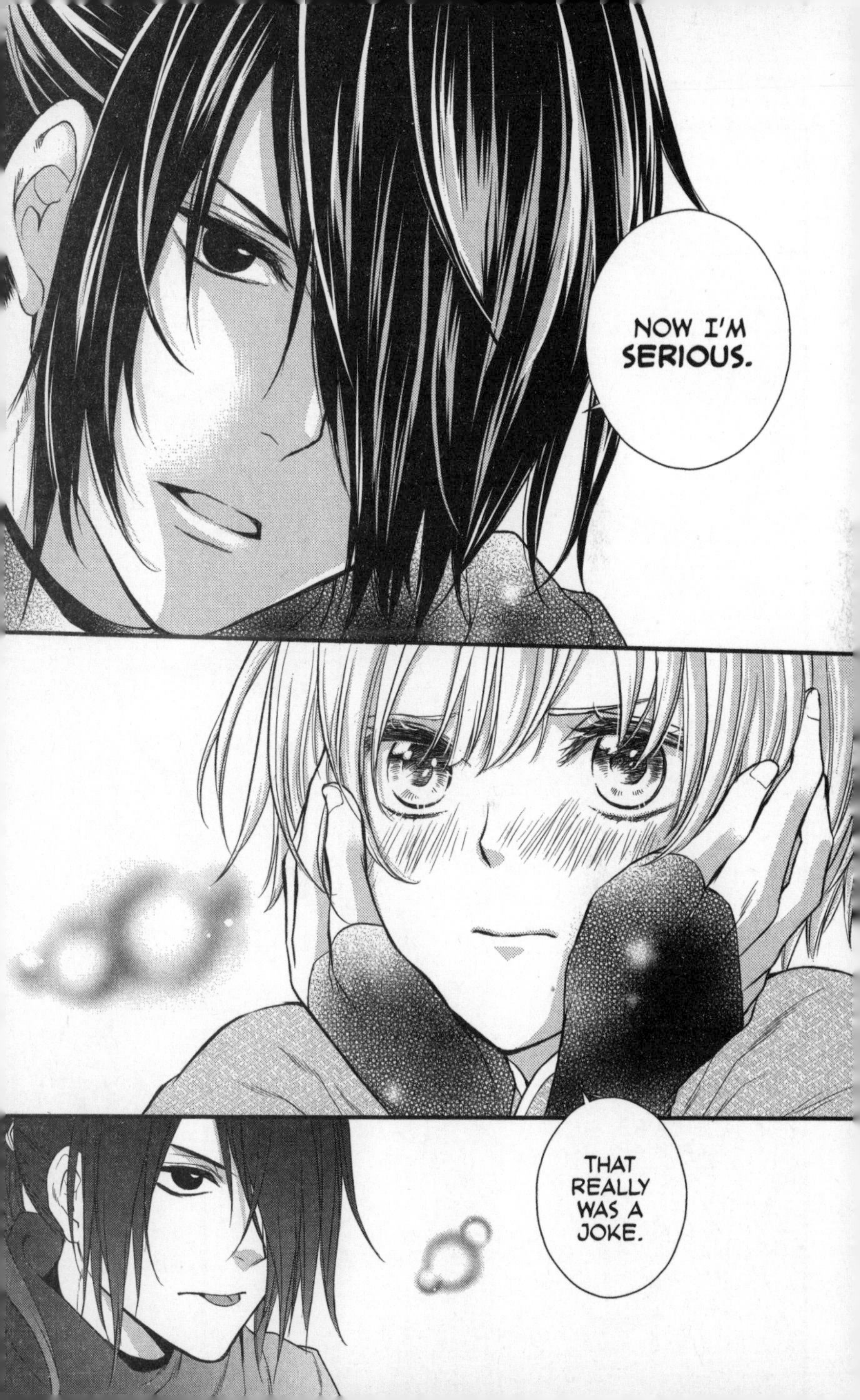
NOW I'M SERIOUS.
THAT REALLY WAS A JOKE.

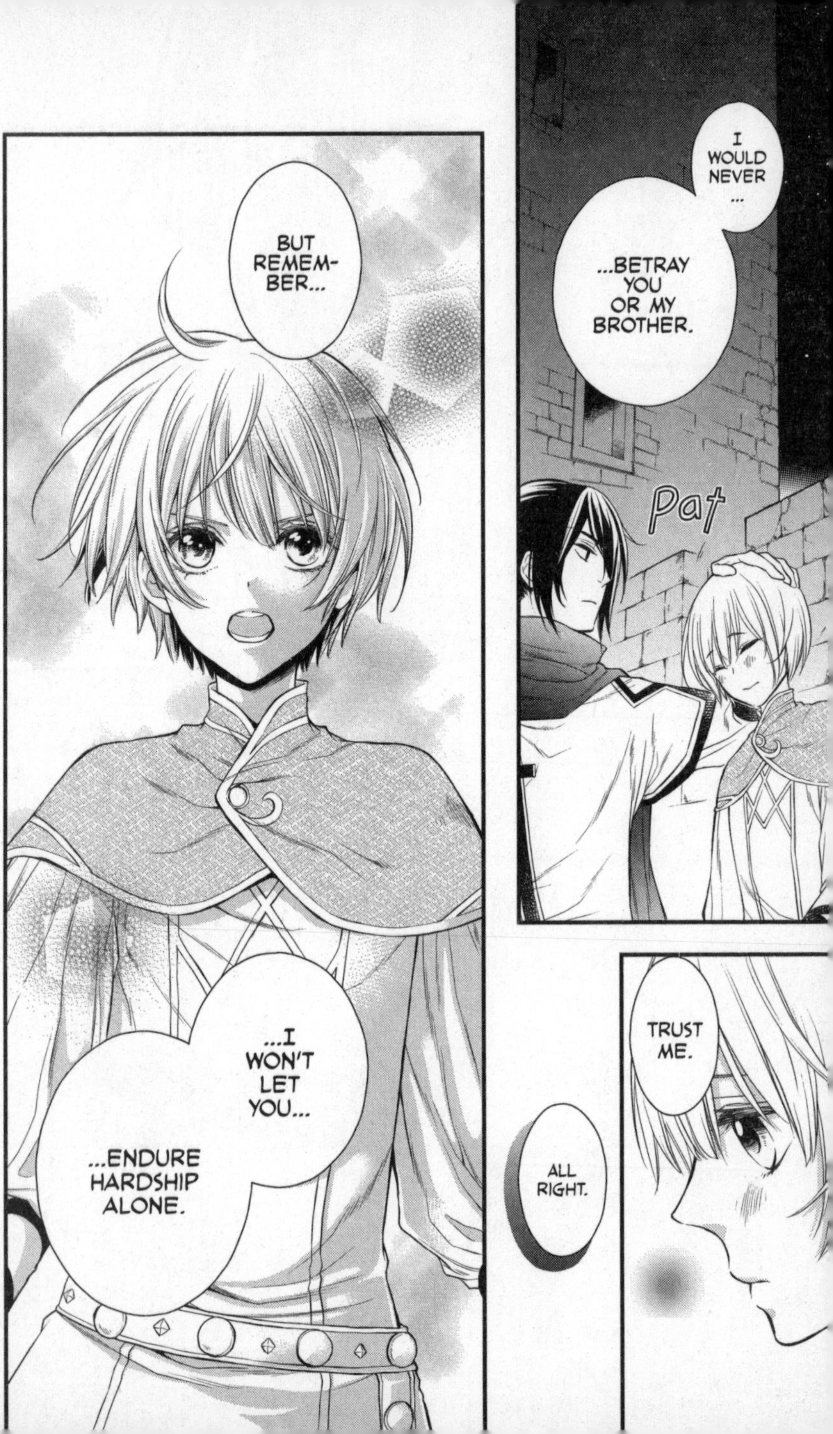
I WOULD NEVER...
...BETRAY YOU OR MY BROTHER.
Pat
TRUST ME.
ALL RIGHT.
BUT REMEM-BER...
...I WON'T LET YOU...
...ENDURE HARDSHIP ALONE.

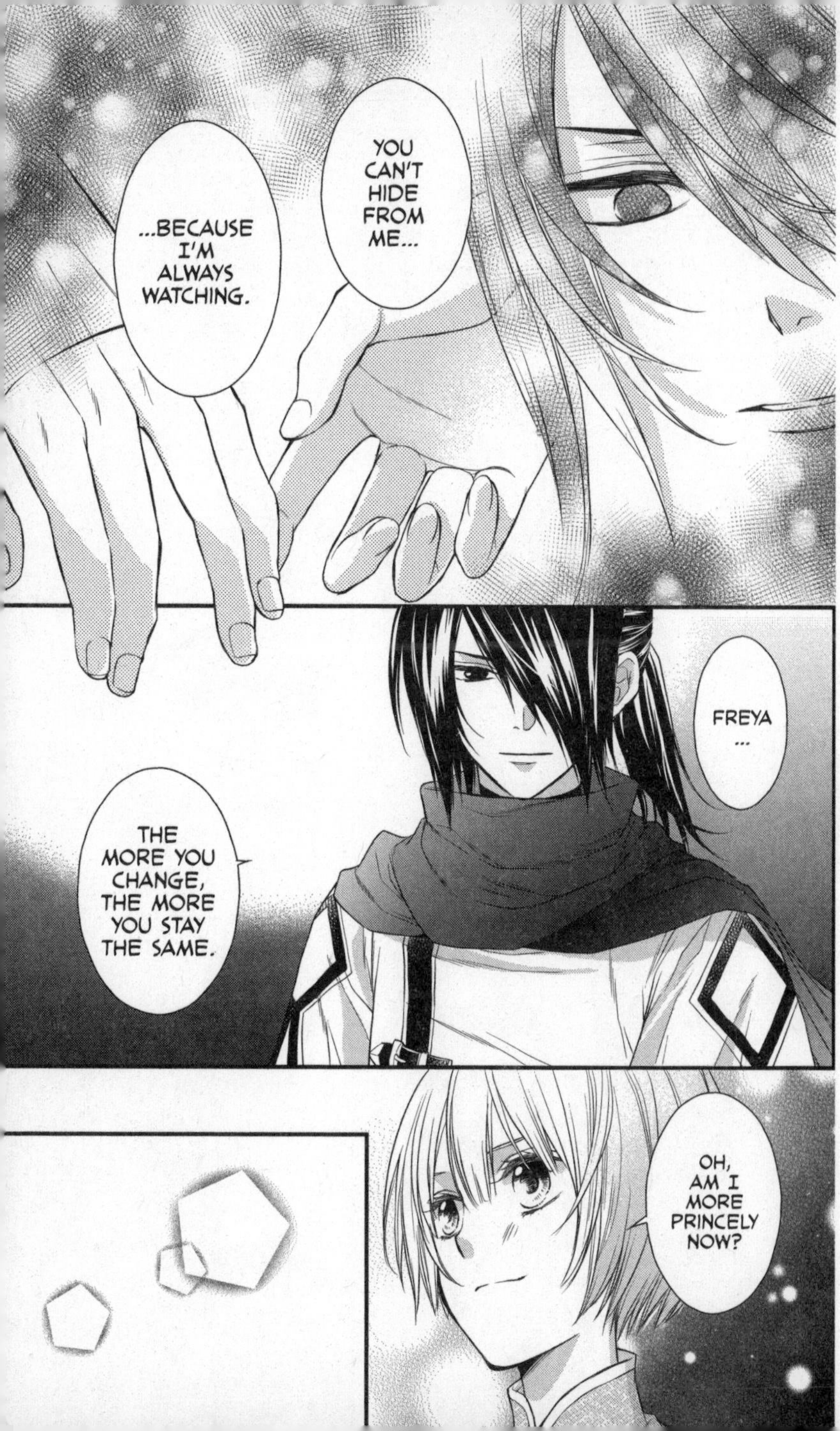
YOU CAN'T HIDE FROM ME...
...BECAUSE I'M ALWAYS WATCHING.
FREYA ...
THE MORE YOU CHANGE, THE MORE YOU STAY THE SAME.
OH, AM I MORE PRINCELY NOW?

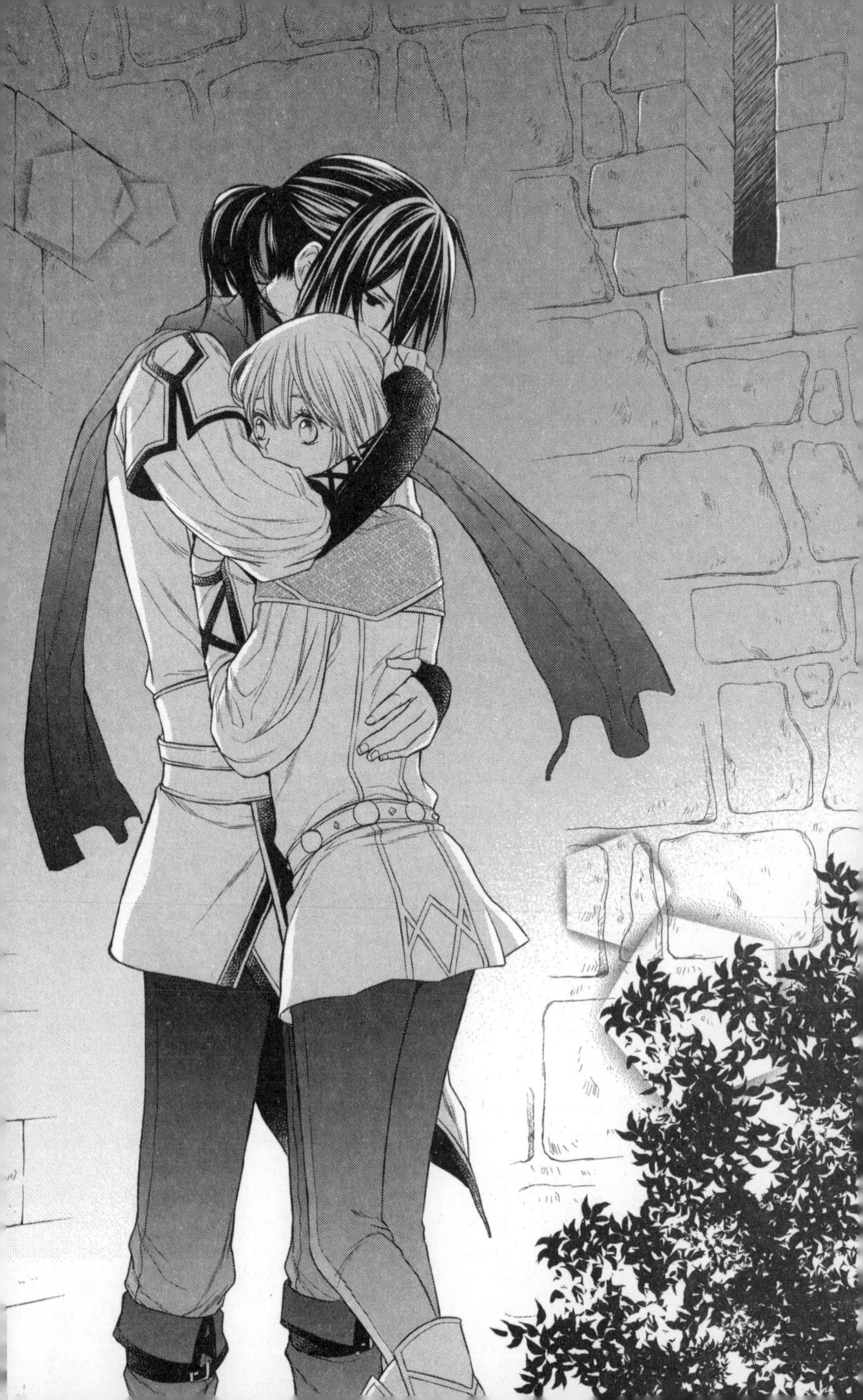

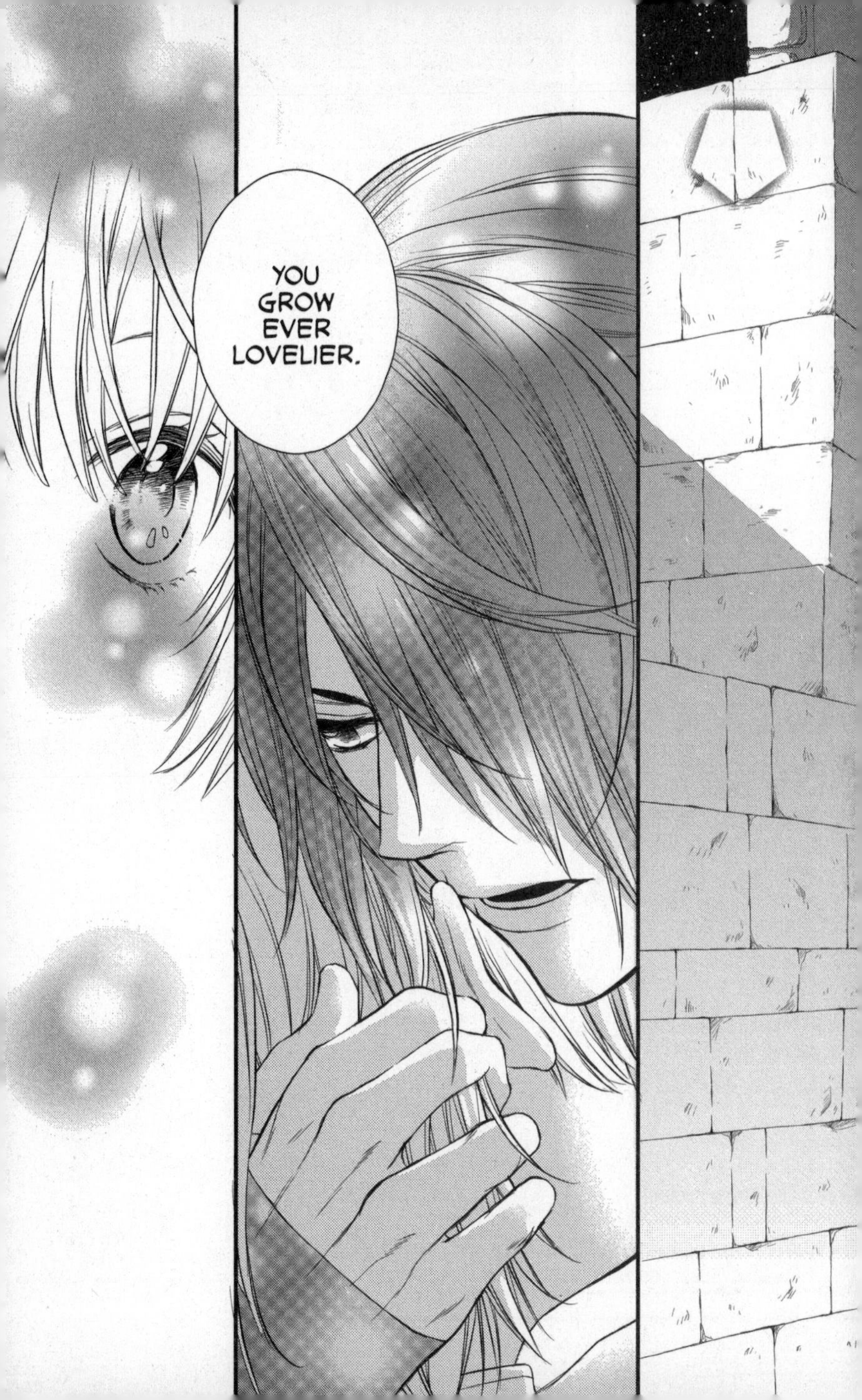
YOU GROW EVER LOVELIER.

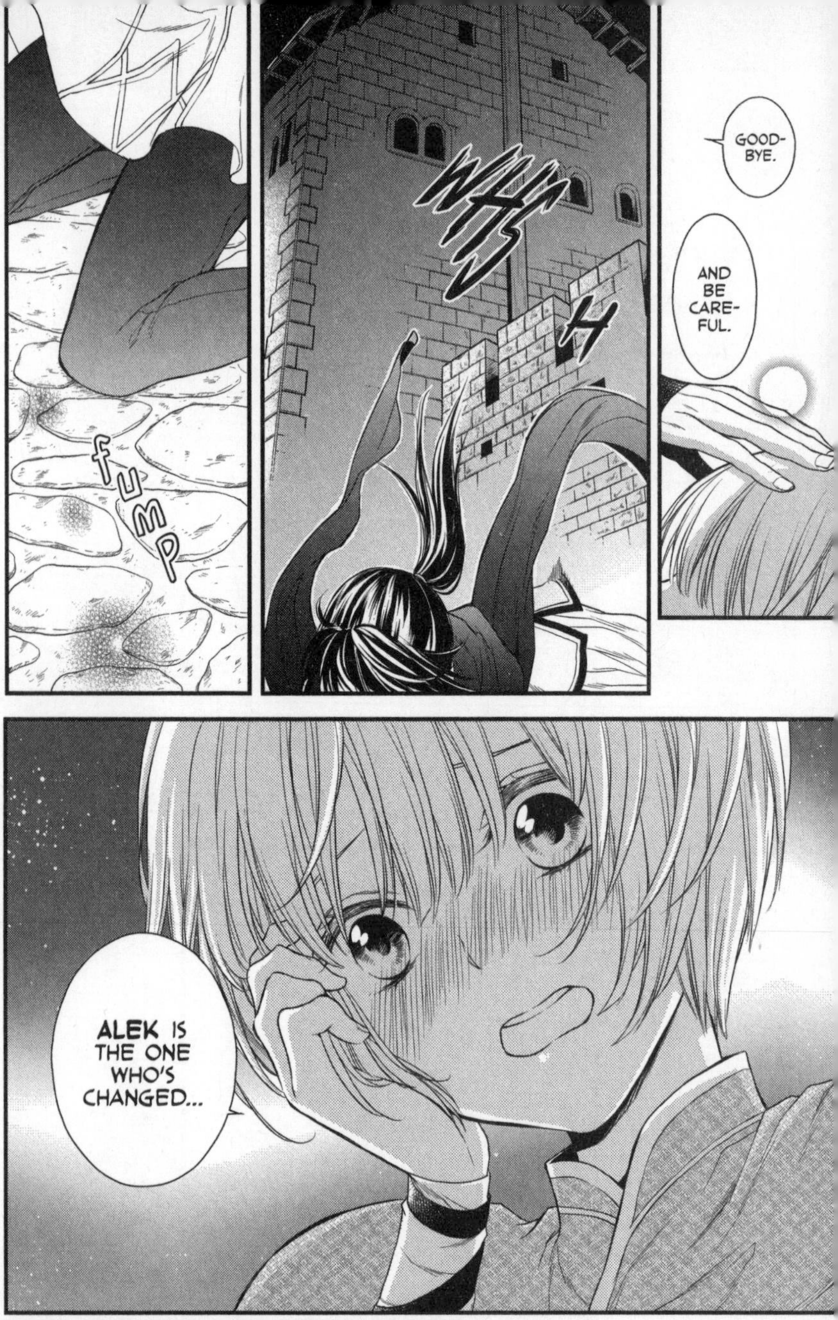
GOOD-BYE.
AND BE CAREFUL.
WHSSH
fump
ALEK IS THE ONE WHO'S CHANGED...

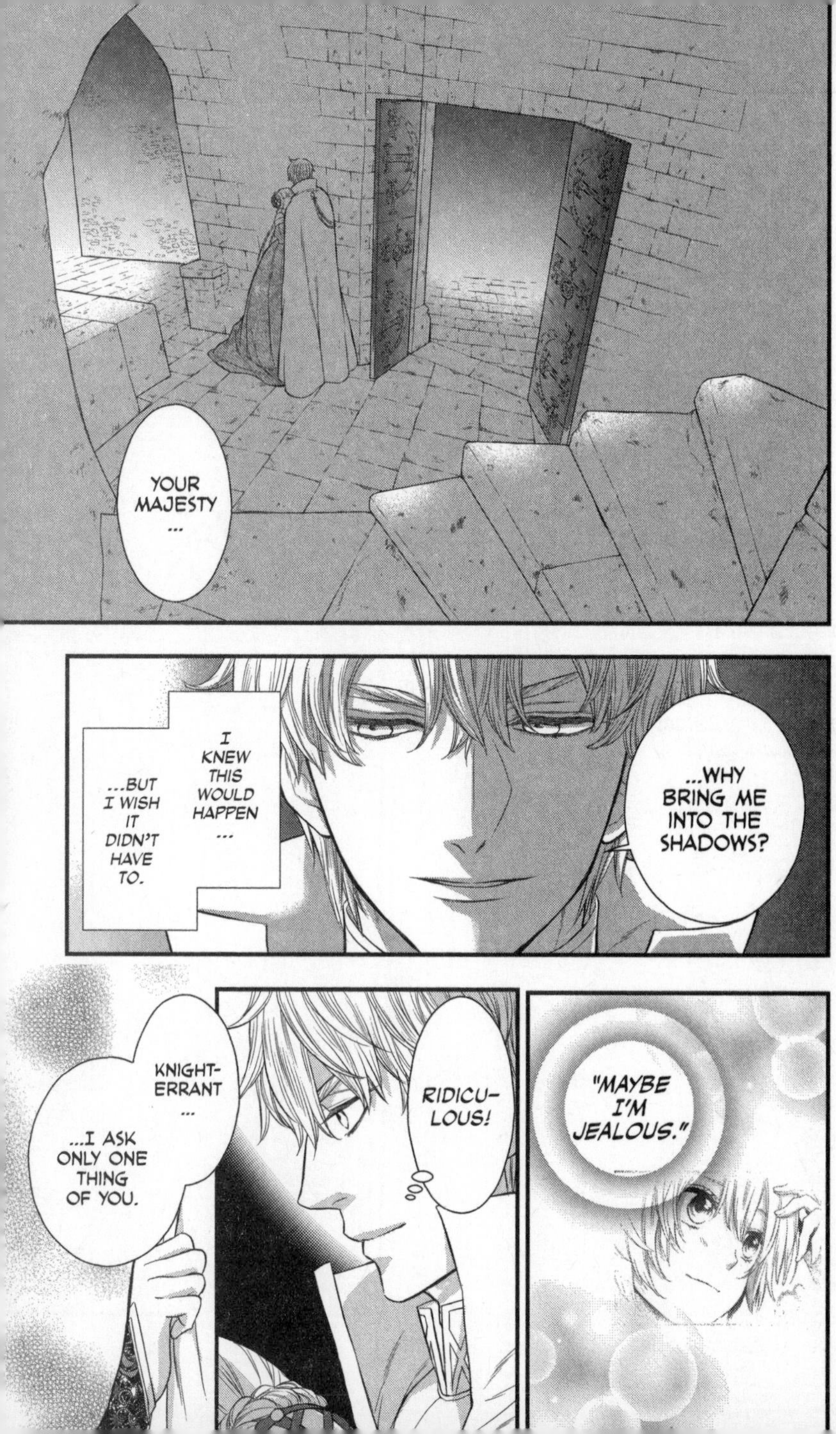
YOUR MAJESTY ...
...WHY BRING ME INTO THE SHADOWS?
I KNEW THIS WOULD HAPPEN ...
...BUT I WISH IT DIDN'T HAVE TO.
"MAYBE I'M JEALOUS."
RIDICU-LOUS!
KNIGHT-ERRANT ...
...I ASK ONLY ONE THING OF YOU.

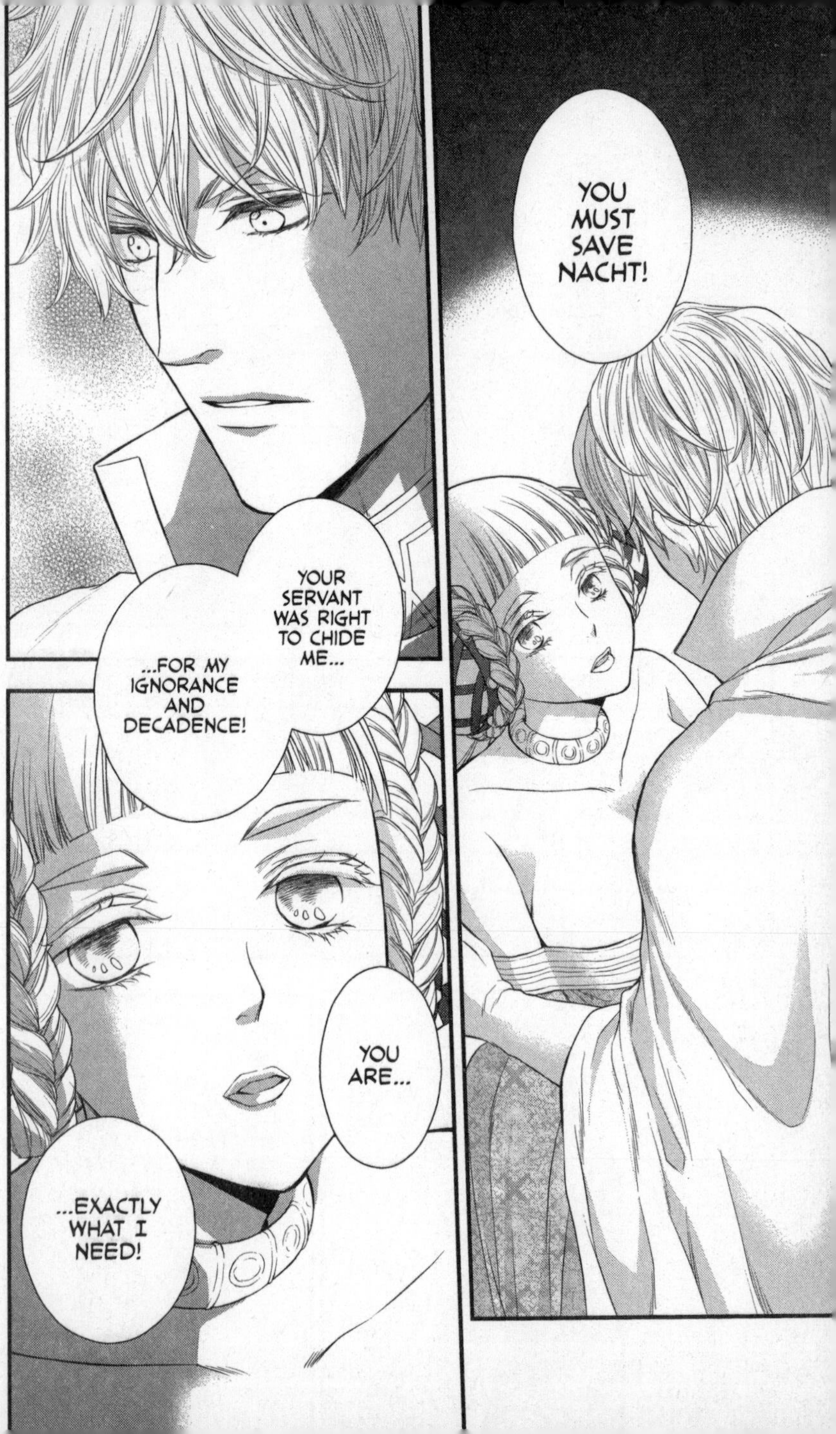
YOU MUST SAVE NACHT!
YOUR SERVANT WAS RIGHT TO CHIDE ME...
...FOR MY IGNORANCE AND DECADENCE!
YOU ARE...
...EXACTLY WHAT I NEED!

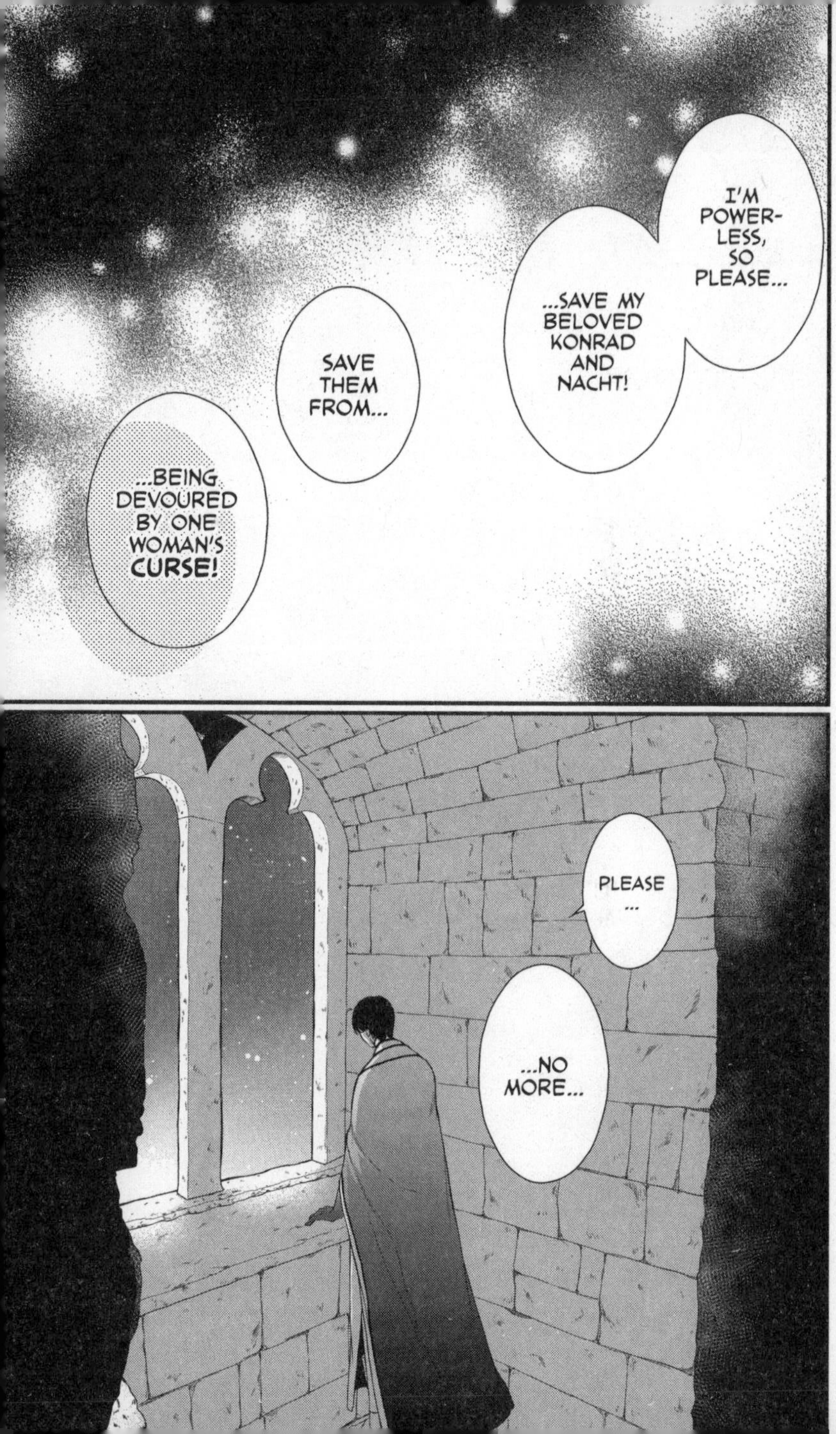
I'M POWER-LESS, SO PLEASE...
...SAVE MY BELOVED KONRAD AND NACHT!
SAVE THEM FROM...
...BEING DEVOURED BY ONE WOMAN'S CURSE!
PLEASE...
...NO MORE...

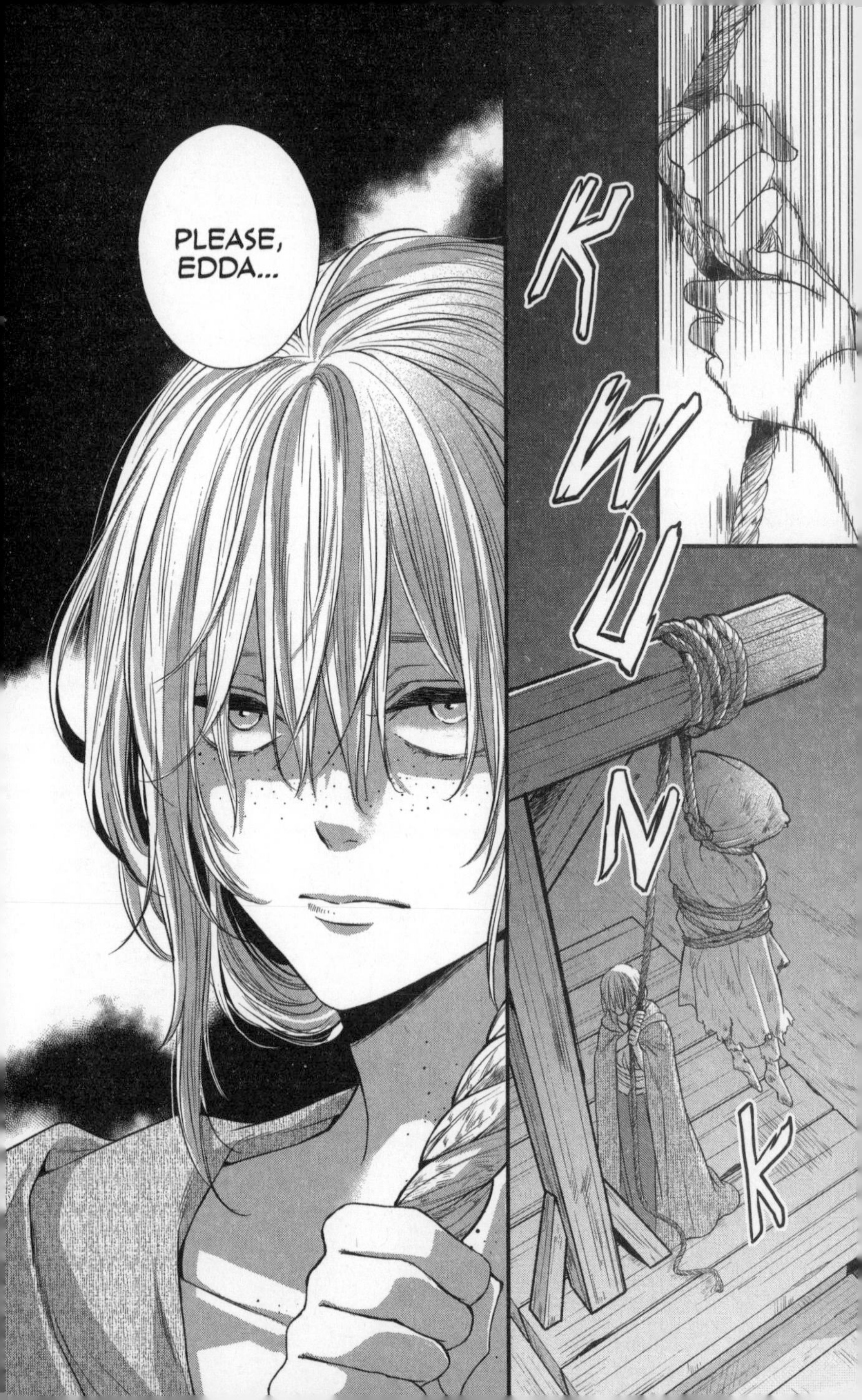
KWUNK
PLEASE, EDDA...

Chapter 15: The Darkness of Schellaberg

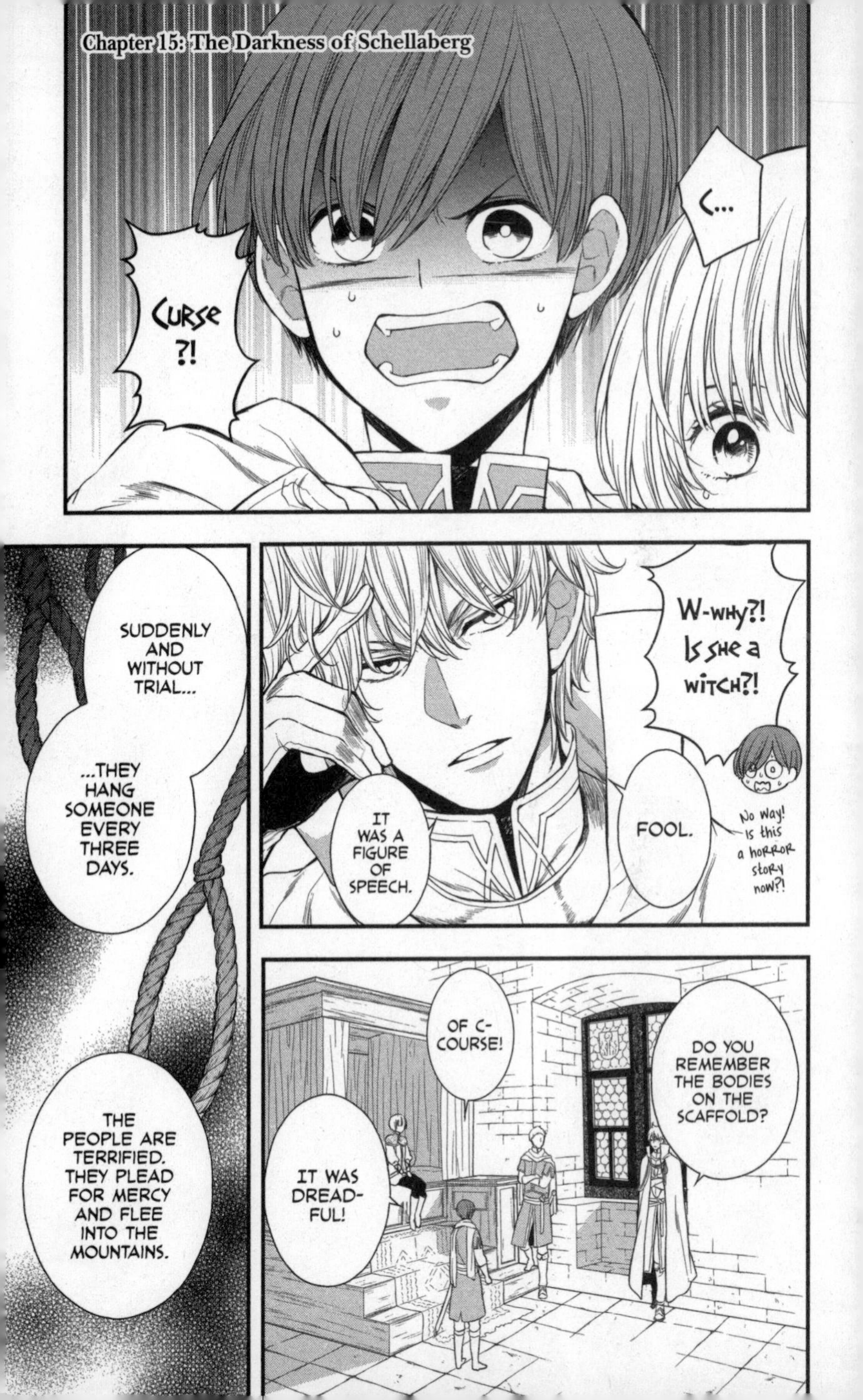
C...
Curse ?!
W-why?! Is she a witch?!
No way! Is this a horror story now?!
FOOL.
IT WAS A FIGURE OF SPEECH.
DO YOU REMEMBER THE BODIES ON THE SCAFFOLD?
OF C-COURSE!
IT WAS DREAD-FUL!
SUDDENLY AND WITHOUT TRIAL...
...THEY HANG SOMEONE EVERY THREE DAYS.
THE PEOPLE ARE TERRIFIED. THEY PLEAD FOR MERCY AND FLEE INTO THE MOUNTAINS.

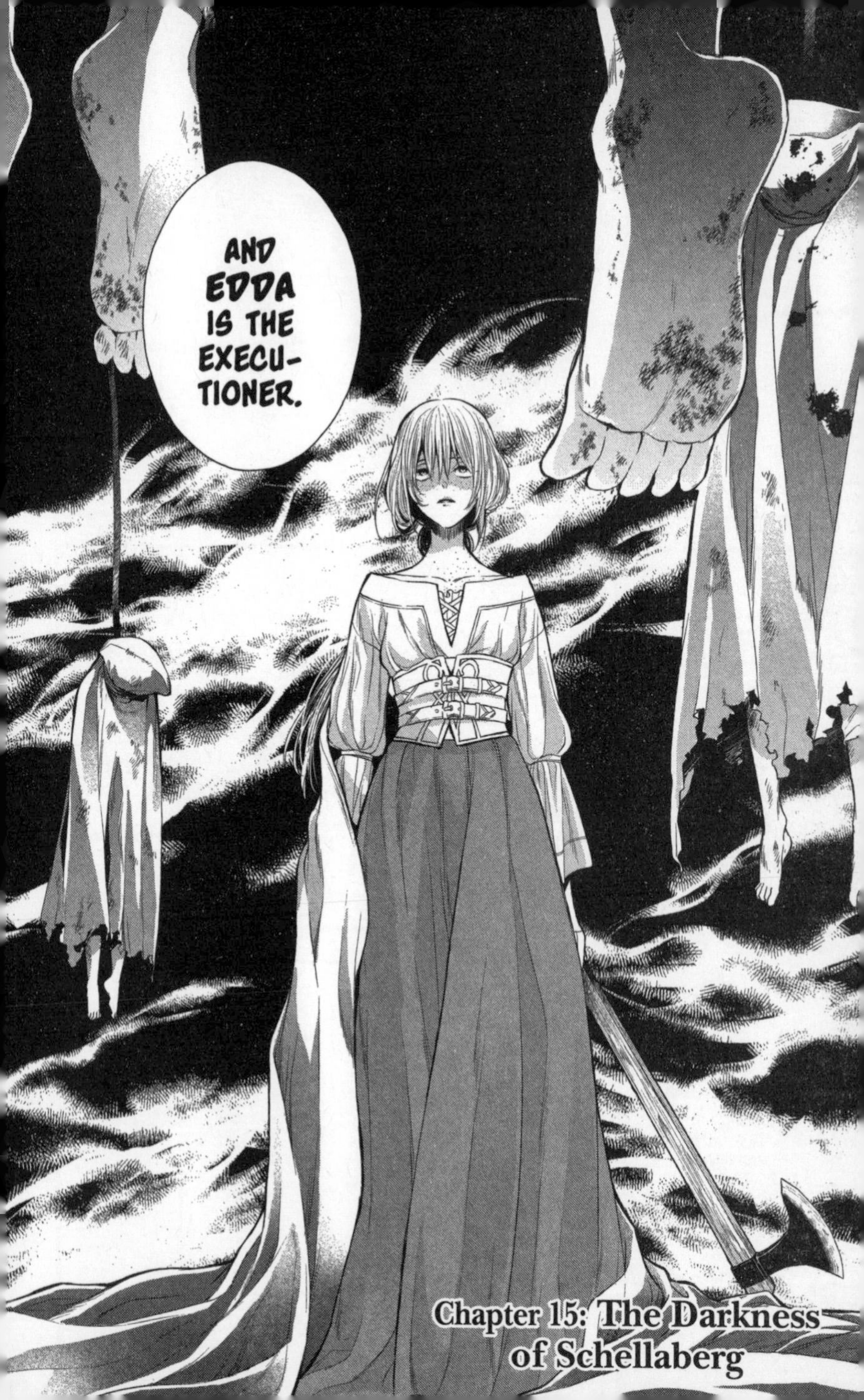
AND EDDA IS THE EXECUTIONER.

Chapter 15: The Darkness of Schellaberg

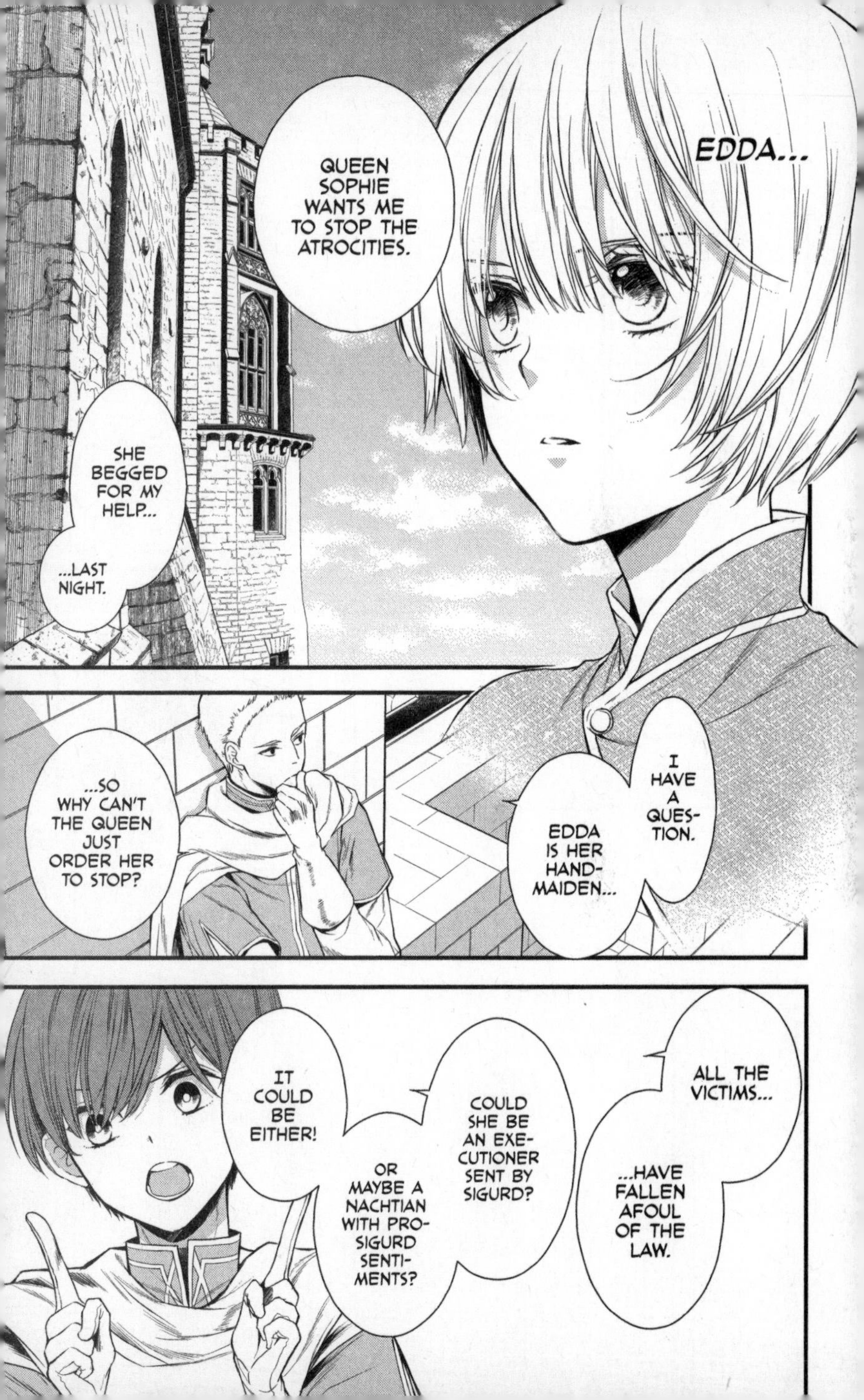
EDDA...
QUEEN SOPHIE WANTS ME TO STOP THE ATROCITIES.
SHE BEGGED FOR MY HELP...
...LAST NIGHT.
I HAVE A QUES-TION.
EDDA IS HER HAND-MAIDEN...
...SO WHY CAN'T THE QUEEN JUST ORDER HER TO STOP?
ALL THE VICTIMS...
...HAVE FALLEN AFOUL OF THE LAW.
COULD SHE BE AN EXE-CUTIONER SENT BY SIGURD?
OR MAYBE A NACHTIAN WITH PRO-SIGURD SENTI-MENTS?
IT COULD BE EITHER!

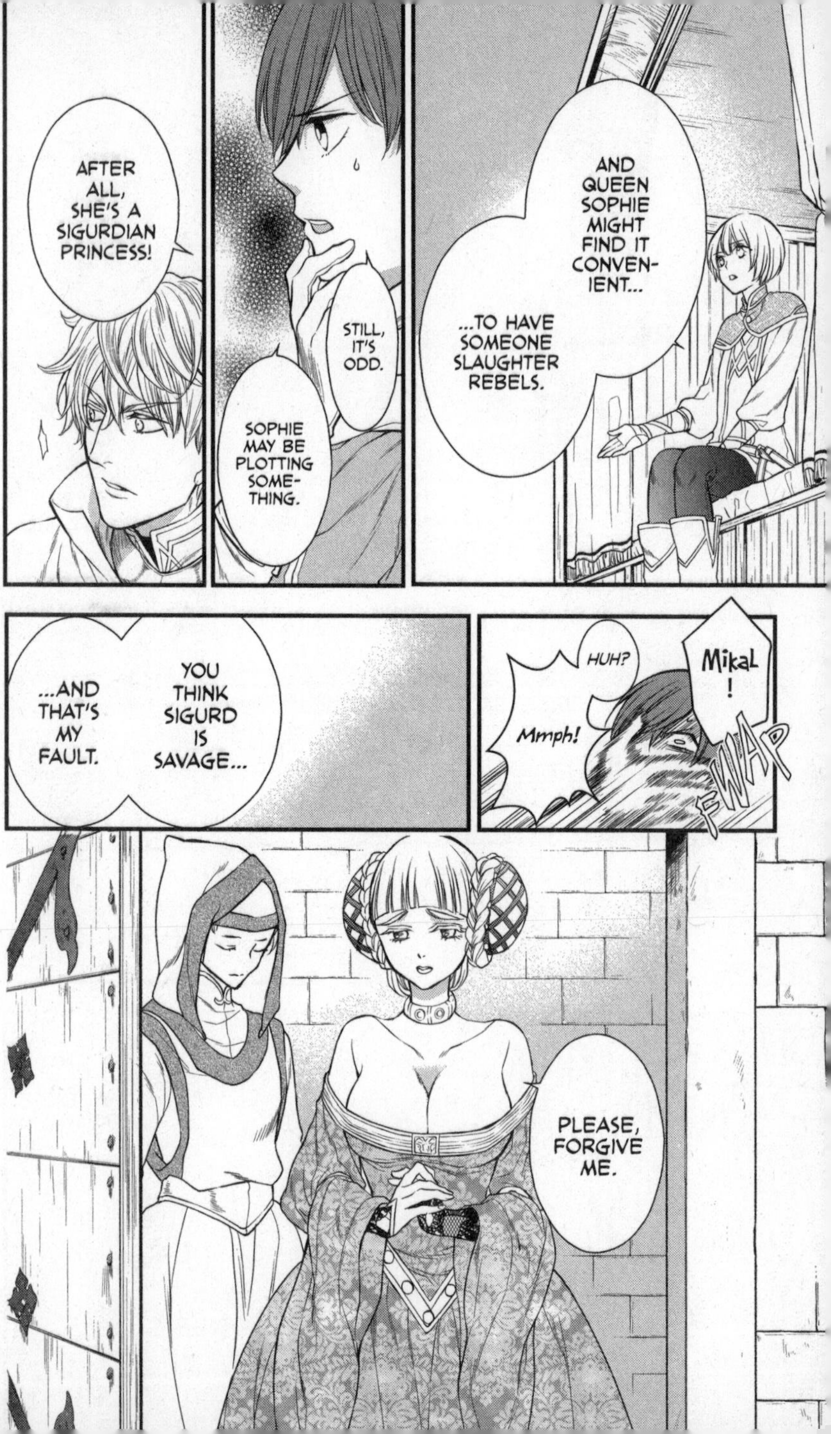
AND QUEEN SOPHIE MIGHT FIND IT CONVENIENT...
...TO HAVE SOMEONE SLAUGHTER REBELS.
STILL, IT'S ODD.
SOPHIE MAY BE PLOTTING SOMETHING.
AFTER ALL, SHE'S A SIGURDIAN PRINCESS!
Mikal!
HUH?
Mmph!
FWAP
YOU THINK SIGURD IS SAVAGE...
...AND THAT'S MY FAULT.
PLEASE, FORGIVE ME.

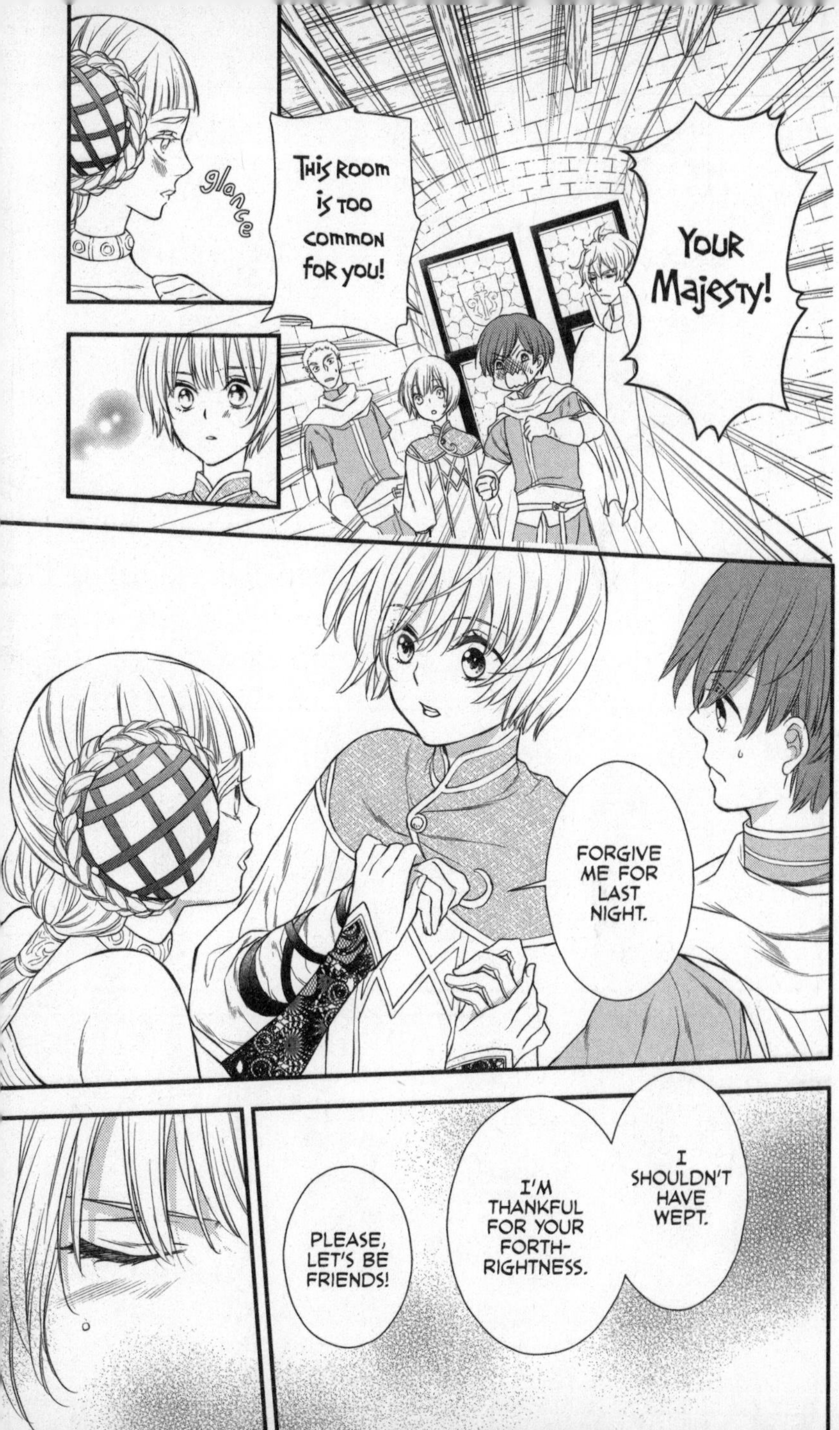
YOUR Majesty!
THIS ROOM IS TOO COMMON FOR YOU!
glance
FORGIVE ME FOR LAST NIGHT.
I SHOULDN'T HAVE WEPT.
I'M THANKFUL FOR YOUR FORTH-RIGHTNESS.
PLEASE, LET'S BE FRIENDS!

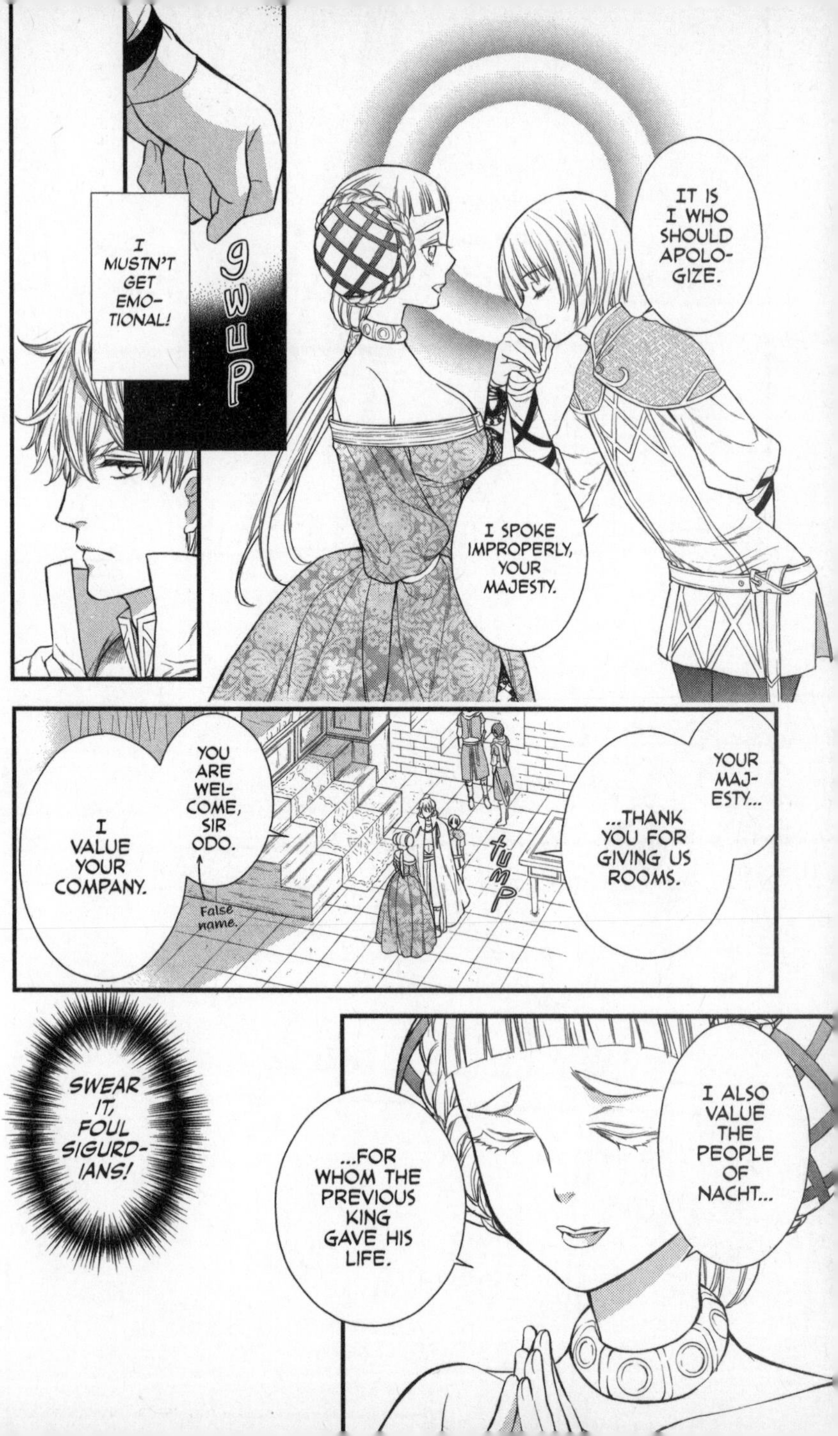
IT IS I WHO SHOULD APOLOGIZE.
I SPOKE IMPROPERLY, YOUR MAJESTY.
GWUP
I MUSTN'T GET EMOTIONAL!
YOUR MAJESTY...
...THANK YOU FOR GIVING US ROOMS.
TUMP
YOU ARE WELCOME, SIR ODO.
False name.
I VALUE YOUR COMPANY.
I ALSO VALUE THE PEOPLE OF NACHT...
...FOR WHOM THE PREVIOUS KING GAVE HIS LIFE.
SWEAR IT, FOUL SIGURDIANS!

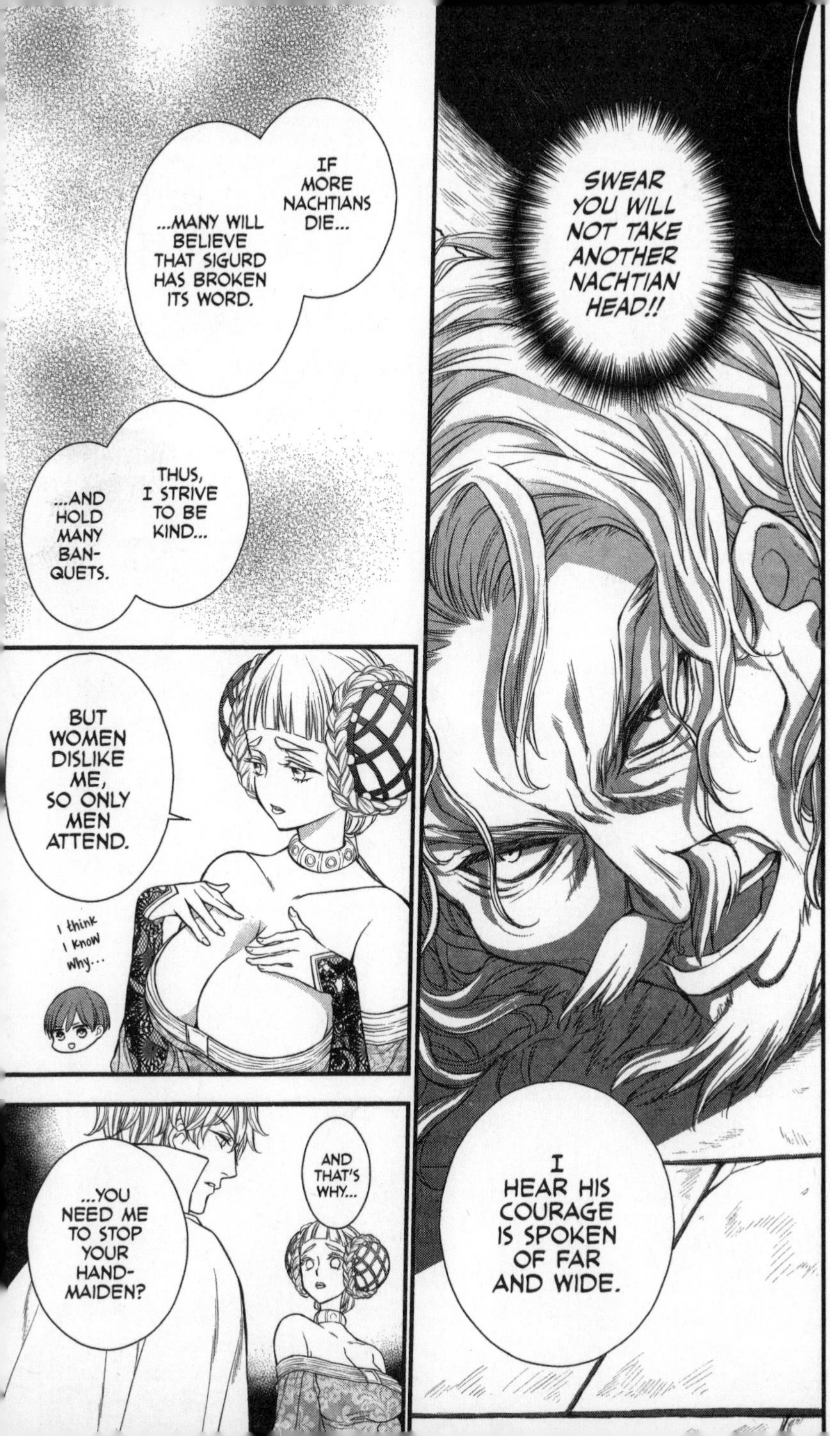
SWEAR YOU WILL NOT TAKE ANOTHER NACHTIAN HEAD!!
I HEAR HIS COURAGE IS SPOKEN OF FAR AND WIDE.
IF MORE NACHTIANS DIE...
...MANY WILL BELIEVE THAT SIGURD HAS BROKEN ITS WORD.
THUS, I STRIVE TO BE KIND...
...AND HOLD MANY BAN-QUETS.
BUT WOMEN DISLIKE ME, SO ONLY MEN ATTEND.
I think I know why...
AND THAT'S WHY...
...YOU NEED ME TO STOP YOUR HAND-MAIDEN?

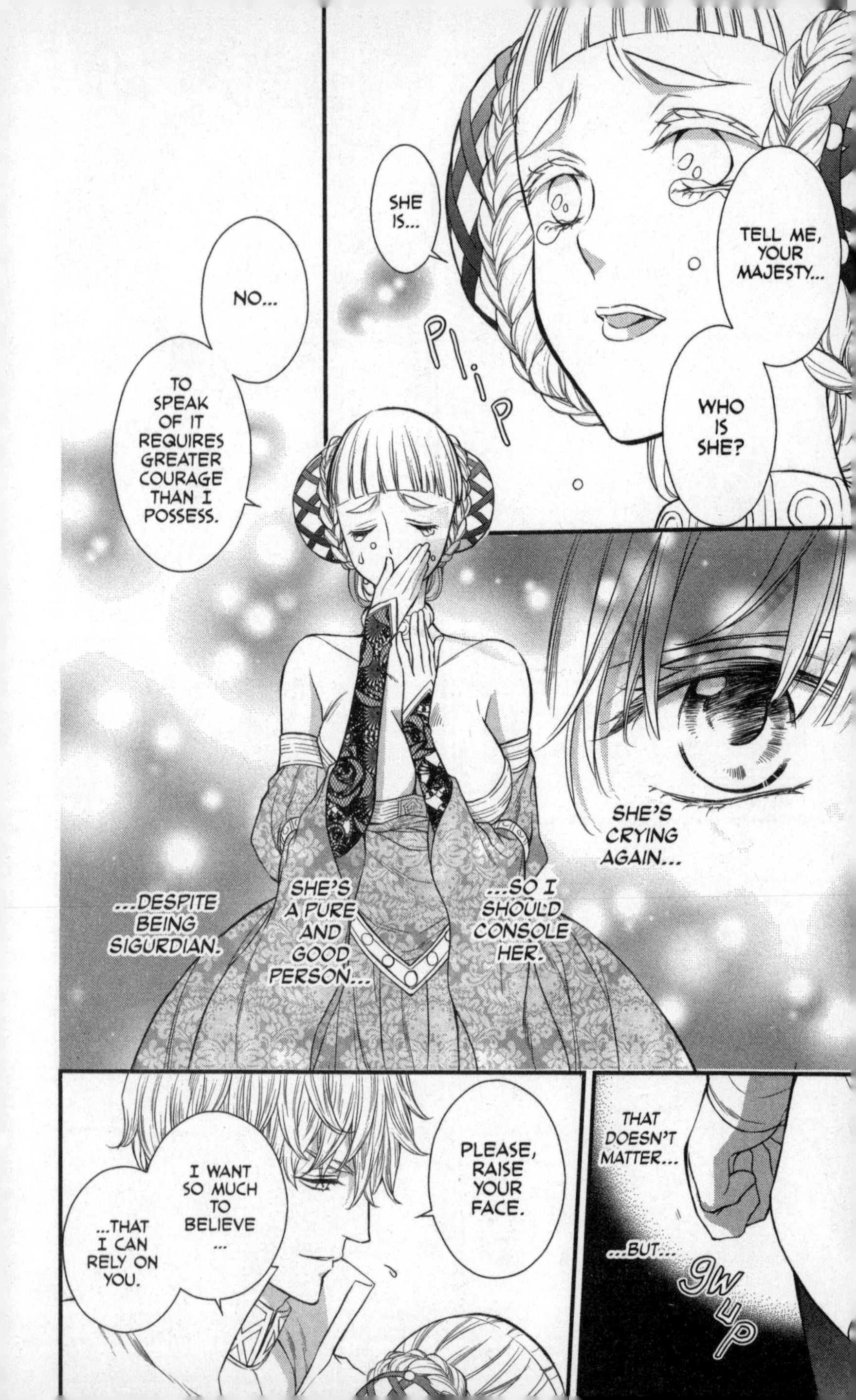
TELL ME, YOUR MAJESTY...
WHO IS SHE?
PLIIP
SHE IS...
NO...
TO SPEAK OF IT REQUIRES GREATER COURAGE THAN I POSSESS.
SHE'S CRYING AGAIN...
...SO I SHOULD CONSOLE HER.
SHE'S A PURE AND GOOD PERSON...
...DESPITE BEING SIGURDIAN.
THAT DOESN'T MATTER...
...BUT...
GWUP
PLEASE, RAISE YOUR FACE.
I WANT SO MUCH TO BELIEVE...
...THAT I CAN RELY ON YOU.

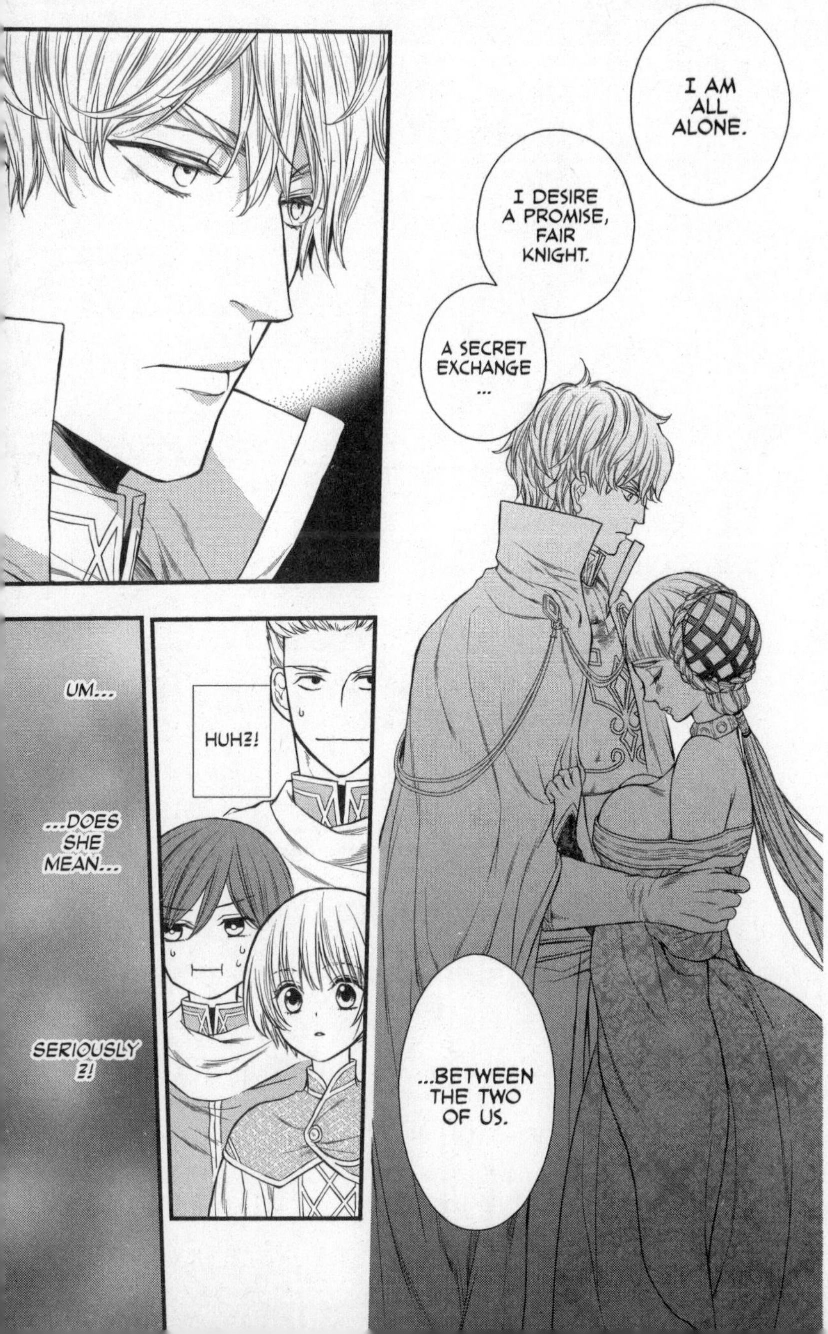
I AM ALL ALONE.
I DESIRE A PROMISE, FAIR KNIGHT.
A SECRET EXCHANGE ...
...BETWEEN THE TWO OF US.
HUH?!
UM...
...DOES SHE MEAN...
SERIOUSLY ?!

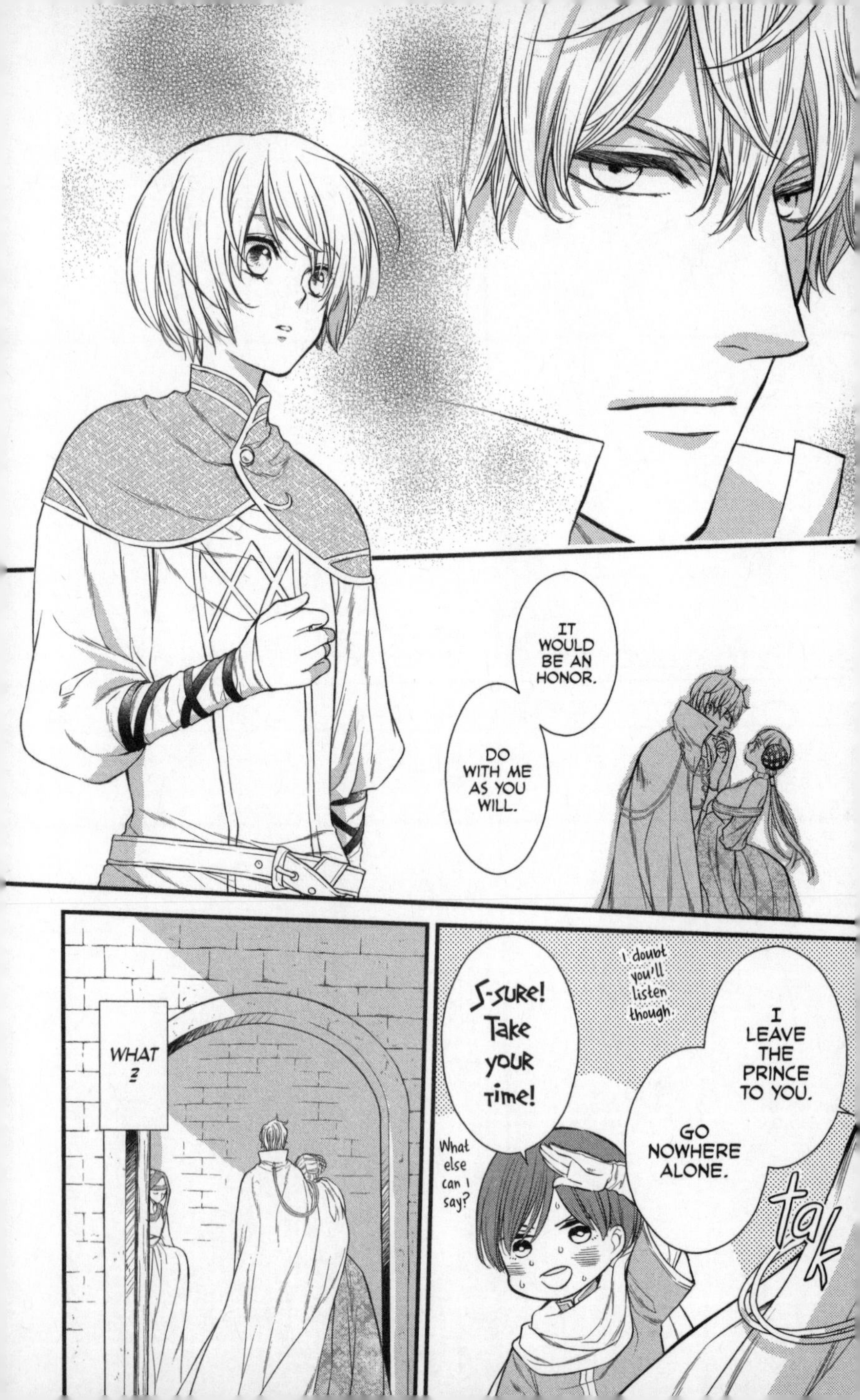
IT WOULD BE AN HONOR.
DO WITH ME AS YOU WILL.
I LEAVE THE PRINCE TO YOU.
GO NOWHERE ALONE.
I doubt you'll listen though.
S-SURE! Take your time!
What else can I say?
tak
WHAT?

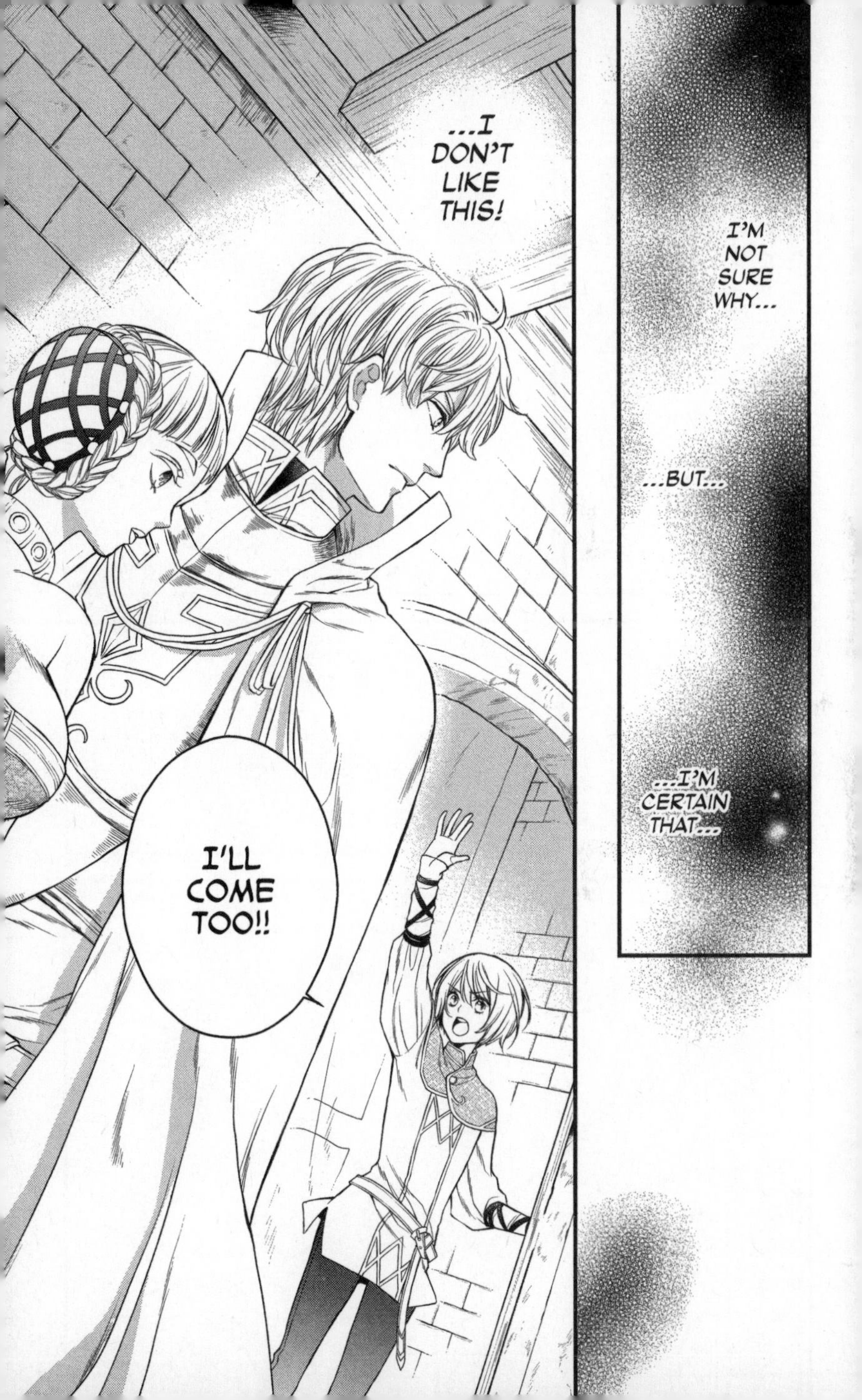
I'M NOT SURE WHY...
...BUT...
...I'M CERTAIN THAT...
...I DON'T LIKE THIS!
I'LL COME TOO!!

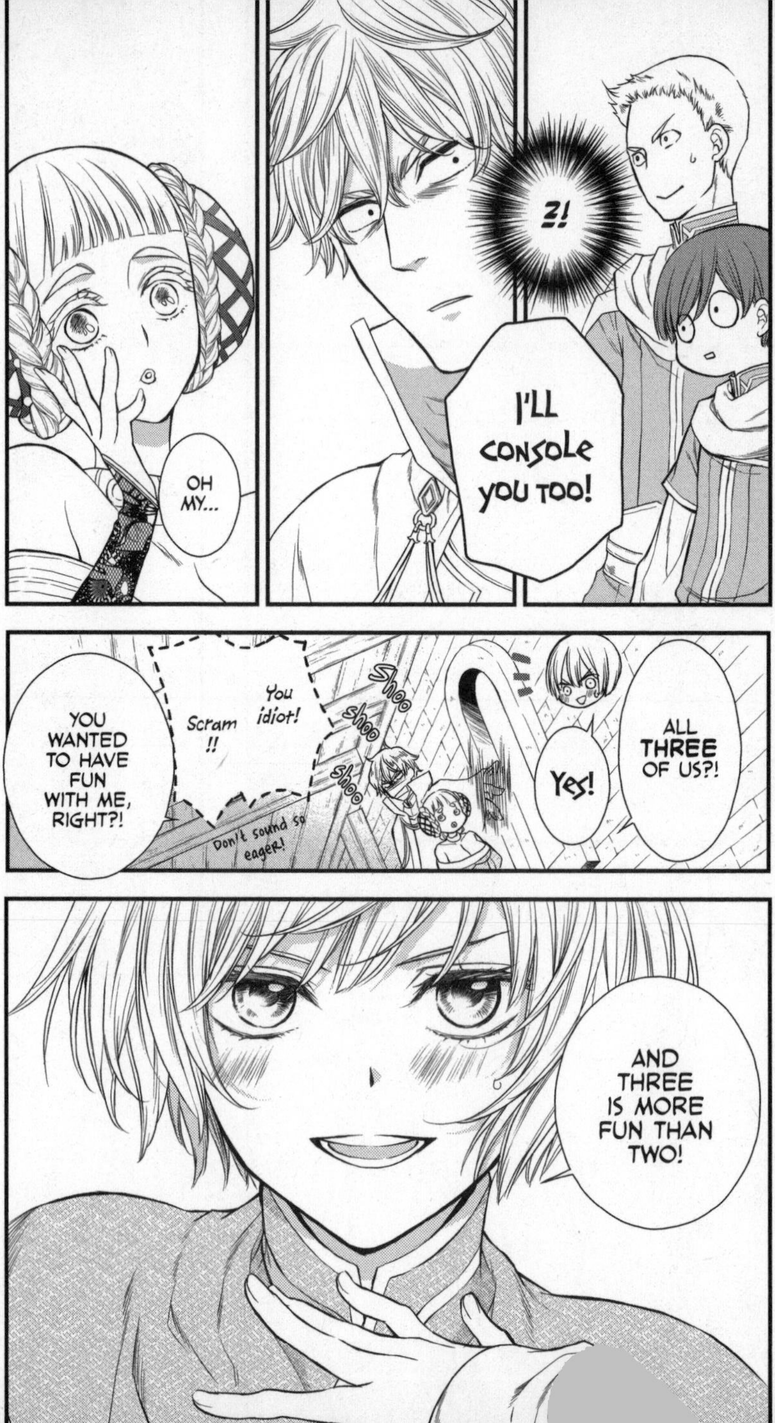
?!
I'LL CONSOLE YOU TOO!
OH MY...
ALL THREE OF US?!
Yes!
Shoo shoo shoo
You idiot!
Scram !!
Don't sound so eager!
YOU WANTED TO HAVE FUN WITH ME, RIGHT?!
AND THREE IS MORE FUN THAN TWO!

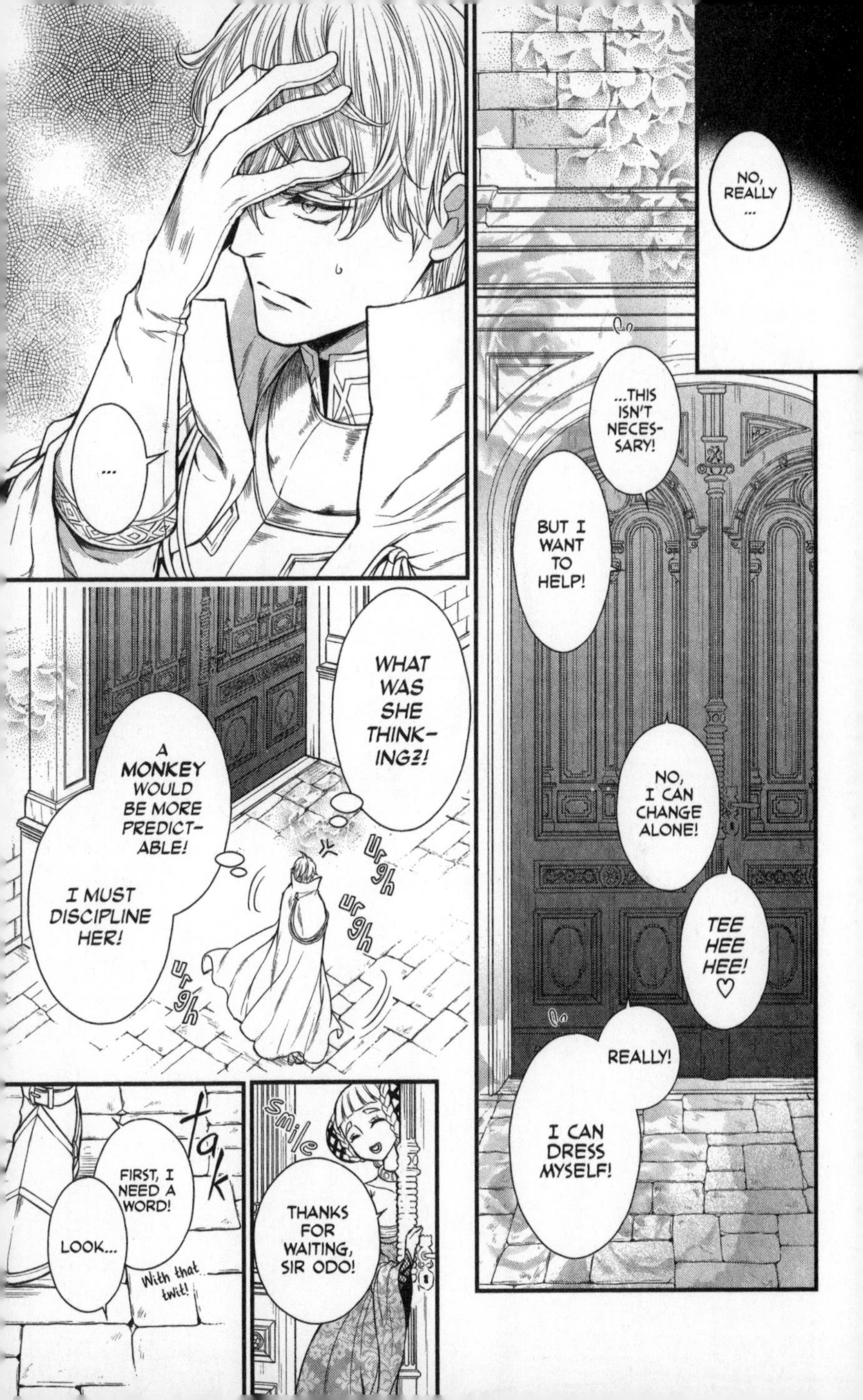
NO, REALLY...
...THIS ISN'T NECES-SARY!
BUT I WANT TO HELP!
NO, I CAN CHANGE ALONE!
TEE HEE HEE! ♡
REALLY!
I CAN DRESS MYSELF!
...
WHAT WAS SHE THINKING?!
A MONKEY WOULD BE MORE PREDICT-ABLE!
I MUST DISCIPLINE HER!
urgh
urgh
urgh
smile
THANKS FOR WAITING, SIR ODO!
tak
FIRST, I NEED A WORD!
LOOK...
With that twit!

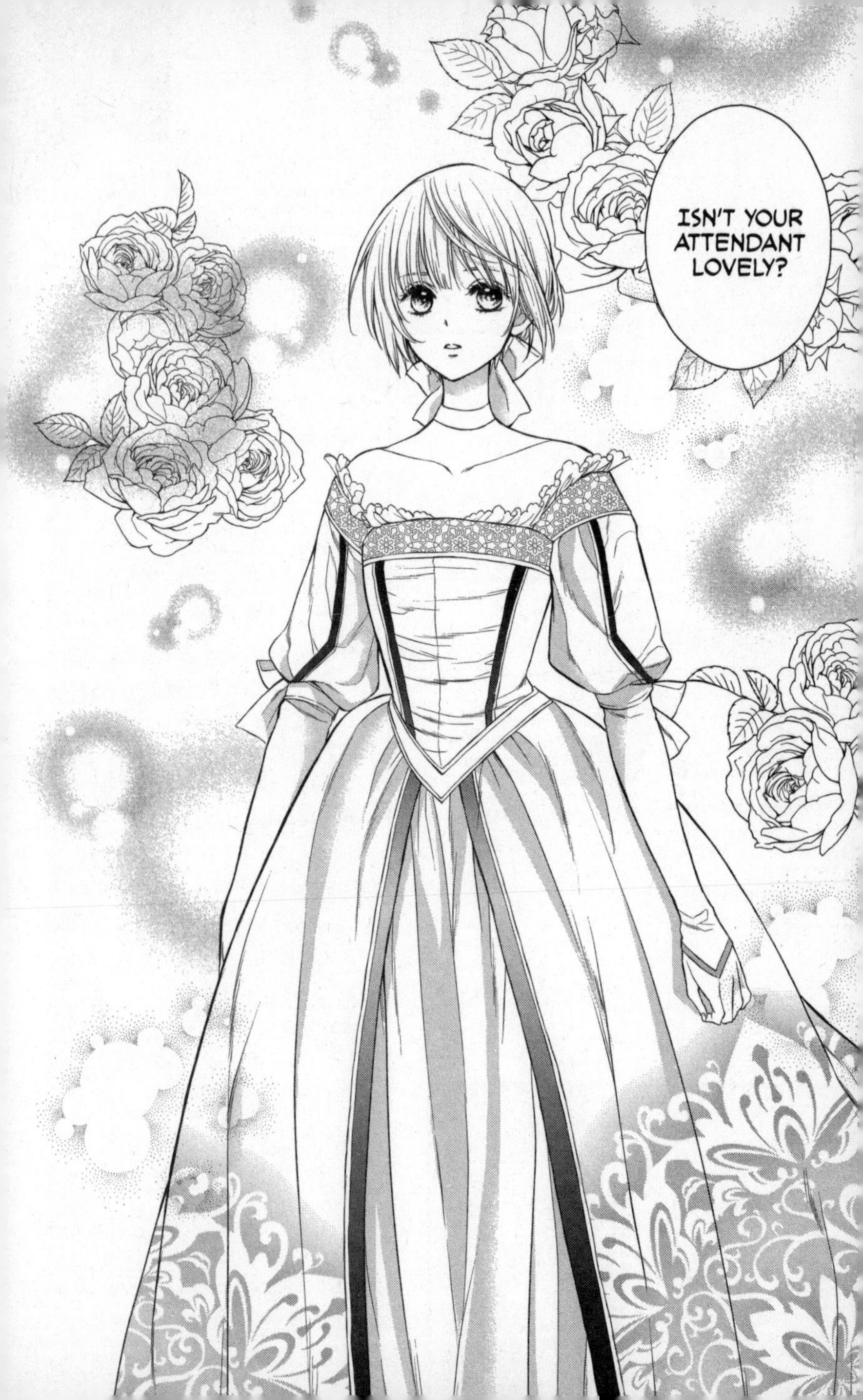
ISN'T YOUR ATTENDANT LOVELY?

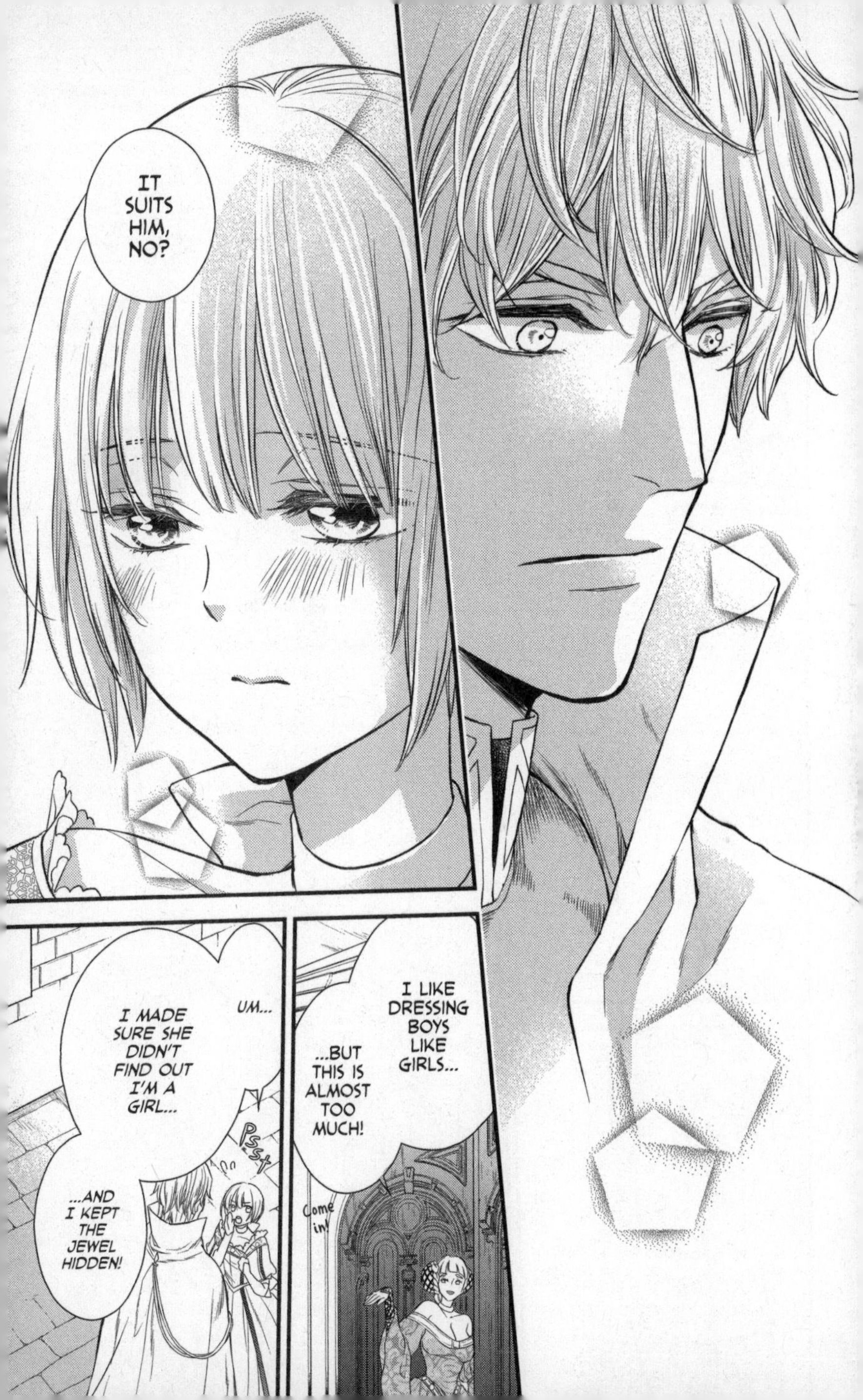
IT SUITS HIM, NO?
I LIKE DRESSING BOYS LIKE GIRLS...
...BUT THIS IS ALMOST TOO MUCH!
Come in!
UM...
I MADE SURE SHE DIDN'T FIND OUT I'M A GIRL...
Psst
...AND I KEPT THE JEWEL HIDDEN!

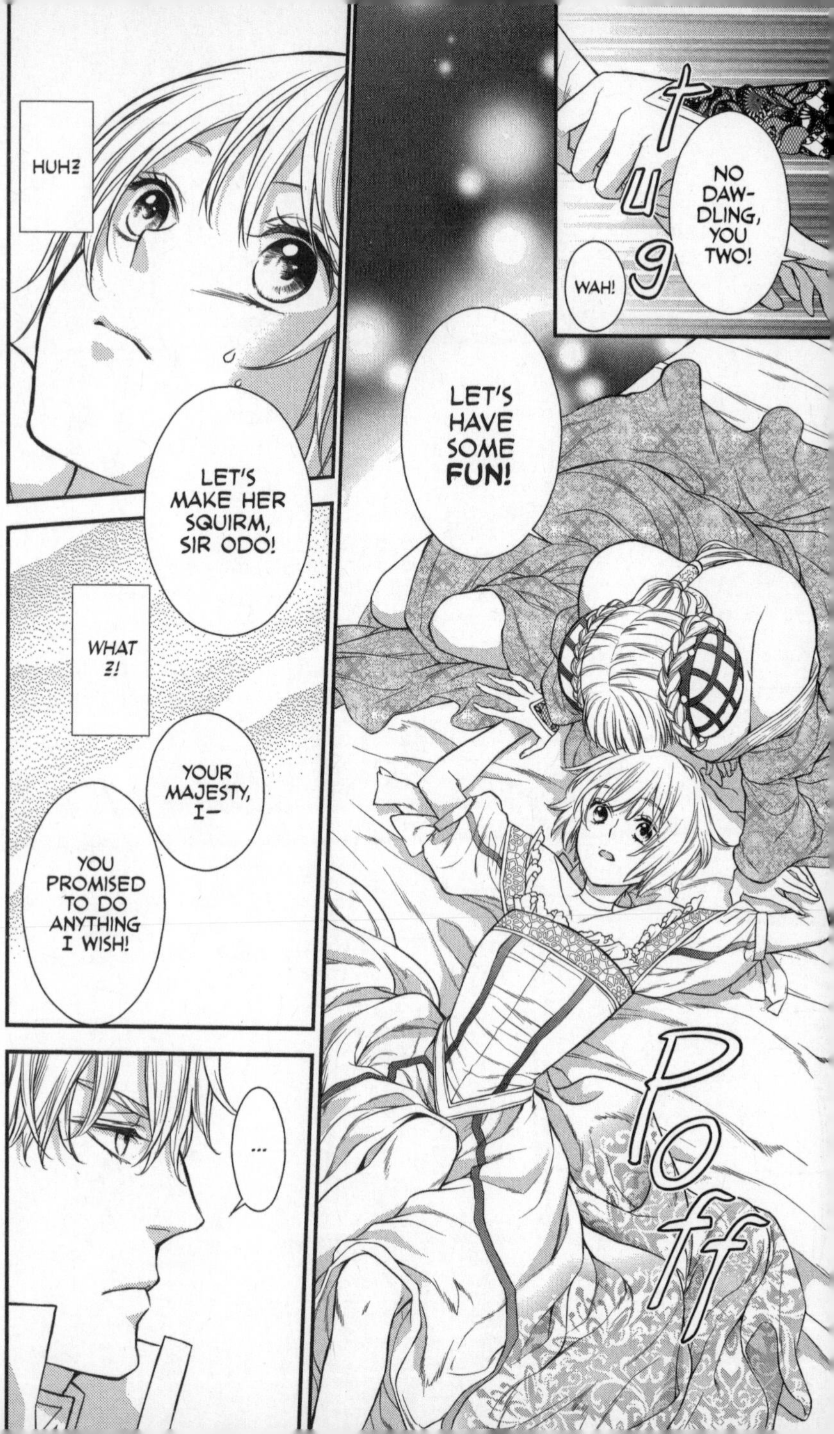
tug
NO DAWDLING, YOU TWO!
WAH!
LET'S HAVE SOME FUN!
LET'S MAKE HER SQUIRM, SIR ODO!
Poff
HUH?
WHAT?!
YOUR MAJESTY, I—
YOU PROMISED TO DO ANYTHING I WISH!
...

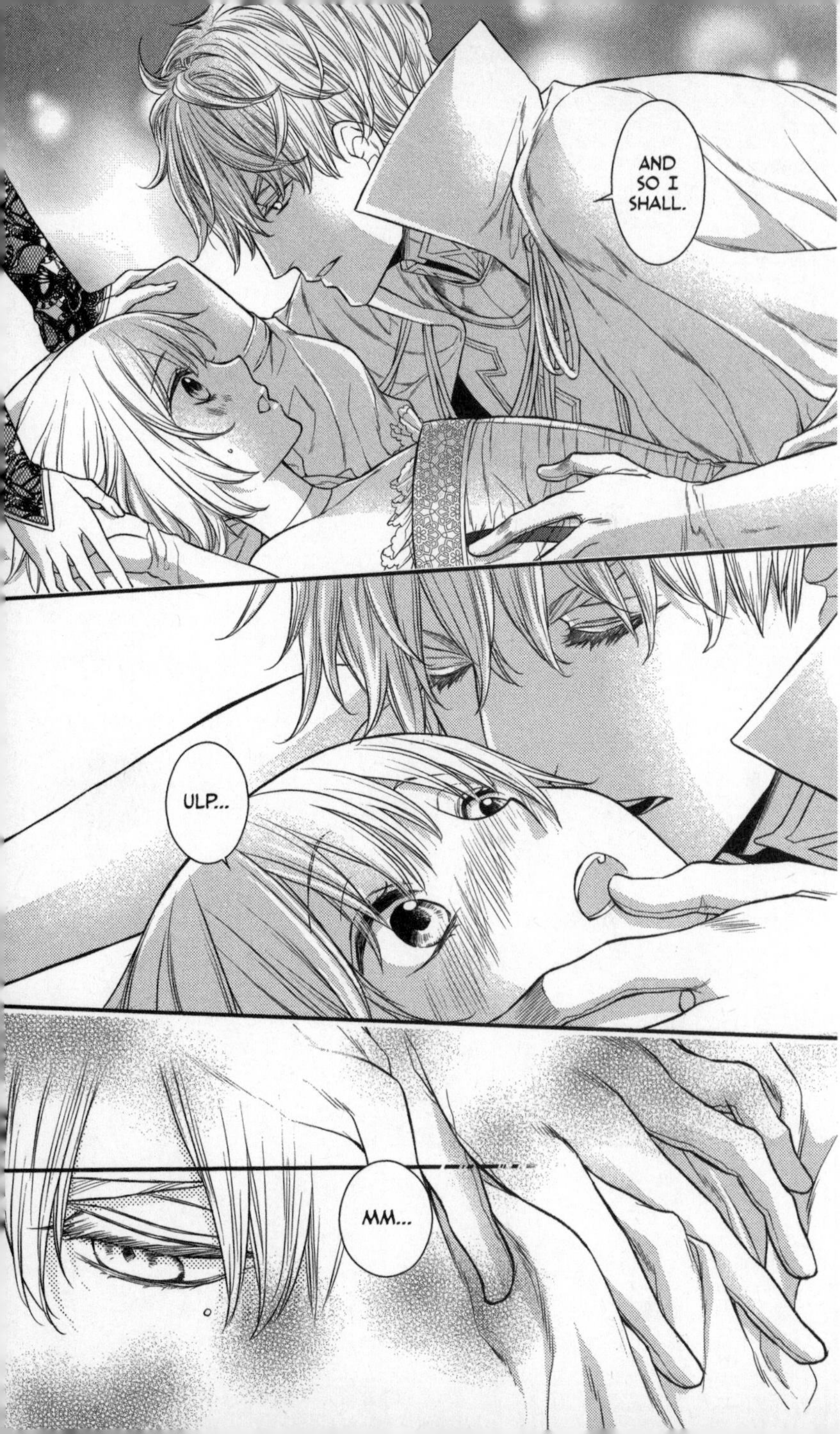
AND SO I SHALL.
ULP...
MM...

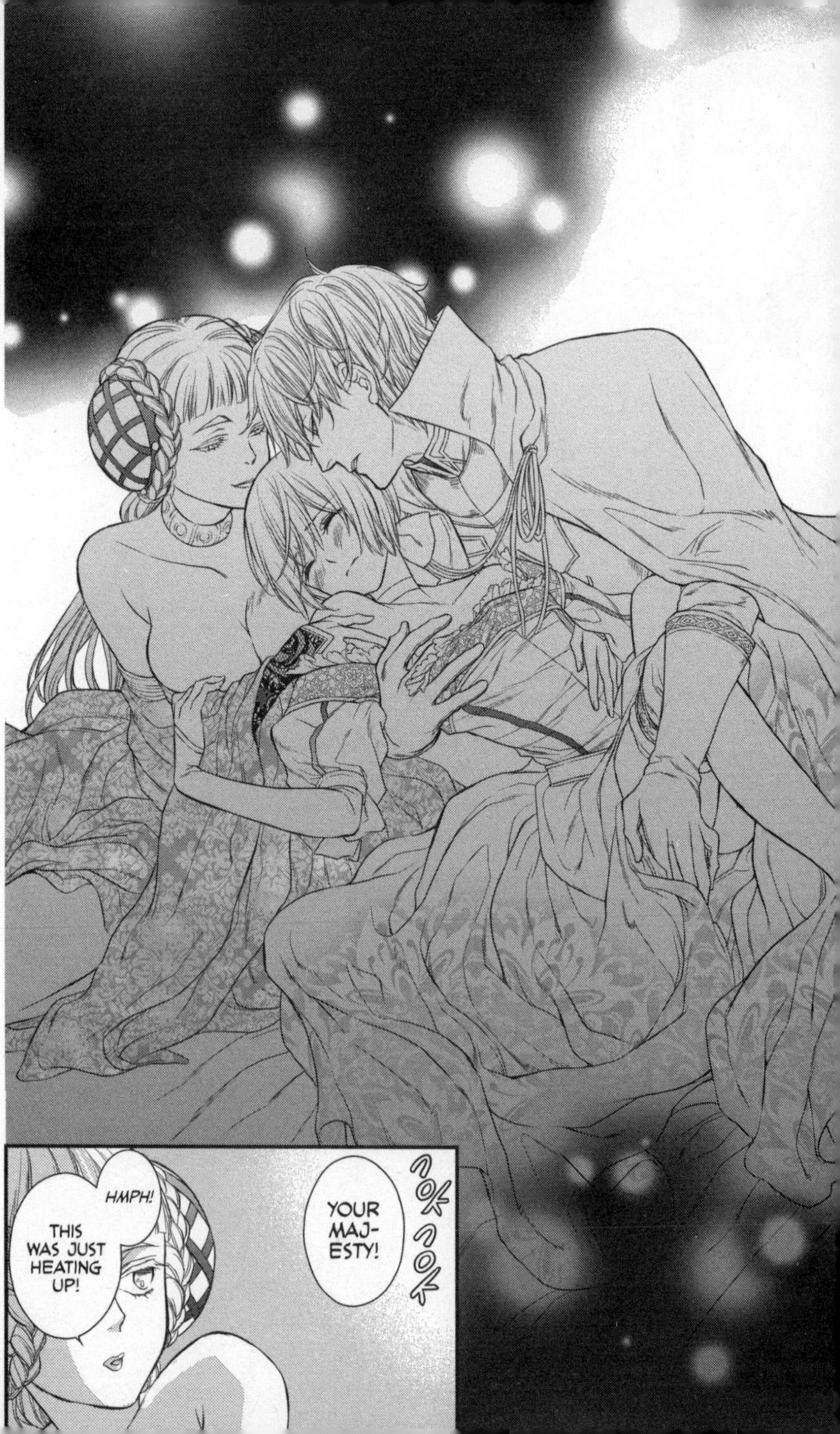
KOK KOK
YOUR MAJ-ESTY!
HMPH!
THIS WAS JUST HEATING UP!

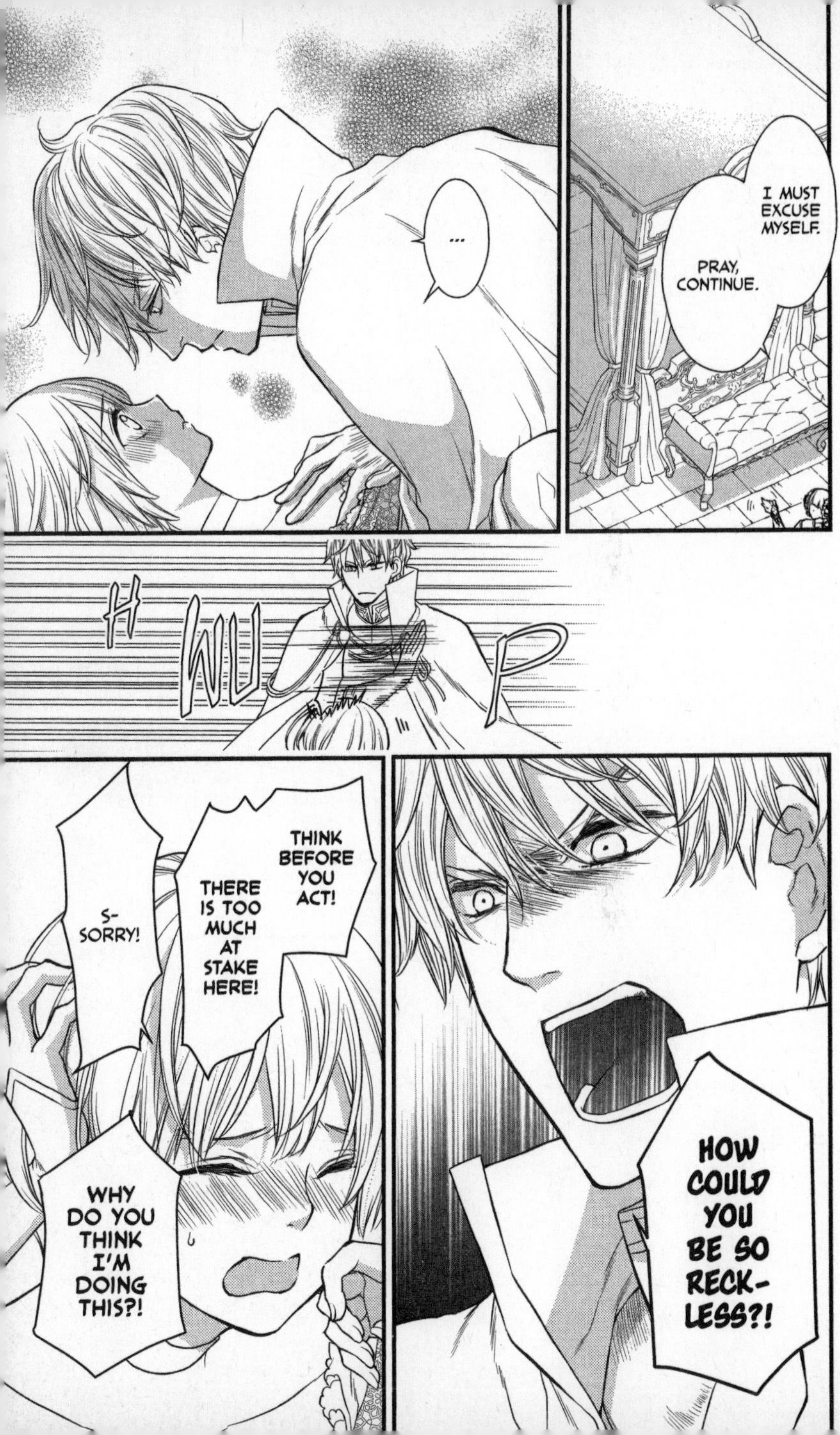
I MUST EXCUSE MYSELF.
PRAY, CONTINUE.
...
HWUP
HOW COULD YOU BE SO RECK-LESS?!
THINK BEFORE YOU ACT!
THERE IS TOO MUCH AT STAKE HERE!
S-SORRY!
WHY DO YOU THINK I'M DOING THIS?!

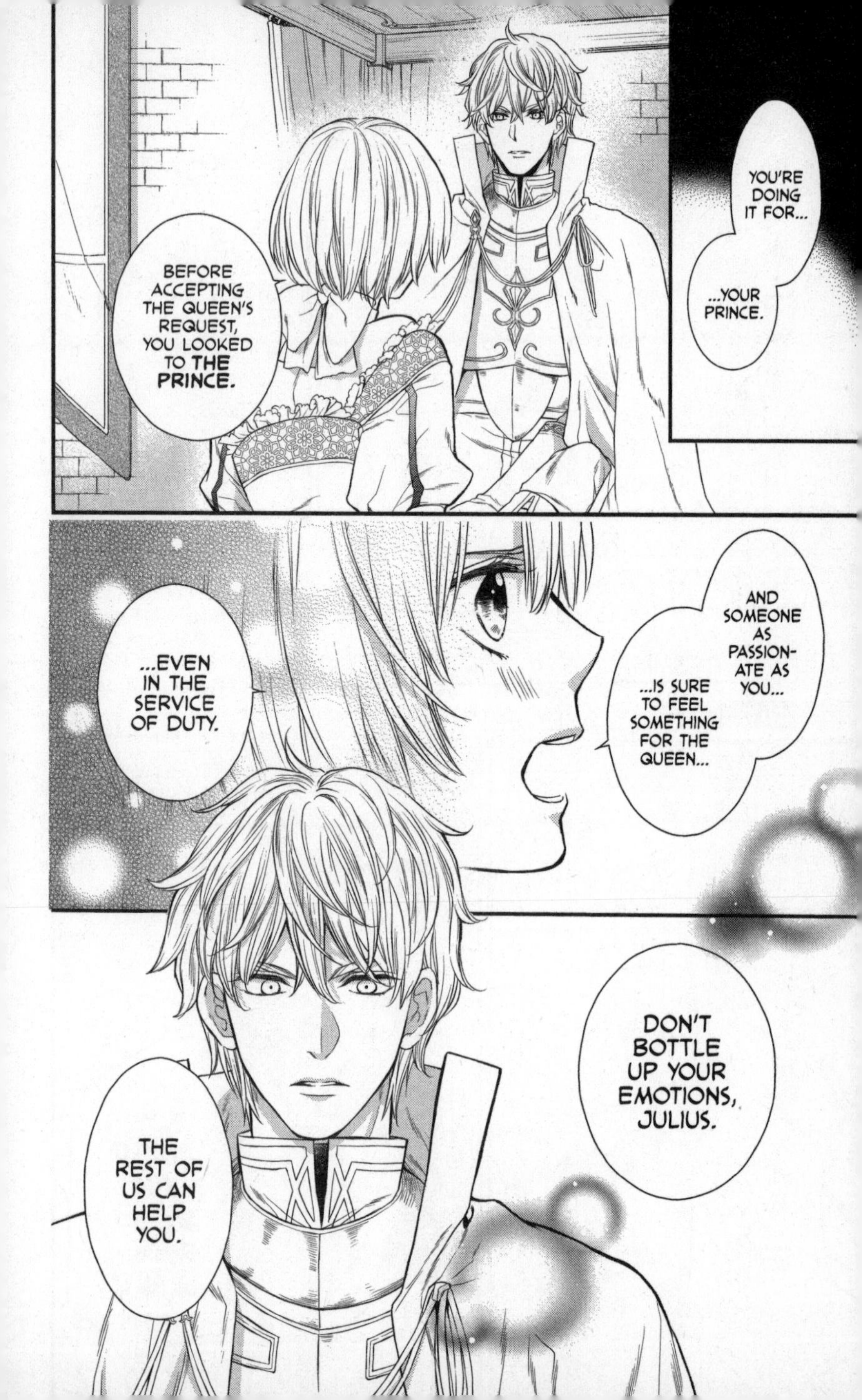
YOU'RE DOING IT FOR...
...YOUR PRINCE.
BEFORE ACCEPTING THE QUEEN'S REQUEST, YOU LOOKED TO THE PRINCE.
AND SOMEONE AS PASSION-ATE AS YOU...
...IS SURE TO FEEL SOMETHING FOR THE QUEEN...
...EVEN IN THE SERVICE OF DUTY.
DON'T BOTTLE UP YOUR EMOTIONS, JULIUS.
THE REST OF US CAN HELP YOU.

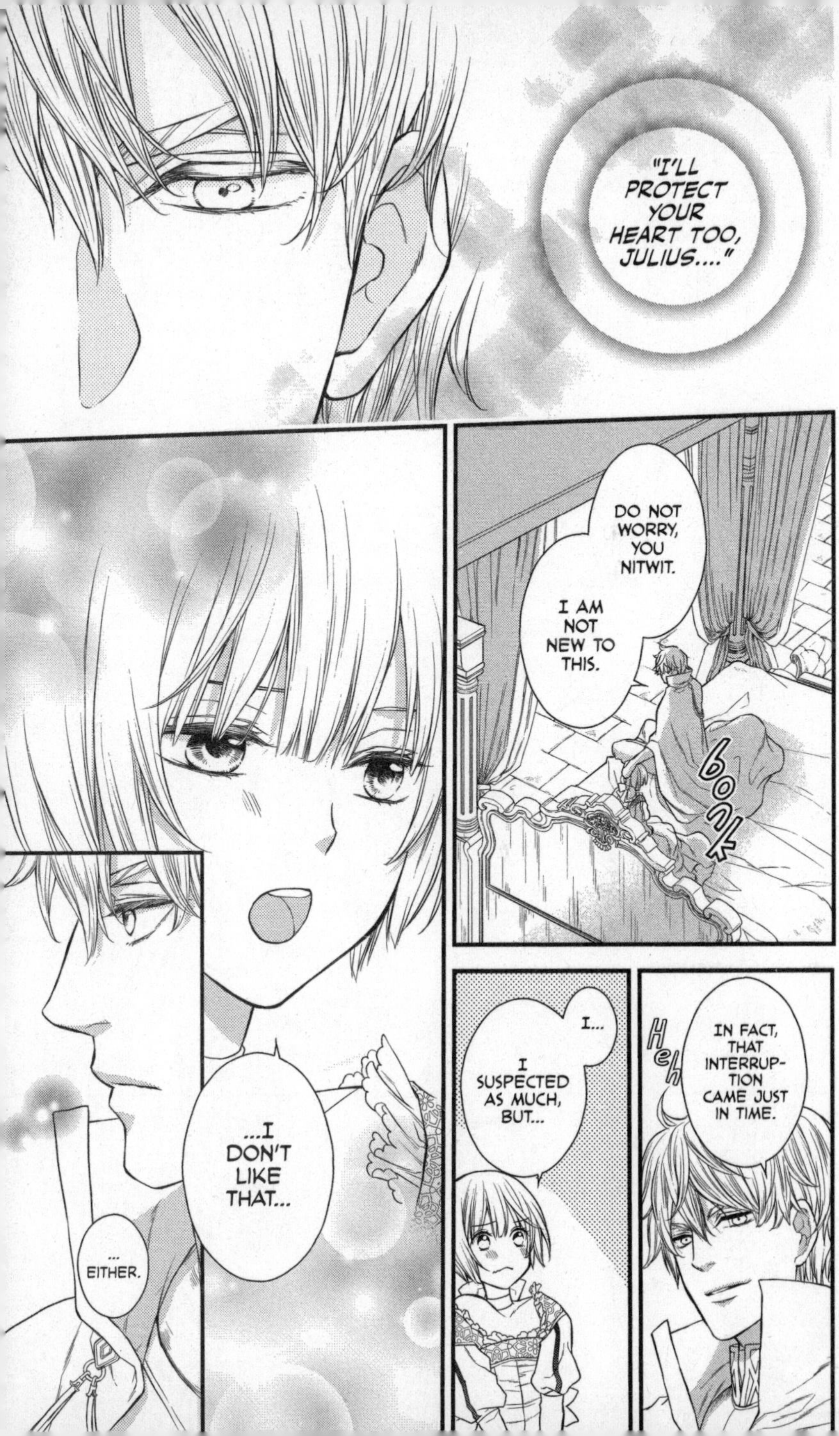
"I'LL PROTECT YOUR HEART TOO, JULIUS...."
DO NOT WORRY, YOU NITWIT.
I AM NOT NEW TO THIS.
bonk
Heh
IN FACT, THAT INTERRUP-TION CAME JUST IN TIME.
I...
I SUSPECTED AS MUCH, BUT...
...I DON'T LIKE THAT...
... EITHER.

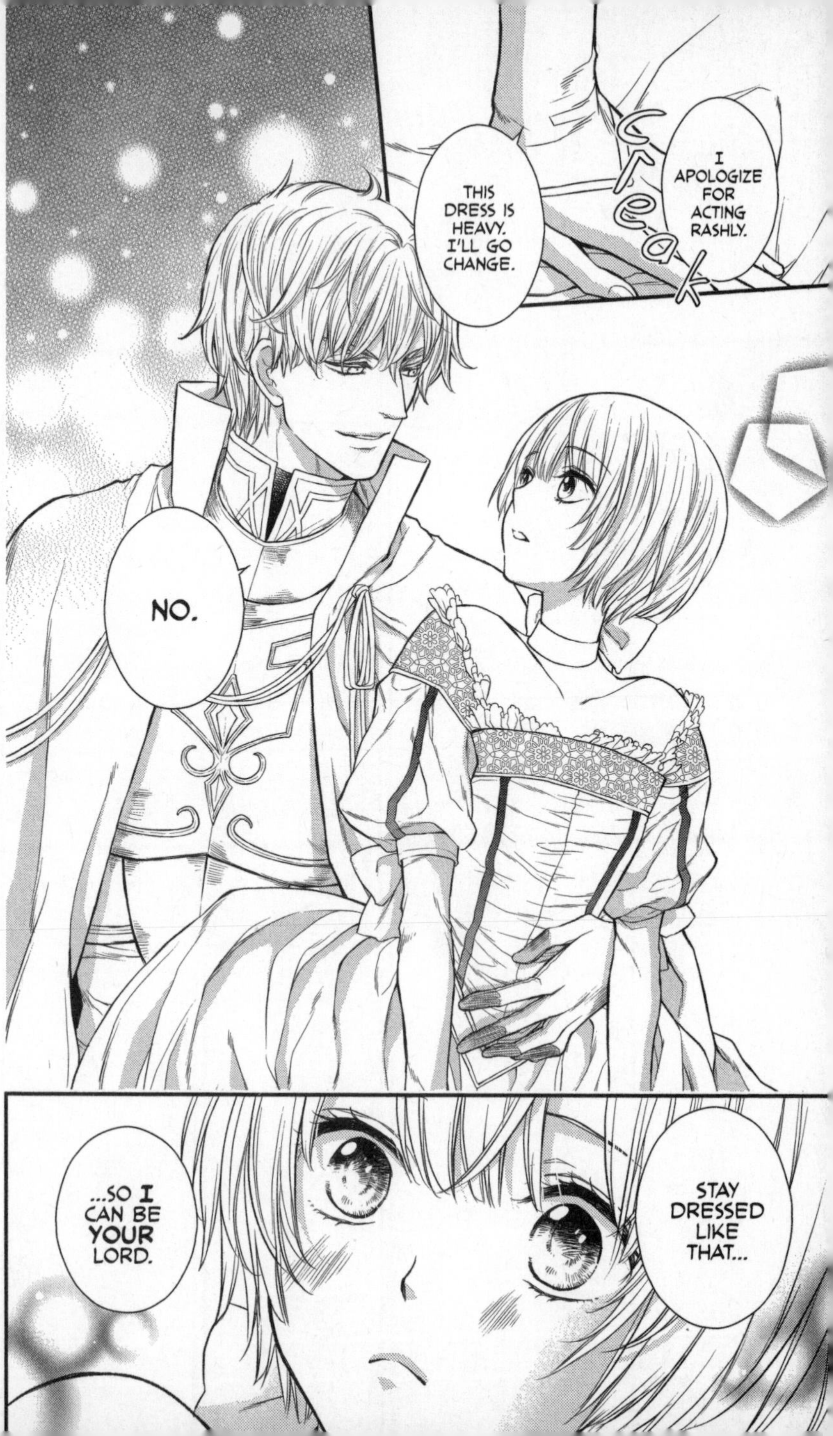
I APOLOGIZE FOR ACTING RASHLY.
creak
THIS DRESS IS HEAVY. I'LL GO CHANGE.
NO.
STAY DRESSED LIKE THAT...
...SO I CAN BE YOUR LORD.

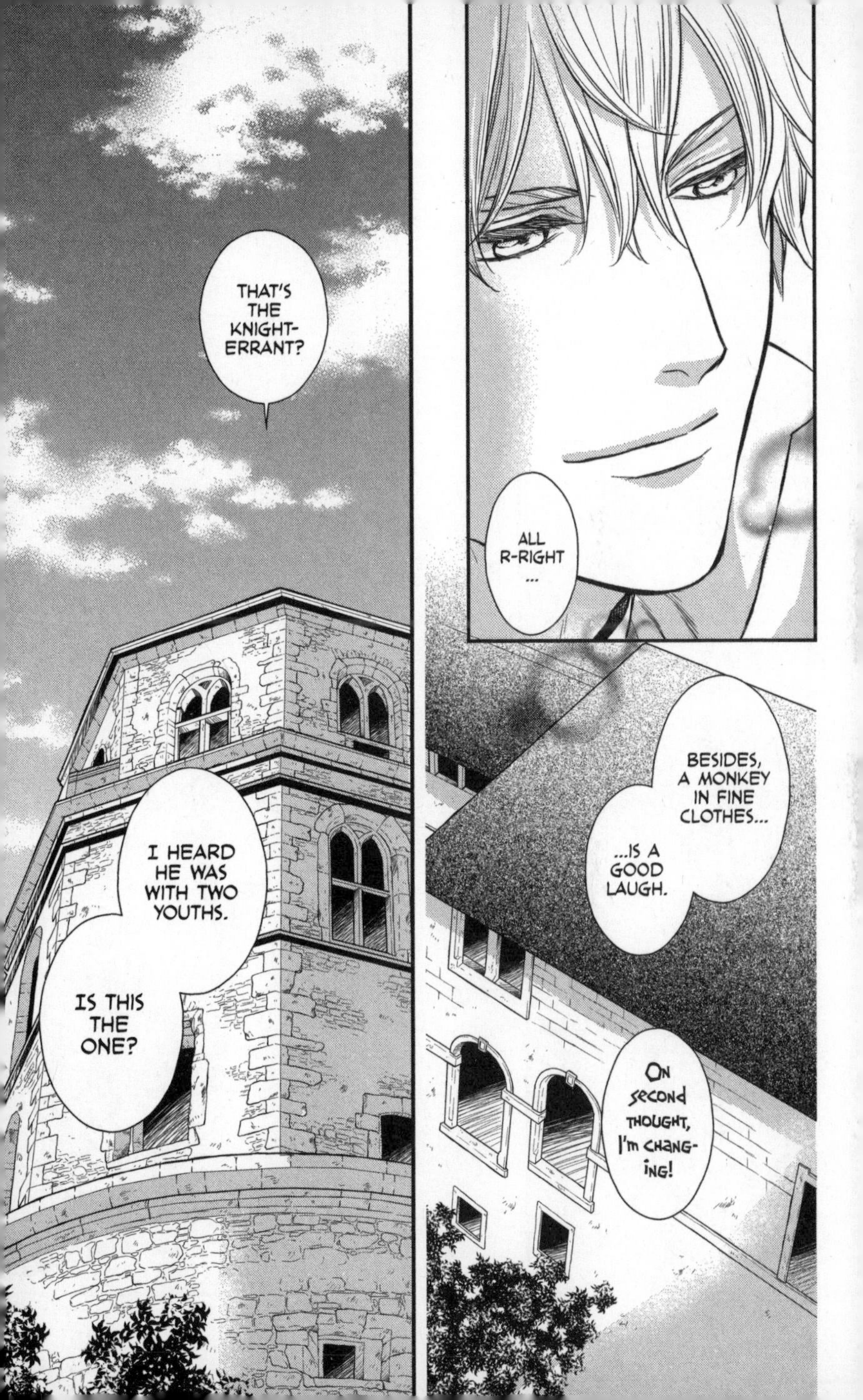
ALL R-RIGHT...
BESIDES, A MONKEY IN FINE CLOTHES...
...IS A GOOD LAUGH.
On second thought, I'm chang-ing!
THAT'S THE KNIGHT-ERRANT?
I HEARD HE WAS WITH TWO YOUTHS.
IS THIS THE ONE?

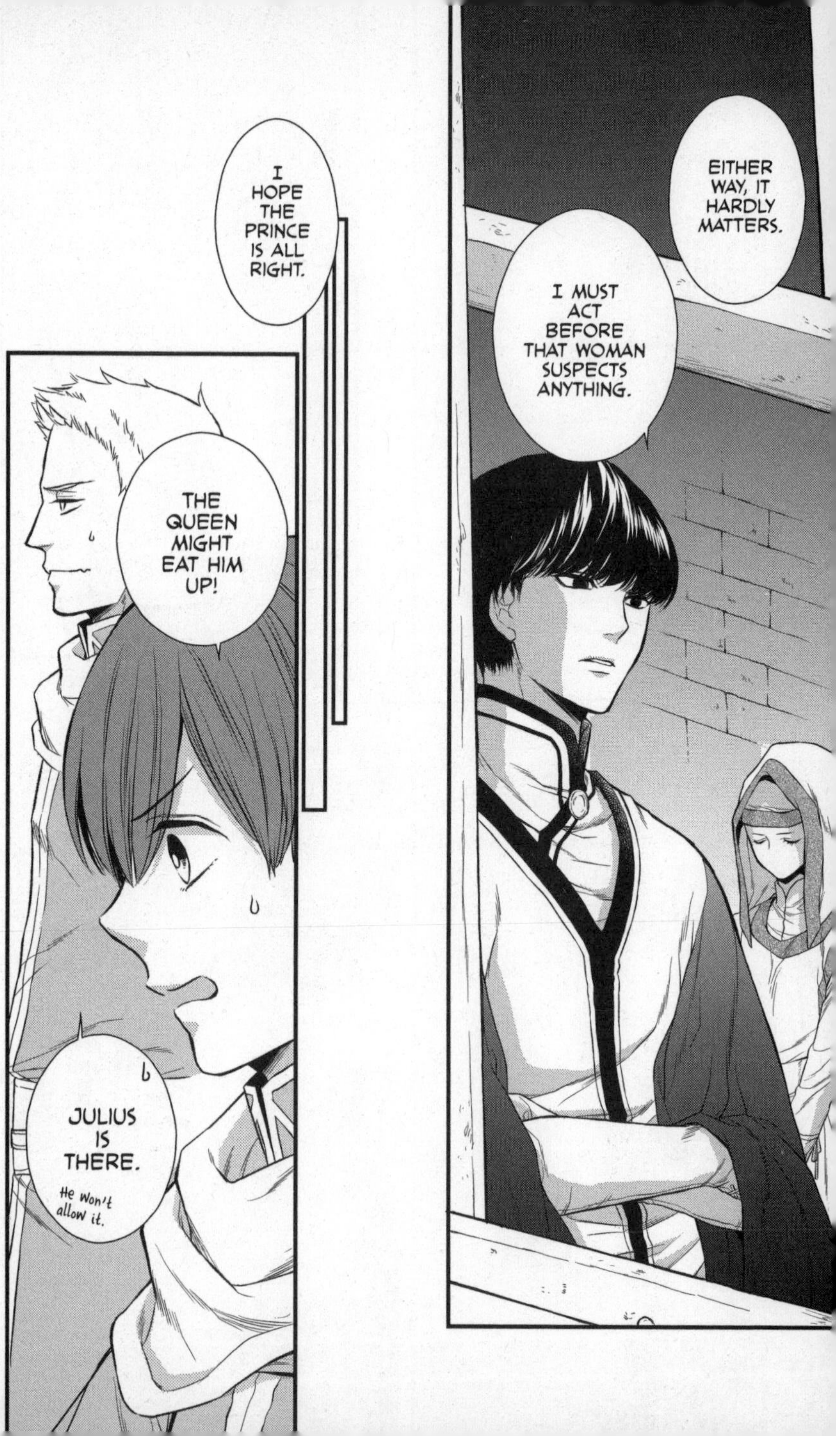
EITHER WAY, IT HARDLY MATTERS.
I MUST ACT BEFORE THAT WOMAN SUSPECTS ANYTHING.
I HOPE THE PRINCE IS ALL RIGHT.
THE QUEEN MIGHT EAT HIM UP!
JULIUS IS THERE.
He won't allow it.

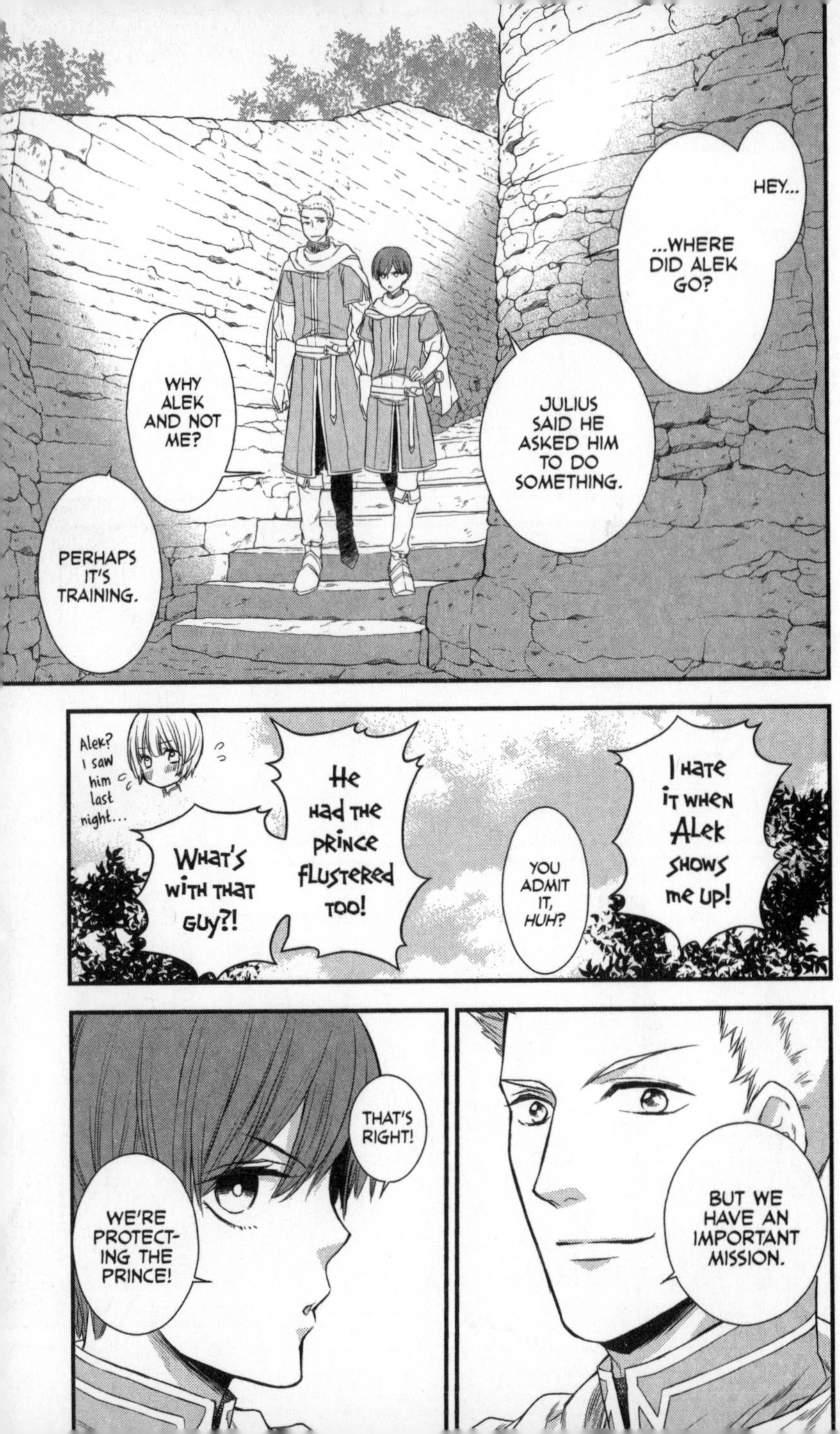
HEY...
...WHERE DID ALEK GO?
JULIUS SAID HE ASKED HIM TO DO SOMETHING.
WHY ALEK AND NOT ME?
PERHAPS IT'S TRAINING.
I hate it when Alek shows me up!
YOU ADMIT IT, HUH?
He had the prince flustered too!
What's with that guy?!
Alek? I saw him last night...
BUT WE HAVE AN IMPORTANT MISSION.
THAT'S RIGHT!
WE'RE PROTECTING THE PRINCE!

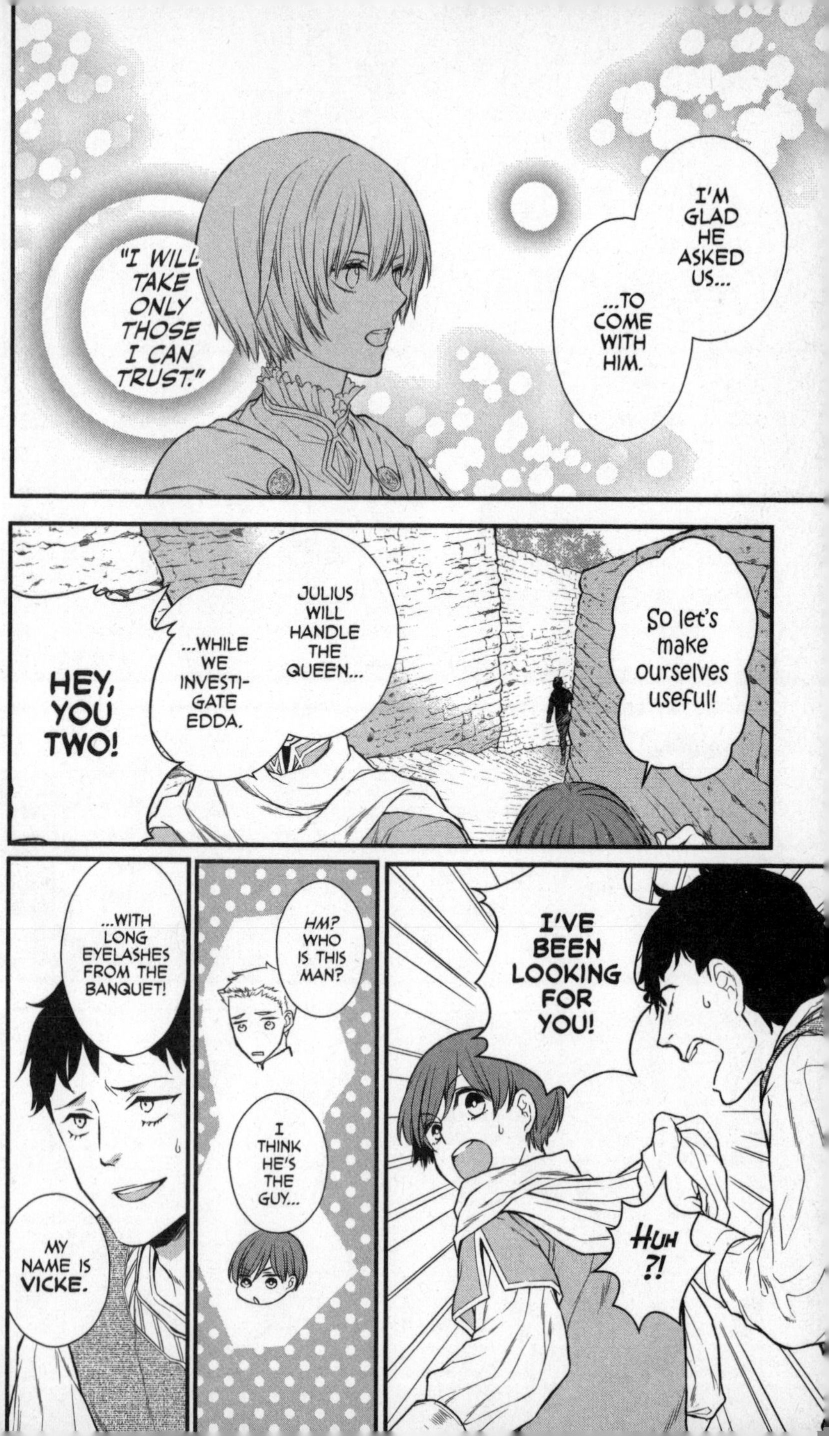
I'M GLAD HE ASKED US...
...TO COME WITH HIM.
"I WILL TAKE ONLY THOSE I CAN TRUST."
So let's make ourselves useful!
JULIUS WILL HANDLE THE QUEEN...
...WHILE WE INVESTIGATE EDDA.
HEY, YOU TWO!
I'VE BEEN LOOKING FOR YOU!
HUH ?!
HM? WHO IS THIS MAN?
I THINK HE'S THE GUY...
...WITH LONG EYELASHES FROM THE BANQUET!
MY NAME IS VICKE.

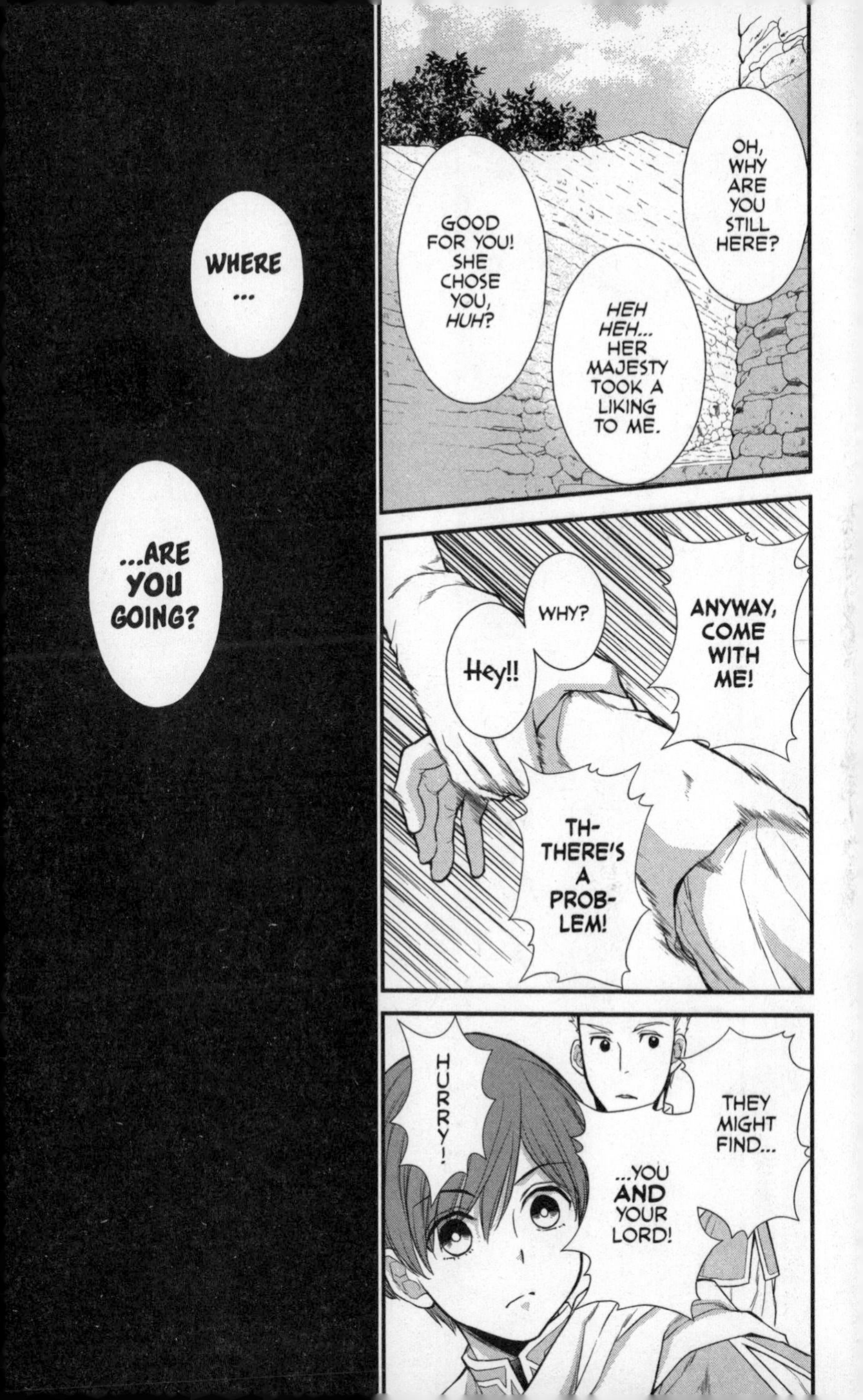
OH, WHY ARE YOU STILL HERE?
HEH HEH... HER MAJESTY TOOK A LIKING TO ME.
GOOD FOR YOU! SHE CHOSE YOU, HUH?
ANYWAY, COME WITH ME!
WHY?
Hey!!
TH-THERE'S A PROBLEM!
THEY MIGHT FIND...
...YOU AND YOUR LORD!
HURRY!
WHERE...
...ARE YOU GOING?

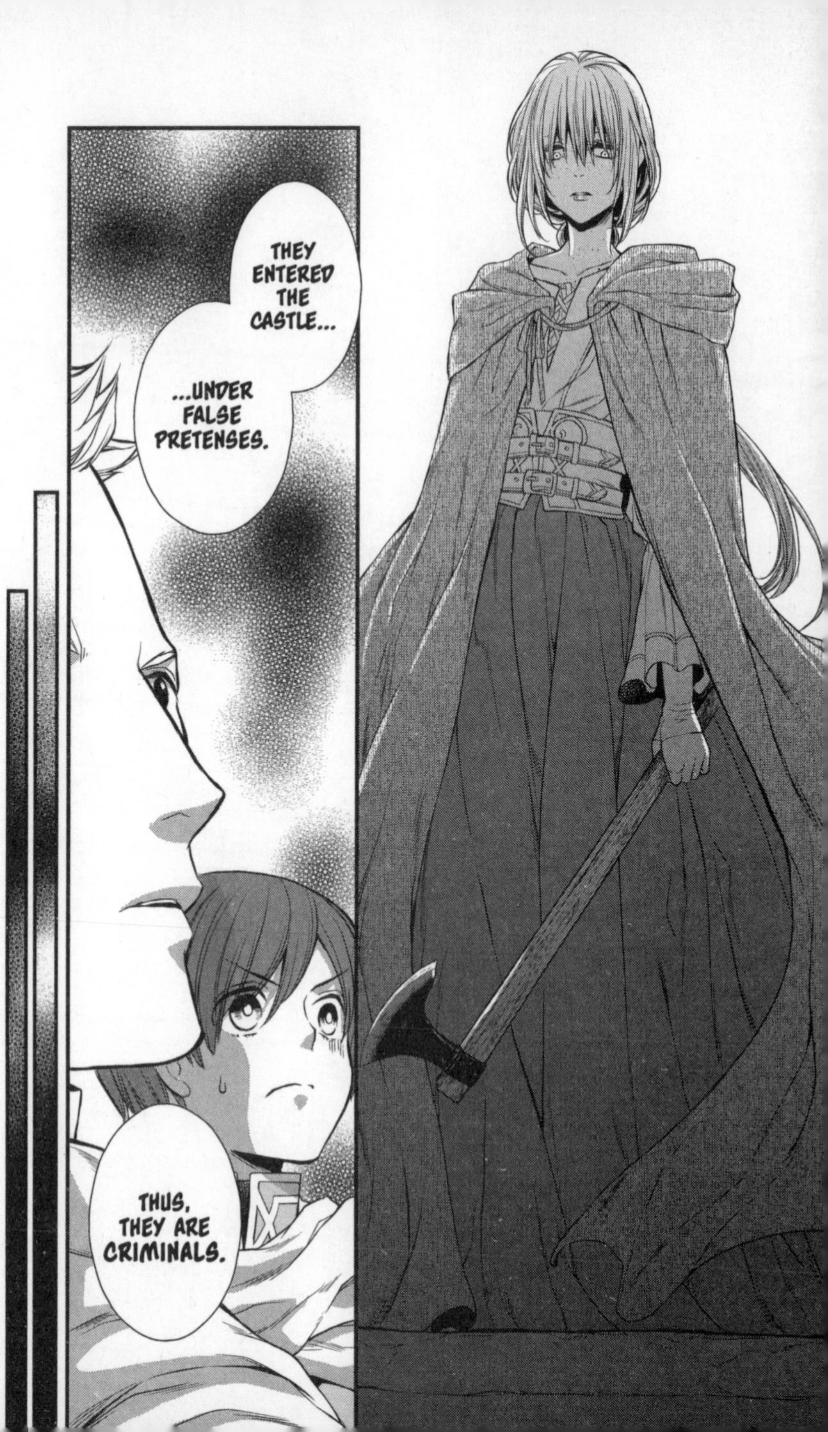
THEY ENTERED THE CASTLE...
...UNDER FALSE PRETENSES.
THUS, THEY ARE CRIMINALS.

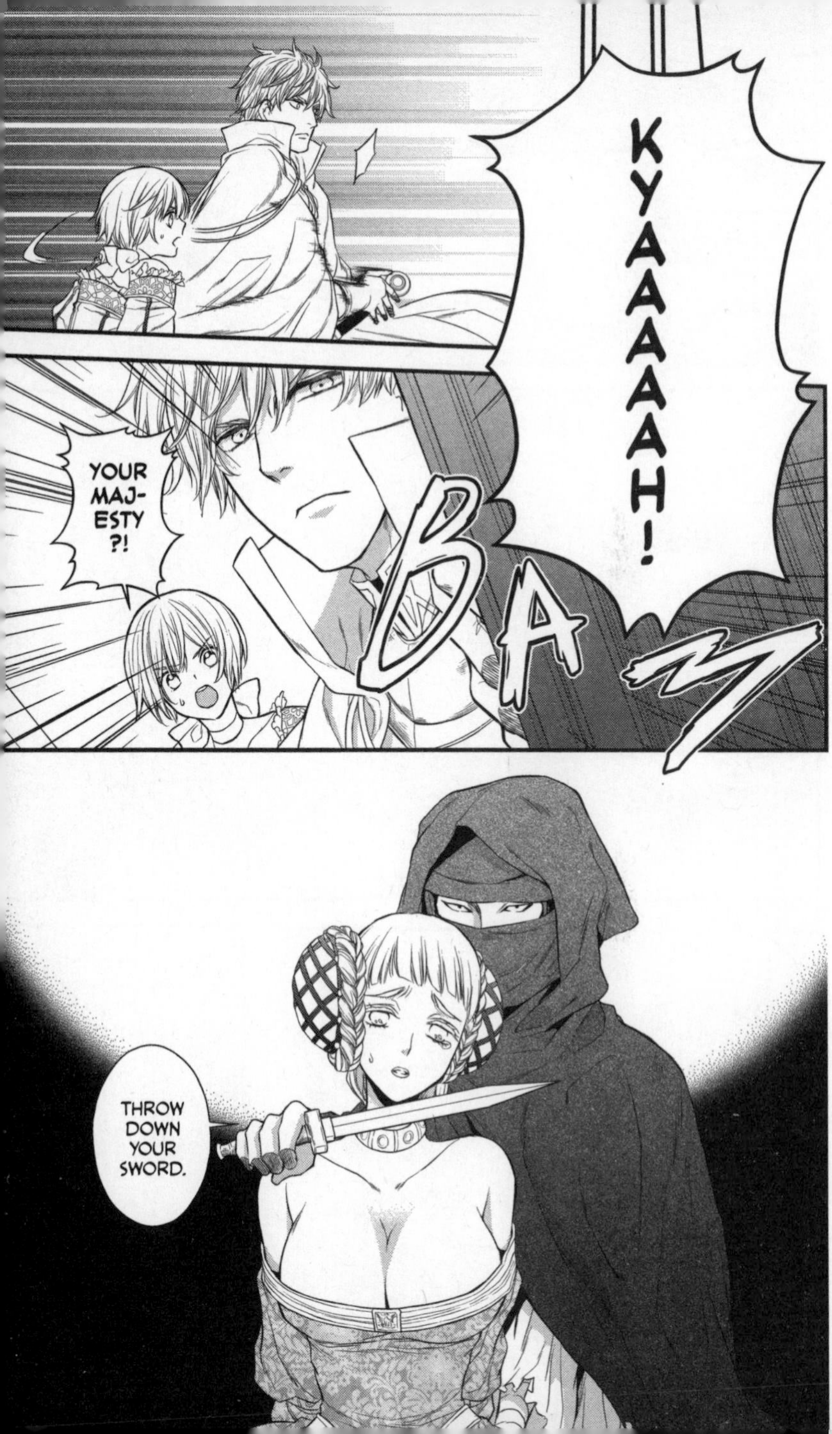
KYAAAAAH!
YOUR MAJ-ESTY?!
BAM
THROW DOWN YOUR SWORD.

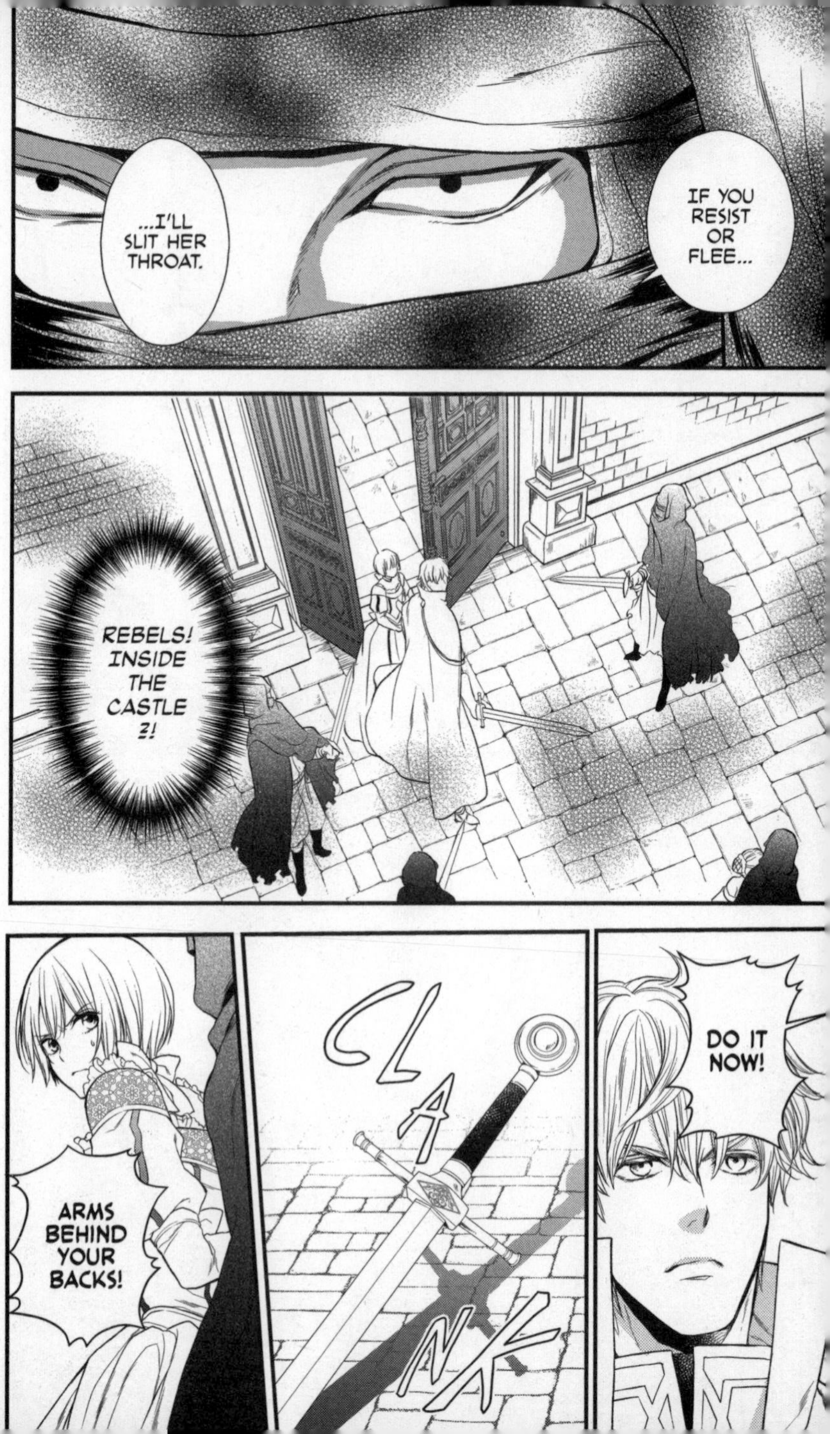
IF YOU RESIST OR FLEE...
...I'LL SLIT HER THROAT.
REBELS! INSIDE THE CASTLE ?!
DO IT NOW!
CLANK
ARMS BEHIND YOUR BACKS!

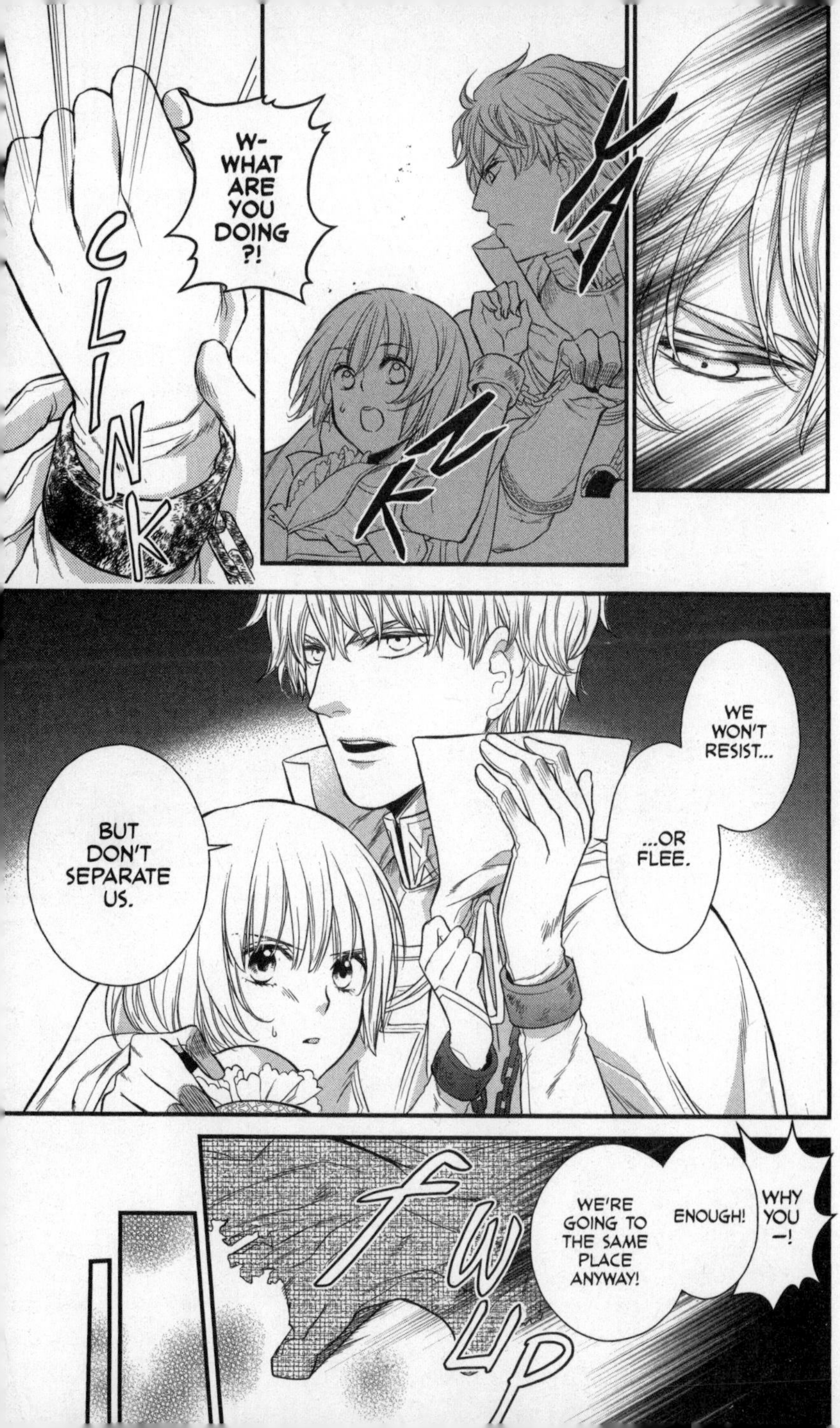
YANK
W-WHAT ARE YOU DOING?!
CLINK
WE WON'T RESIST...
...OR FLEE.
BUT DON'T SEPARATE US.
WHY YOU—!
ENOUGH!
WE'RE GOING TO THE SAME PLACE ANYWAY!
FWUP

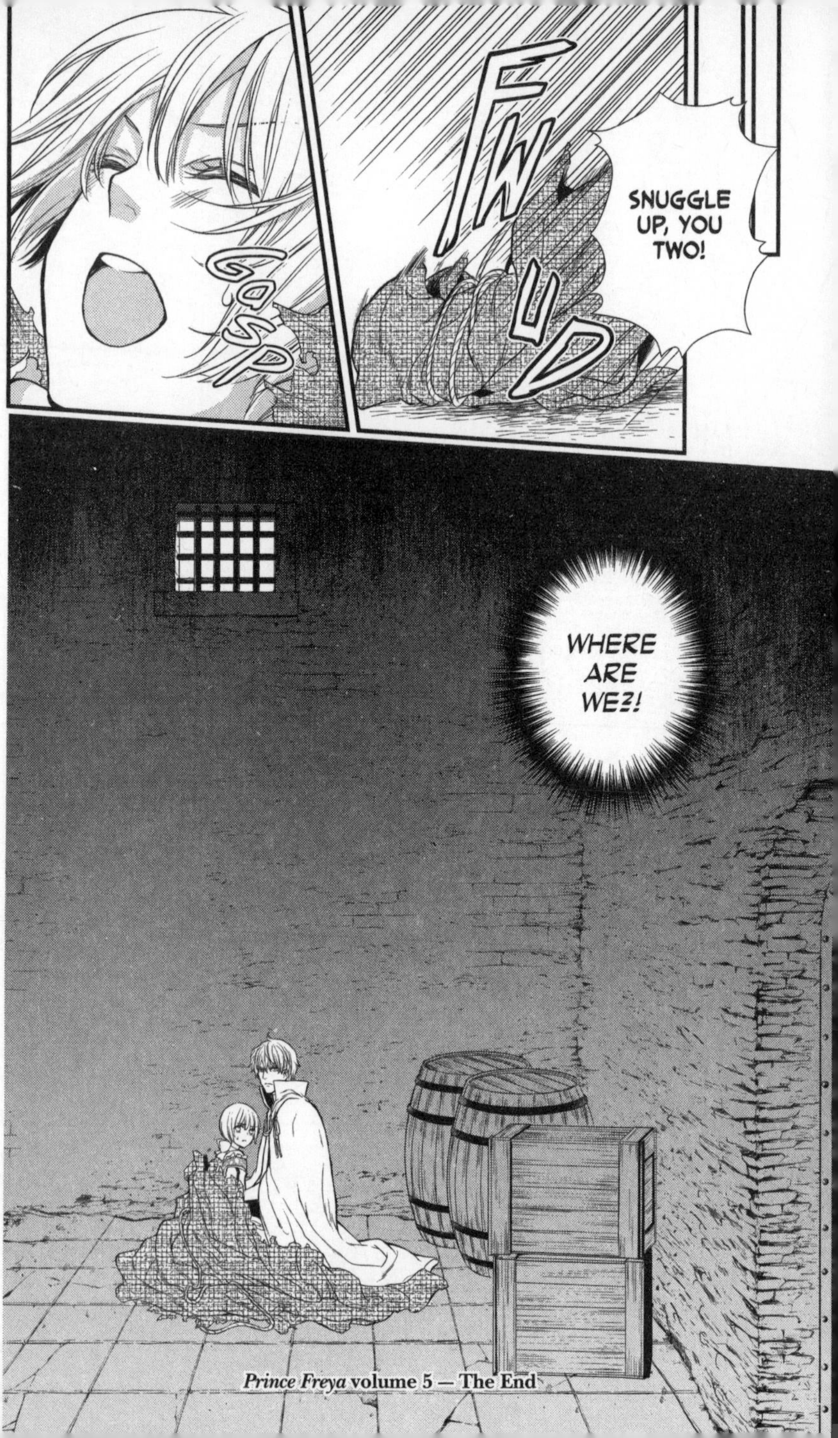
SNUGGLE UP, YOU TWO!
FWUD
GASP
WHERE ARE WE?!
Prince Freya volume 5 — The End

Bonus Chapter: Memories

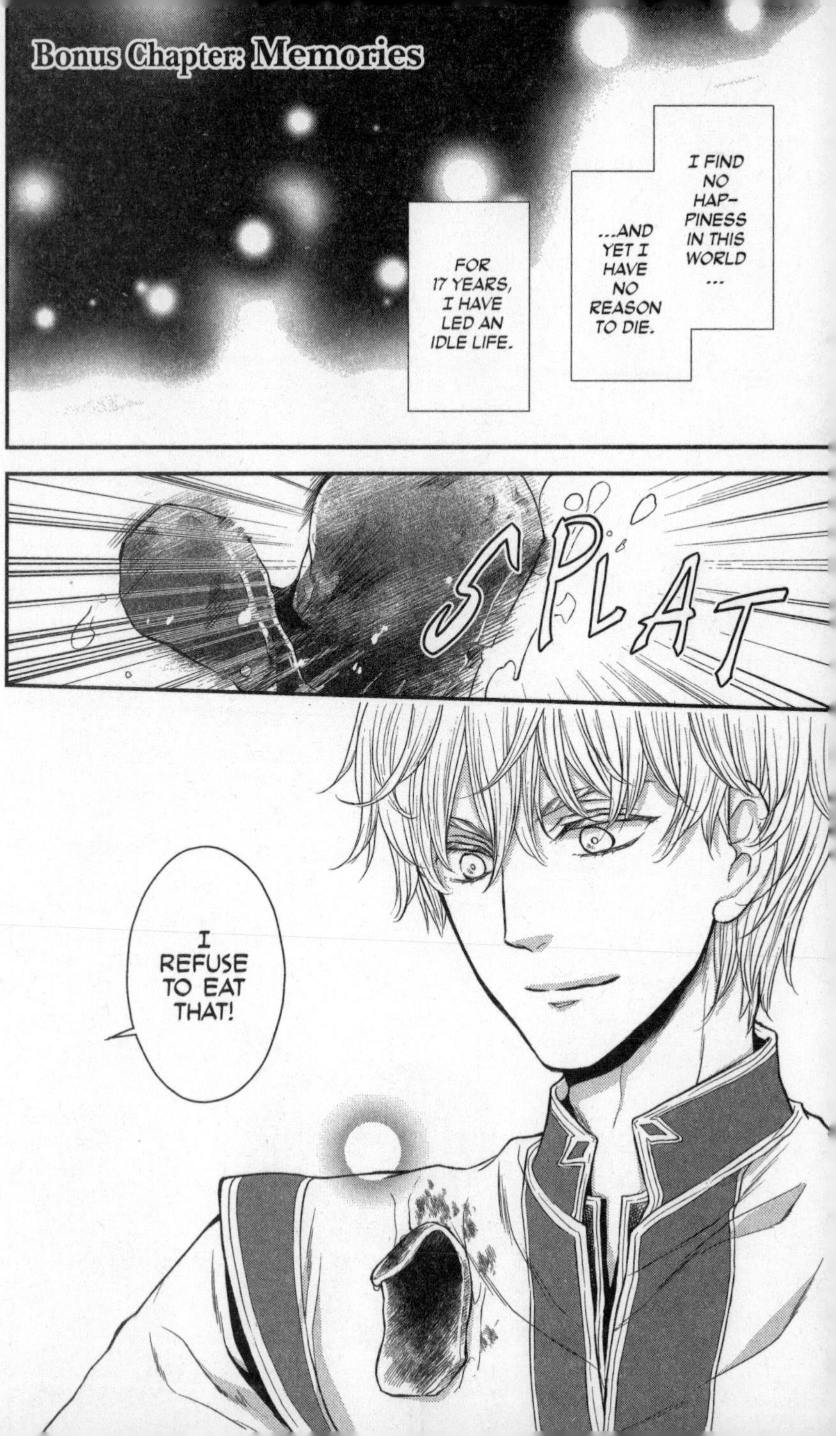
I FIND NO HAPPINESS IN THIS WORLD...
...AND YET I HAVE NO REASON TO DIE.
FOR 17 YEARS, I HAVE LED AN IDLE LIFE.
SPLAT
I REFUSE TO EAT THAT!

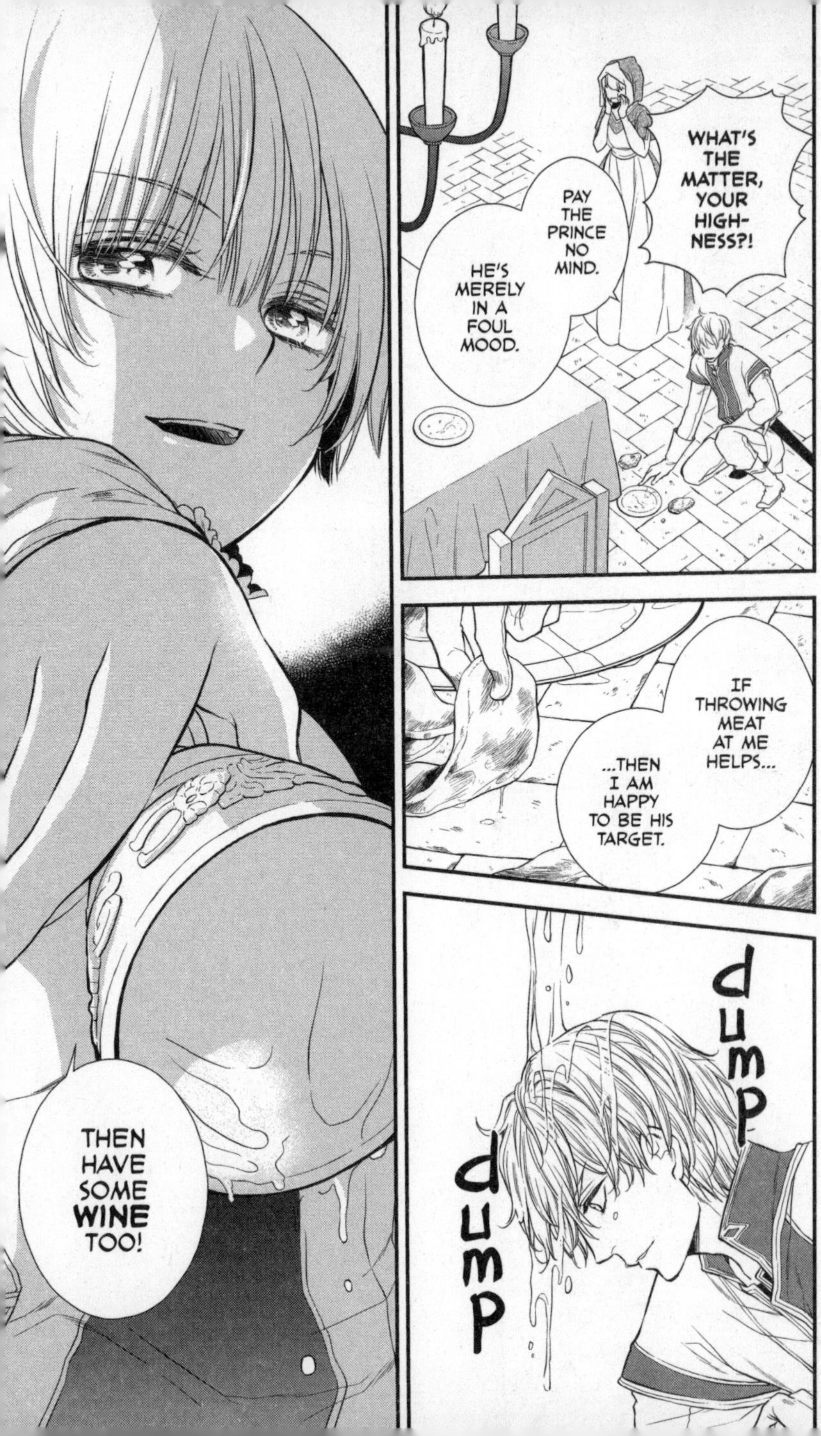
WHAT'S THE MATTER, YOUR HIGHNESS?!
PAY THE PRINCE NO MIND.
HE'S MERELY IN A FOUL MOOD.
IF THROWING MEAT AT ME HELPS...
...THEN I AM HAPPY TO BE HIS TARGET.
dump
dump
THEN HAVE SOME **WINE** TOO!

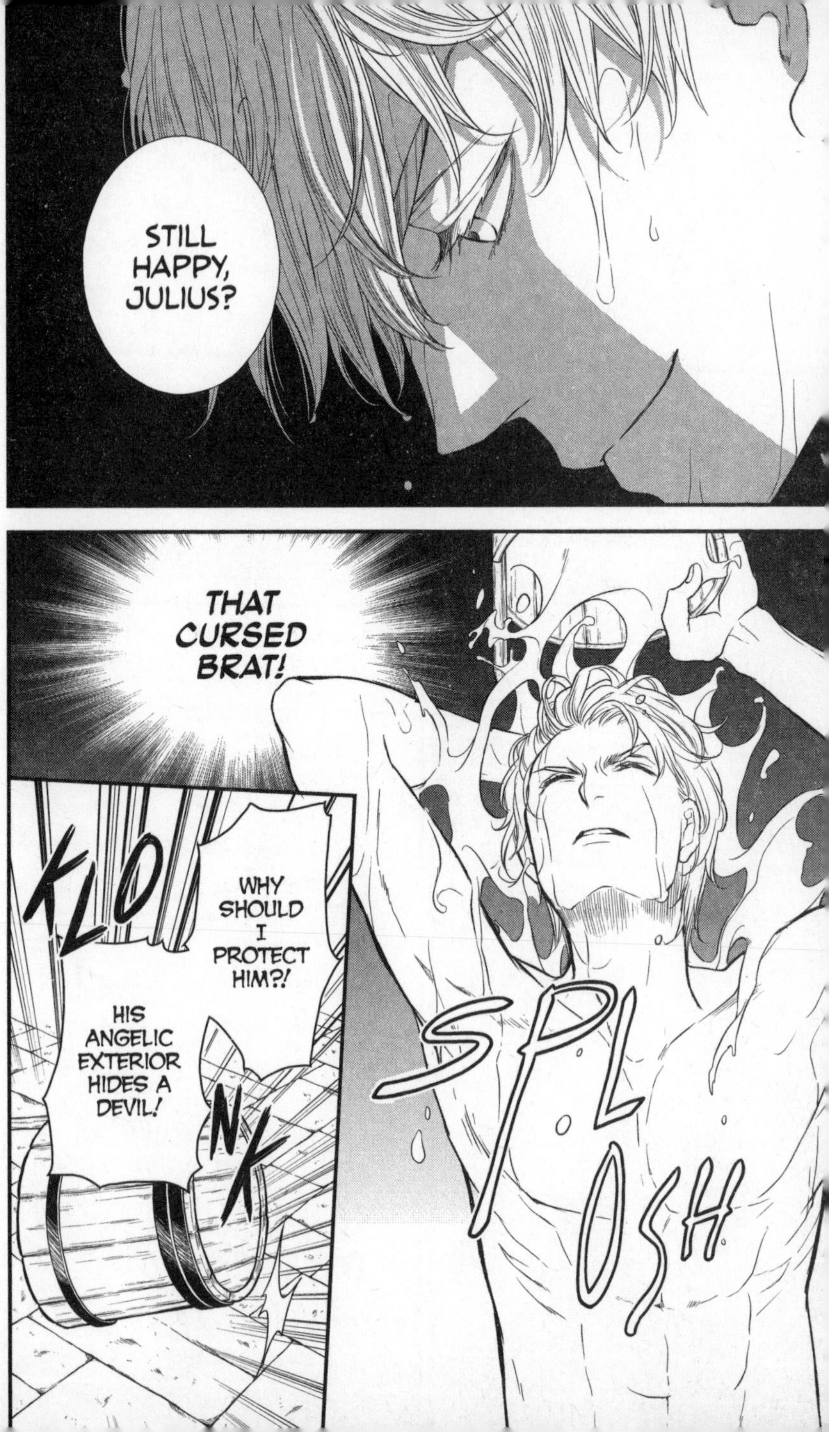
STILL HAPPY, JULIUS?
THAT CURSED BRAT!
SPLOSH
KLONK
WHY SHOULD I PROTECT HIM?!
HIS ANGELIC EXTERIOR HIDES A DEVIL!

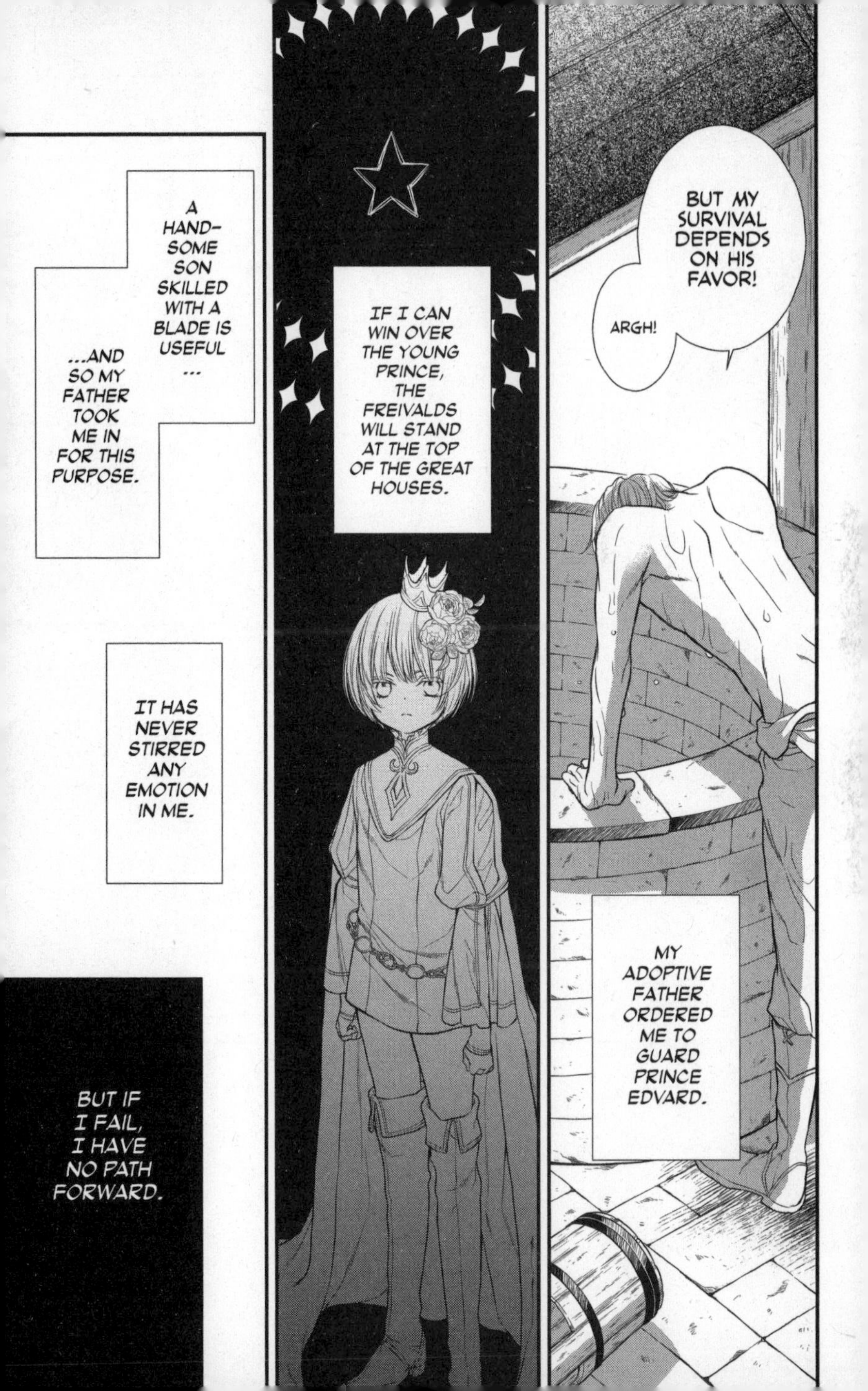
BUT MY SURVIVAL DEPENDS ON HIS FAVOR!
ARGH!
MY ADOPTIVE FATHER ORDERED ME TO GUARD PRINCE EDVARD.
IF I CAN WIN OVER THE YOUNG PRINCE, THE FREIVALDS WILL STAND AT THE TOP OF THE GREAT HOUSES.
A HAND-SOME SON SKILLED WITH A BLADE IS USEFUL ...
...AND SO MY FATHER TOOK ME IN FOR THIS PURPOSE.
IT HAS NEVER STIRRED ANY EMOTION IN ME.
BUT IF I FAIL, I HAVE NO PATH FORWARD.

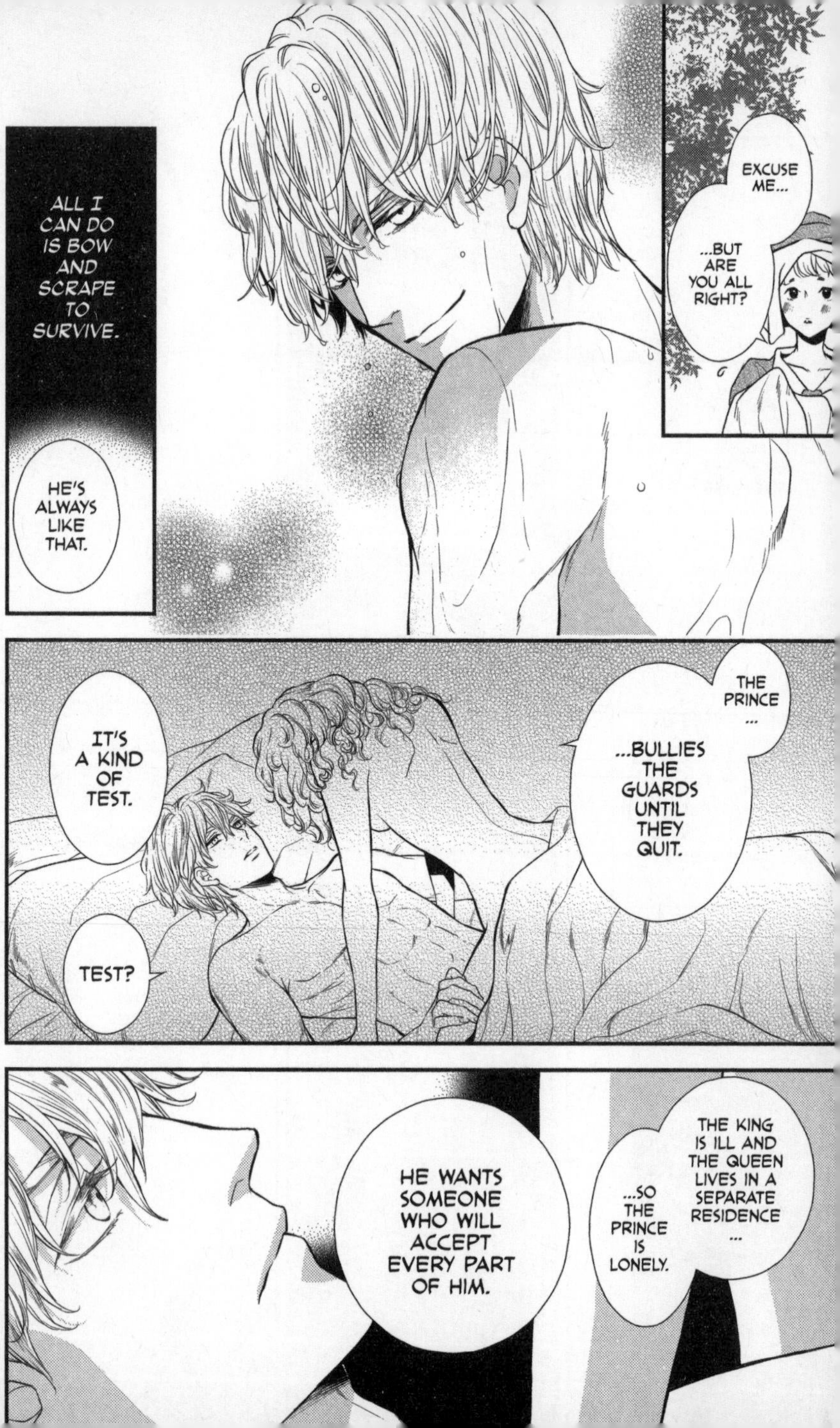
EXCUSE ME...
...BUT ARE YOU ALL RIGHT?
ALL I CAN DO IS BOW AND SCRAPE TO SURVIVE.
HE'S ALWAYS LIKE THAT.
THE PRINCE ...
...BULLIES THE GUARDS UNTIL THEY QUIT.
IT'S A KIND OF TEST.
TEST?
THE KING IS ILL AND THE QUEEN LIVES IN A SEPARATE RESIDENCE ...
...SO THE PRINCE IS LONELY.
HE WANTS SOMEONE WHO WILL ACCEPT EVERY PART OF HIM.

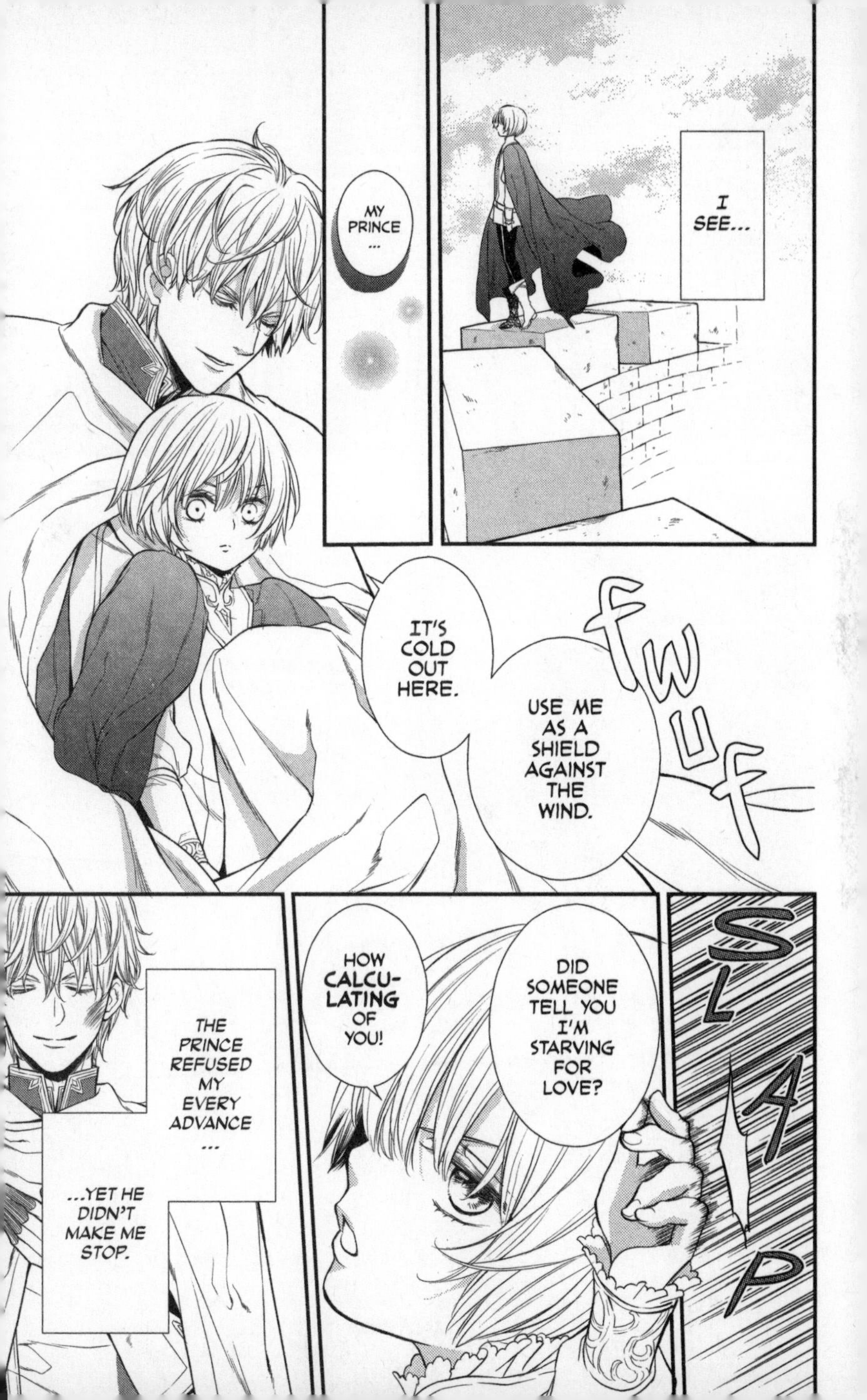
I SEE...
MY PRINCE ...
FWUF
IT'S COLD OUT HERE.
USE ME AS A SHIELD AGAINST THE WIND.
SLAP
DID SOMEONE TELL YOU I'M STARVING FOR LOVE?
HOW CALCULATING OF YOU!
THE PRINCE REFUSED MY EVERY ADVANCE ...
...YET HE DIDN'T MAKE ME STOP.

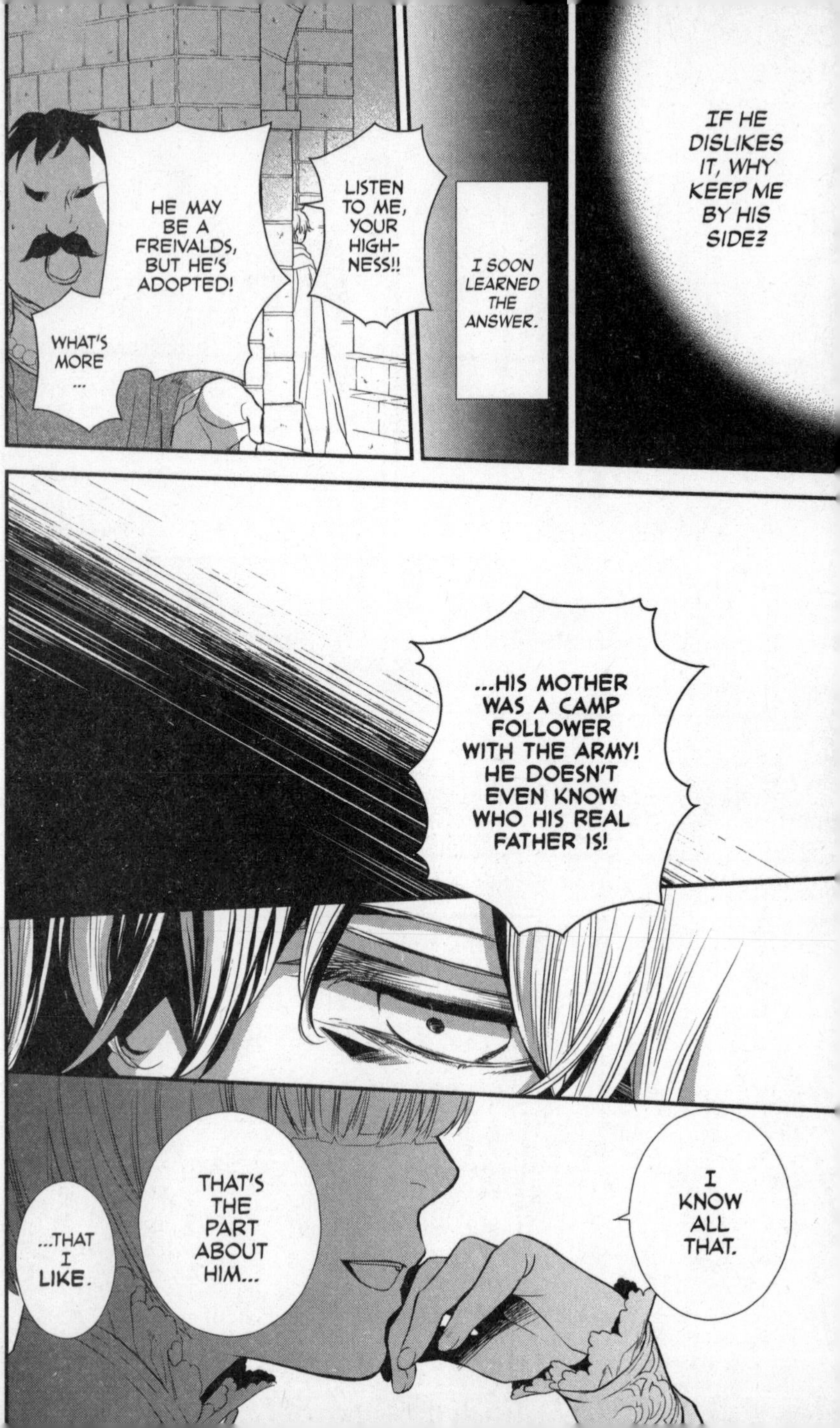
IF HE DISLIKES IT, WHY KEEP ME BY HIS SIDE?
I SOON LEARNED THE ANSWER.
LISTEN TO ME, YOUR HIGHNESS!!
HE MAY BE A FREIVALDS, BUT HE'S ADOPTED!
WHAT'S MORE ...
...HIS MOTHER WAS A CAMP FOLLOWER WITH THE ARMY! HE DOESN'T EVEN KNOW WHO HIS REAL FATHER IS!
I KNOW ALL THAT.
THAT'S THE PART ABOUT HIM...
...THAT I LIKE.

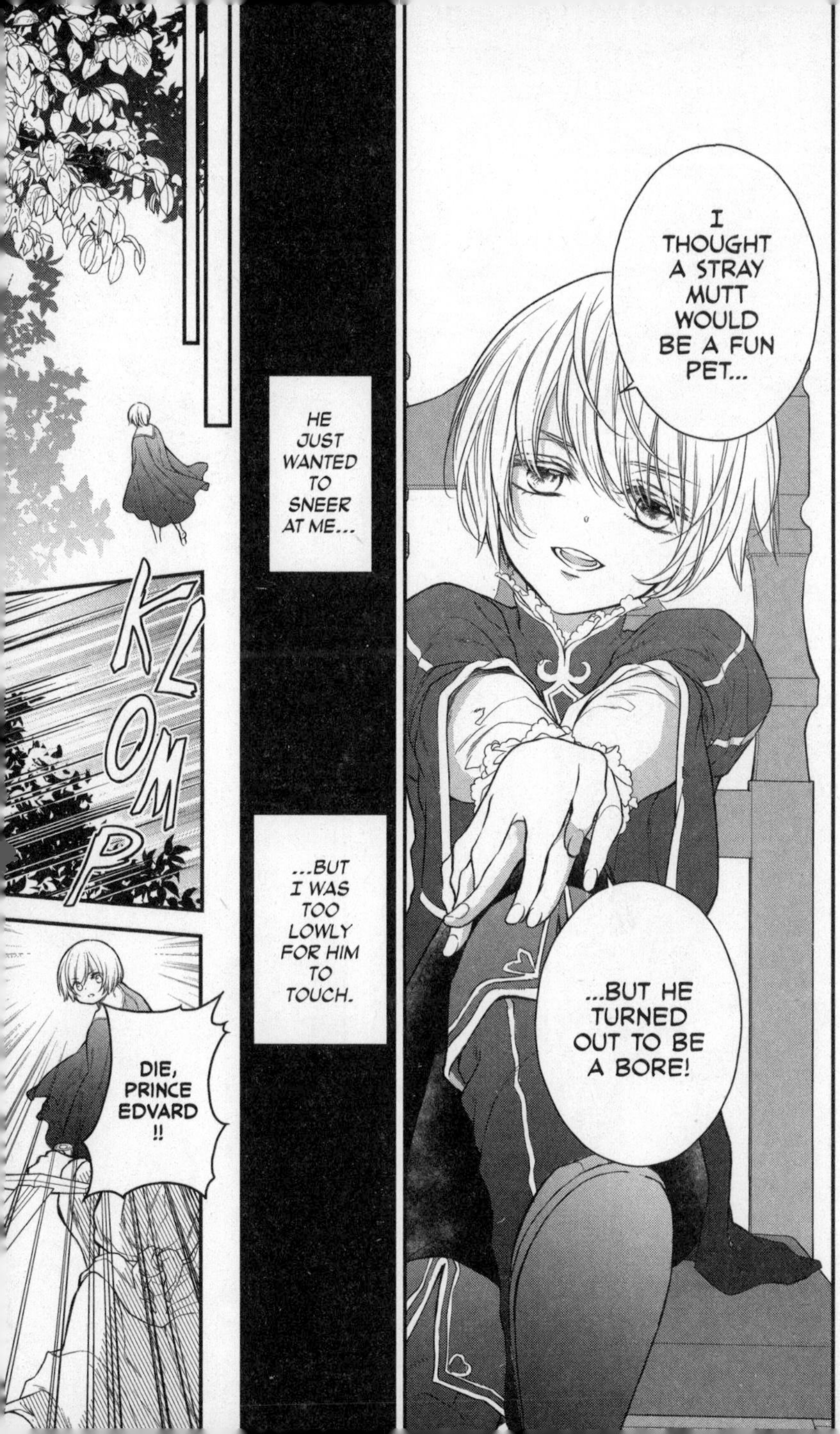
I THOUGHT A STRAY MUTT WOULD BE A FUN PET...
...BUT HE TURNED OUT TO BE A BORE!
HE JUST WANTED TO SNEER AT ME...
...BUT I WAS TOO LOWLY FOR HIM TO TOUCH.
KLOMP
DIE, PRINCE EDVARD!!

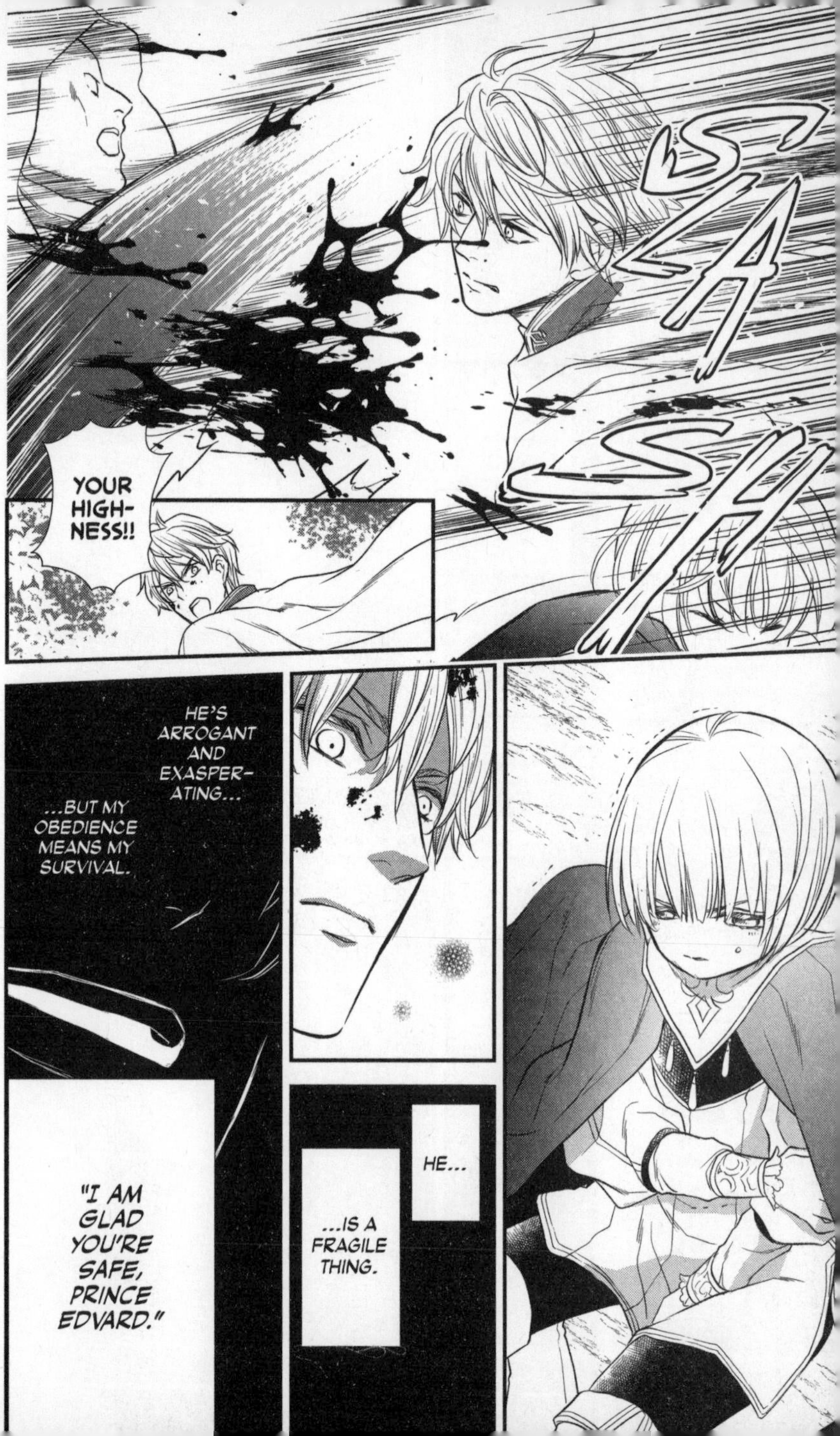
SASH
YOUR HIGHNESS!!
HE'S ARROGANT AND EXASPERATING...
...BUT MY OBEDIENCE MEANS MY SURVIVAL.
HE...
...IS A FRAGILE THING.
"I AM GLAD YOU'RE SAFE, PRINCE EDVARD."

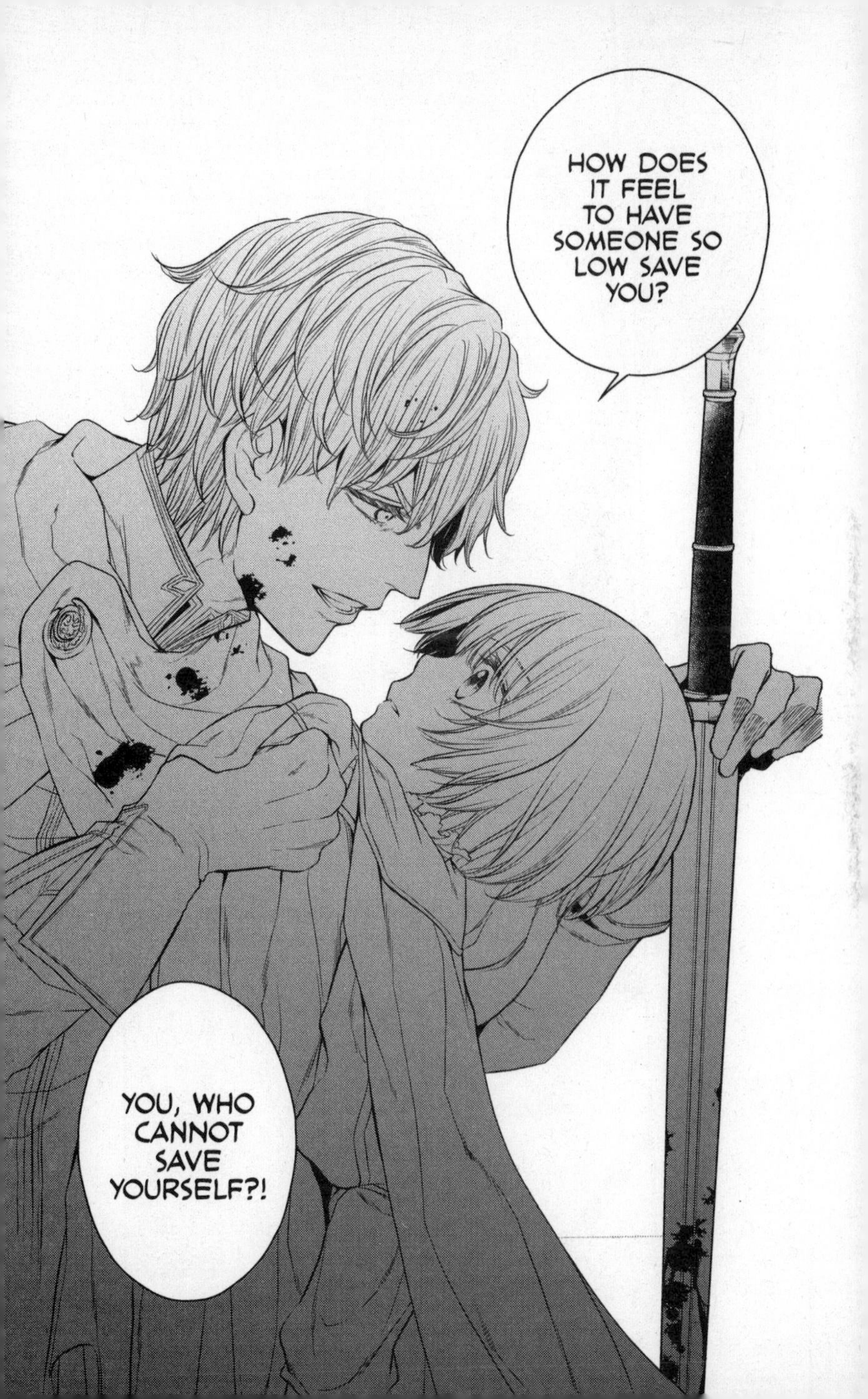
HOW DOES IT FEEL TO HAVE SOMEONE SO LOW SAVE YOU?
YOU, WHO CANNOT SAVE YOURSELF?!

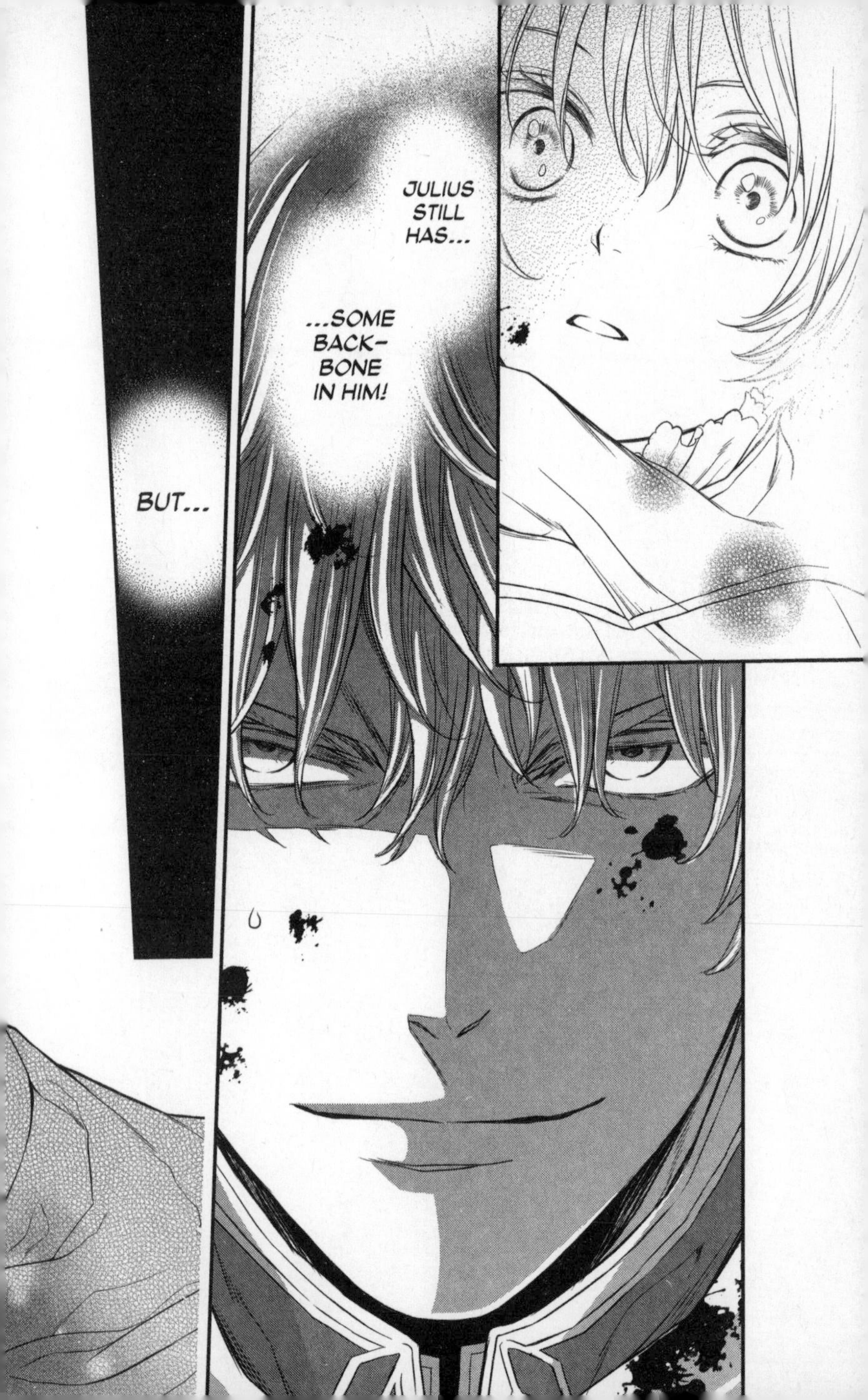
JULIUS STILL HAS...
...SOME BACK-BONE IN HIM!
BUT...

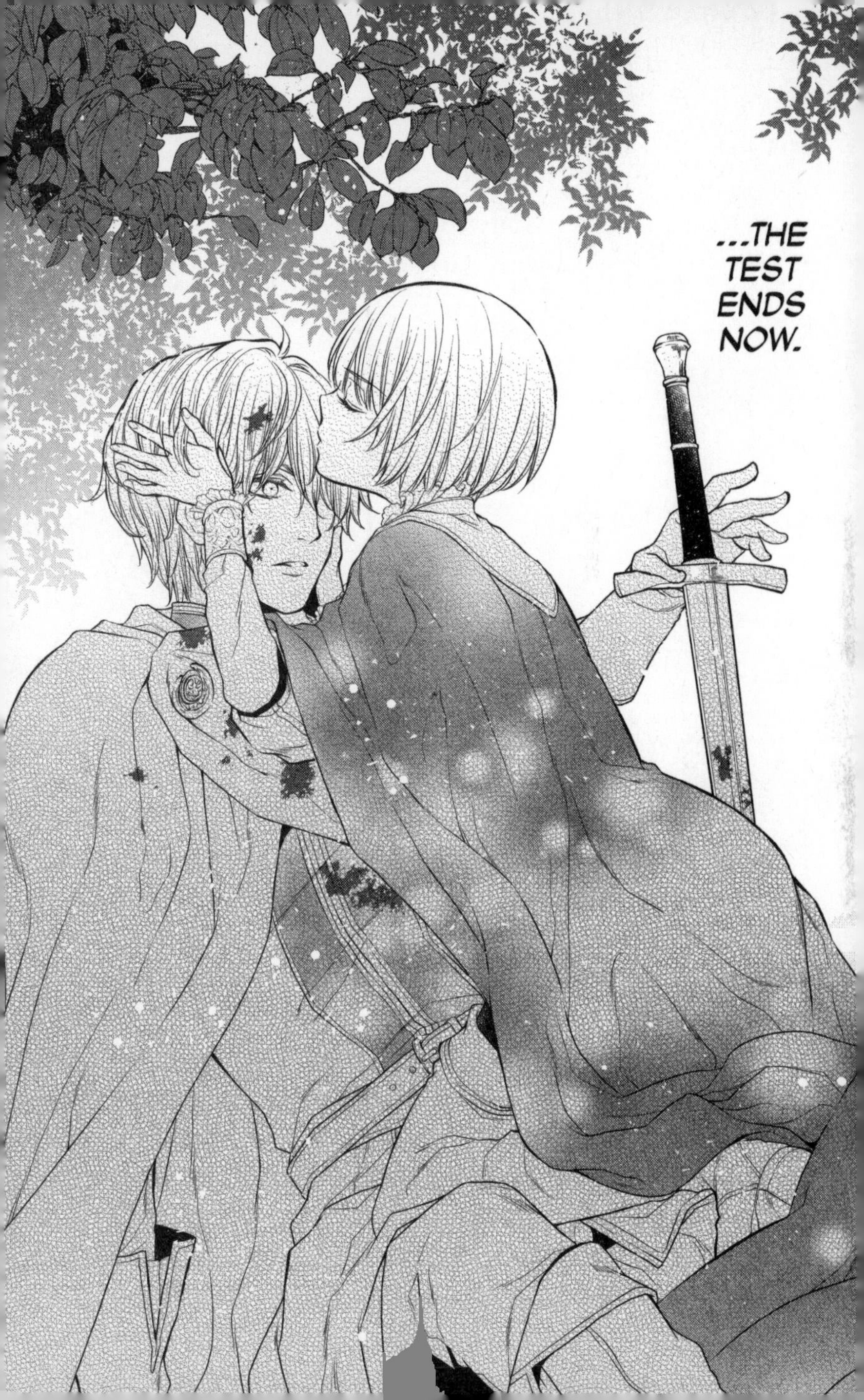
...THE TEST ENDS NOW.

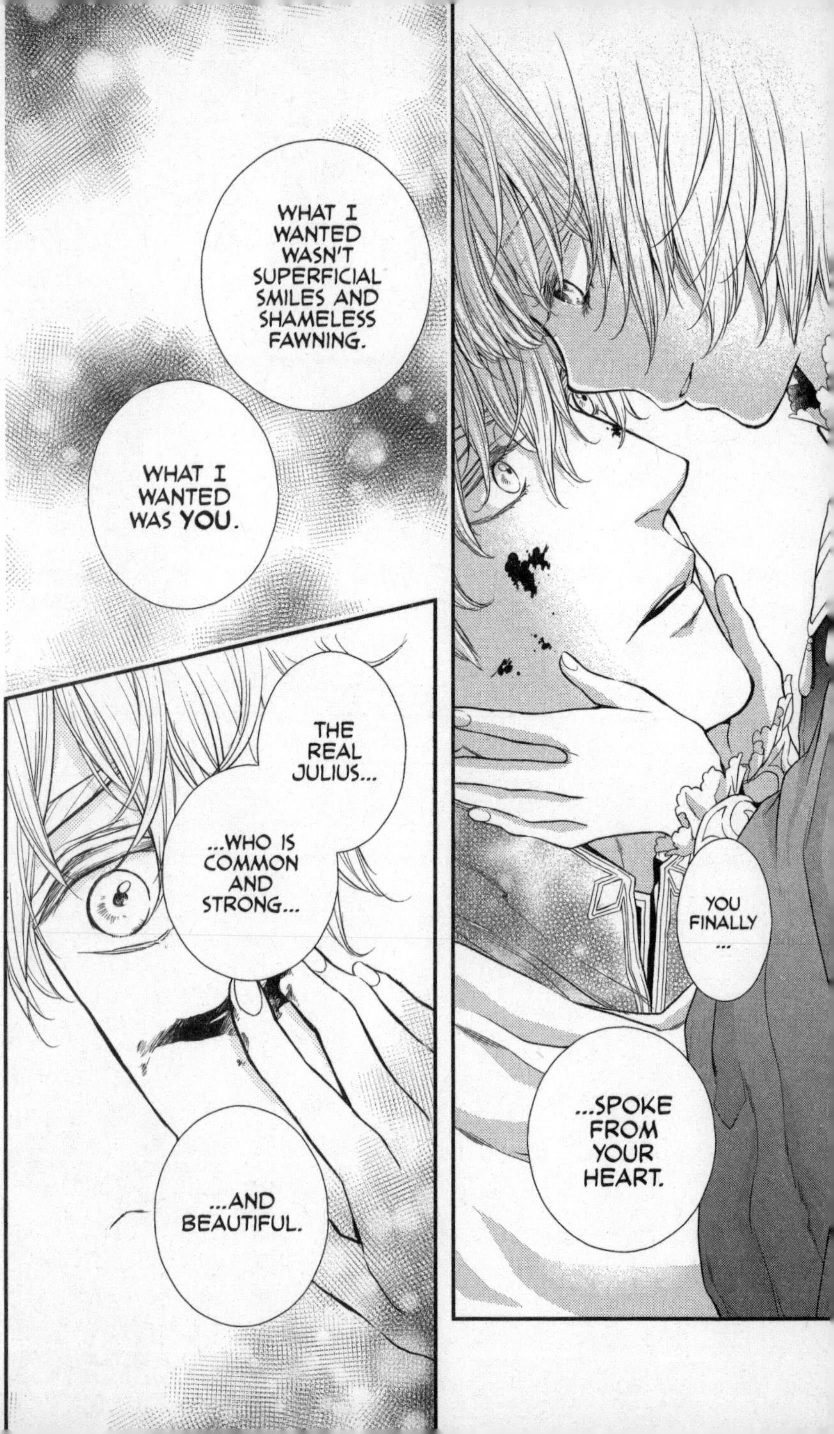
YOU FINALLY ...
...SPOKE FROM YOUR HEART.
WHAT I WANTED WASN'T SUPERFICIAL SMILES AND SHAMELESS FAWNING.
WHAT I WANTED WAS YOU.
THE REAL JULIUS...
...WHO IS COMMON AND STRONG...
...AND BEAUTIFUL.

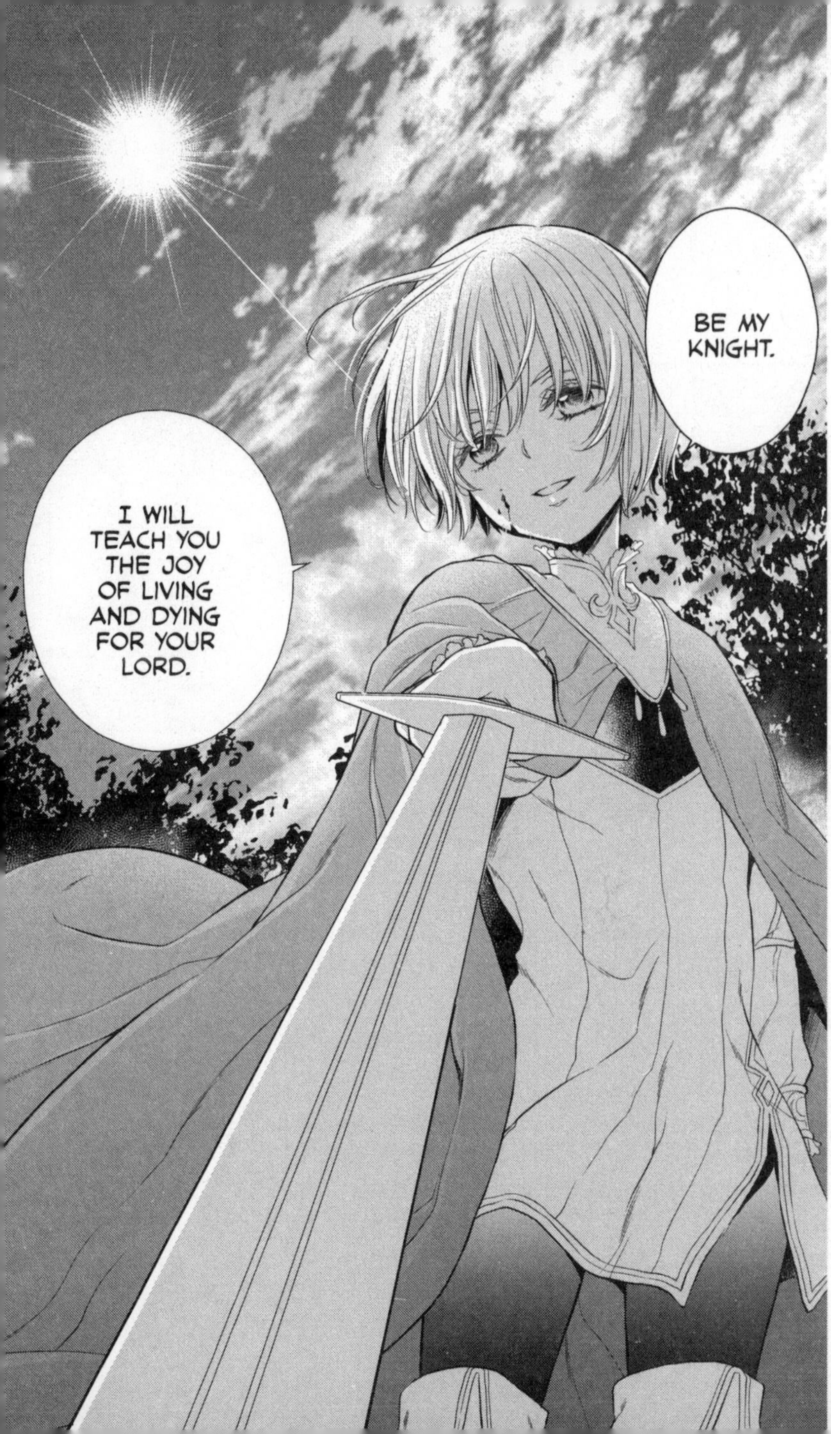
BE MY KNIGHT.
I WILL TEACH YOU THE JOY OF LIVING AND DYING FOR YOUR LORD.

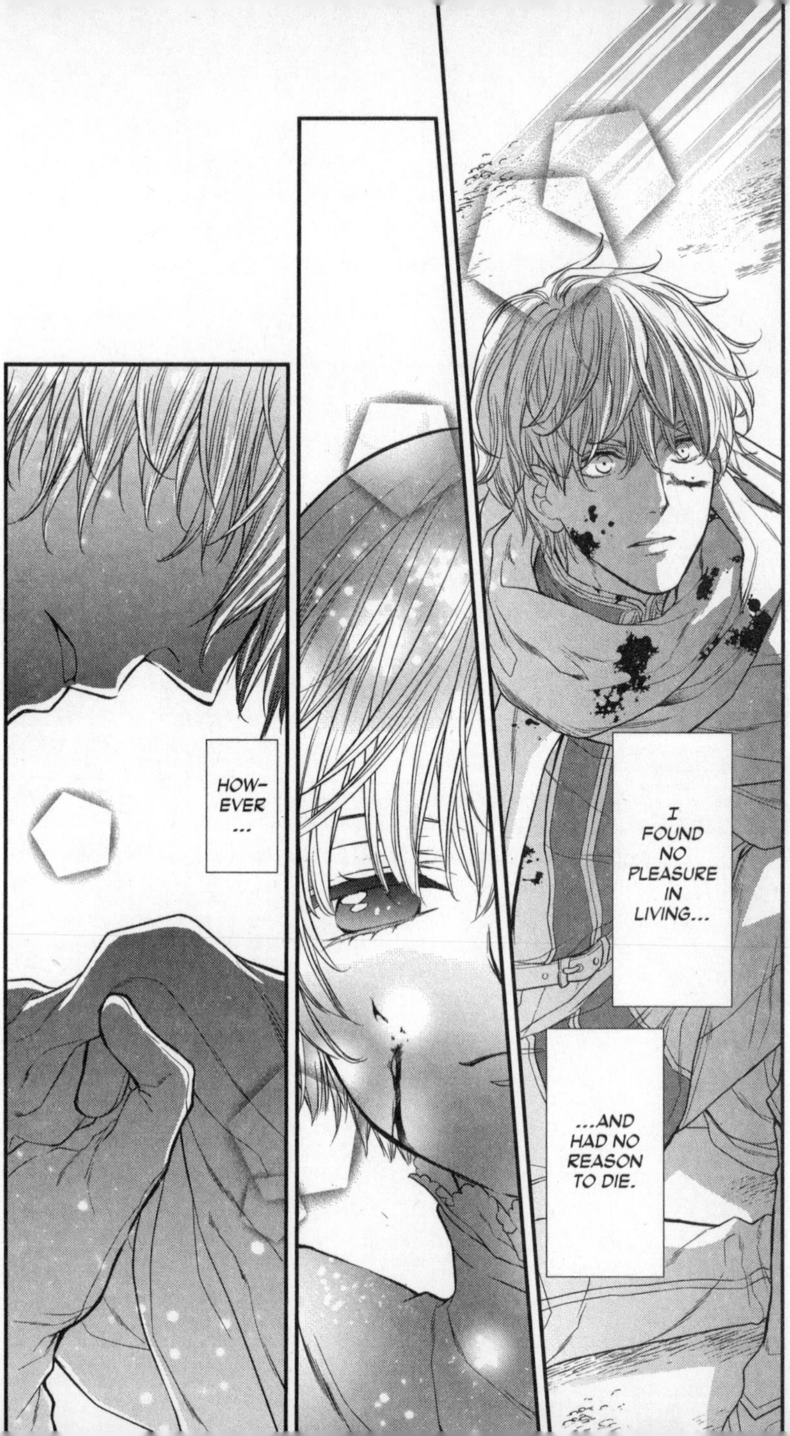
I FOUND NO PLEASURE IN LIVING...
...AND HAD NO REASON TO DIE.
HOW-EVER...

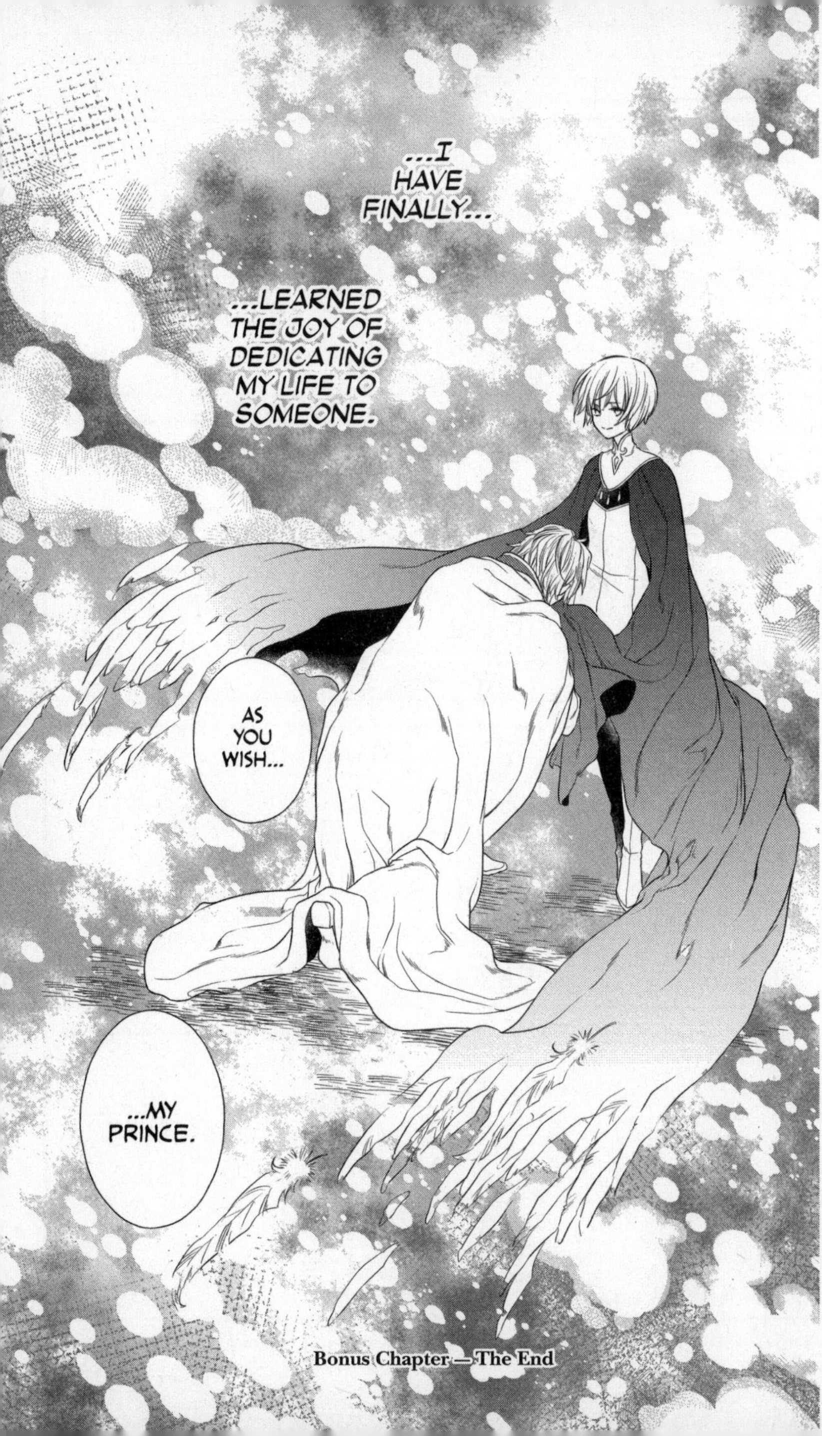
...I HAVE FINALLY...
...LEARNED THE JOY OF DEDICATING MY LIFE TO SOMEONE.
AS YOU WISH...
...MY PRINCE.

Bonus Chapter — The End

Afterword

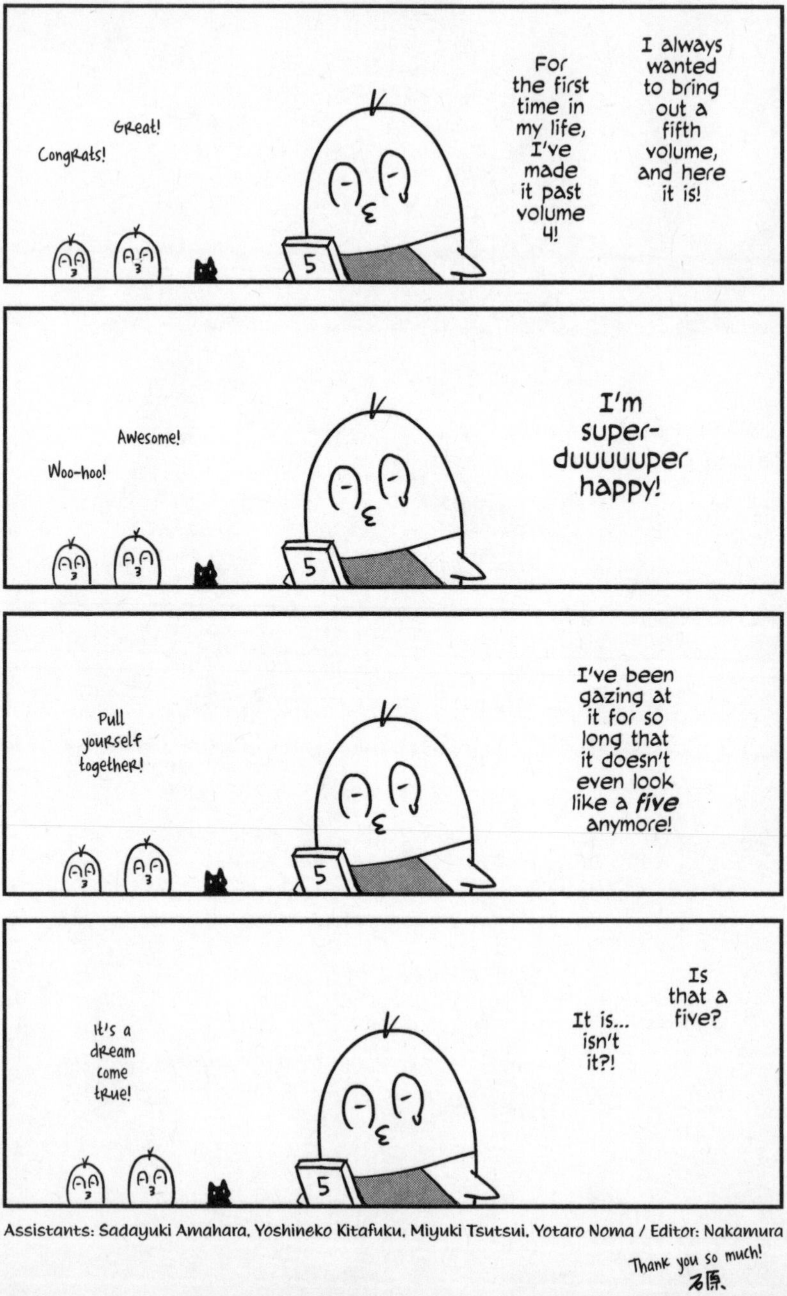
I always wanted to bring out a fifth volume, and here it is!
For the first time in my life, I've made it past volume 4!
Great!
Congrats!
I'm super-duuuuuper happy!
Awesome!
Woo-hoo!
I've been gazing at it for so long that it doesn't even look like a *five* anymore!
Pull yourself together!
Is that a five?
It is... isn't it?!
It's a dream come true!

Assistants: Sadayuki Amahara, Yoshineko Kitafuku, Miyuki Tsutsui, Yotaro Noma / Editor: Nakamura

Thank you so much!
石原

Thank you for purchasing *Prince Freya* volume 5. It's been a while since I've drawn fluff, and I got to do a lot of that in this volume. It's so much fun drawing dresses and frills.

KEIKO ISHIHARA

Born on April 14, Keiko Ishihara began her manga career with *Keisan Desu Kara* (It's All Calculated). Her other works include *Strange Dragon*, which was serialized in the magazine *LaLa*, and *The Heiress and the Chauffeur*, published by VIZ Media. Ishihara is from Hyogo Prefecture, and she loves cats.

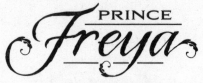

PRINCE Freya

VOLUME 5 · SHOJO BEAT EDITION

STORY AND ART BY
KEIKO ISHIHARA

ENGLISH TRANSLATION & ADAPTATION John Werry
TOUCH-UP ART & LETTERING Sabrina Heep
DESIGN Shawn Carrico
EDITOR Pancha Diaz

Printed in the U.S.A.

Published by VIZ Media, LLC
P.O. Box 77010
San Francisco, CA 94107

10 9 8 7 6 5 4 3 2 1
First printing, September 2021

ratings.viz.com RATED T+ OLDER TEEN

PARENTAL ADVISORY
PRINCE FREYA is rated T+ for Older Teen and is recommended for ages 16 and up. This volume contains death, violence and sexual situations.

VIZ MEDIA
viz.com

Shojo Beat
shojobeat.com

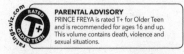

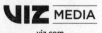

This is the last page.

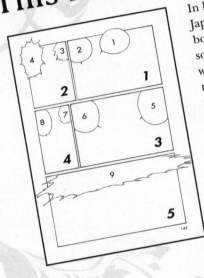

In keeping with the original Japanese comic format, this book reads from right to left—so action, sound effects, and word balloons are completely reversed. This preserves the orientation of the original artwork—plus, it's fun! Check out the diagram shown here to get the hang of things, and then turn to the other side of the book to get started!